Economic Policy and Household Welfare during Crisis and Adjustment in Tanzania

Economic Policy and Household Welfare during Crisis and Adjustment in Tanzania

Alexander H. Sarris
Rogier van den Brink

Published for
Cornell University Food and Nutrition Policy Program
by New York University Press
New York and London

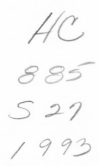

NEW YORK UNIVERSITY PRESS
New York and London

Library of Congress Cataloging-in-Publication Data
Sarris, Alexander.
Economic policy and household welfare during crisis and adjustment
in Tanzania / Alexander H. Sarris, Rogier van den Brink.
p. cm.
The result of a collaborative research program between the Cornell
University Food and Nutrition Policy Program (CFNPP) and the
Economic Research Bureau (ERP) of the University of Dar es Salaam.
ISBN 0-8147-7982-4
1. Tanzania—Economic policy. 2. Households—Tanzania.
I. Brink, Rogerius Johannes Eugenius van den, 1958–   II. Cornell
University Food and Nutrition Policy Program.   III. Title.
HC885.S27   1993
338.9678—dc20   93-10756
                            CIP

New York University Press books are printed on acid-free paper,
and their binding materials are chosen for strength and durability.

Manufactured in the United States of America

10 9 8 7 6 5 4 3 2 1

CONTENTS

List of Tables

List of Figures

Abbreviations

AGSASU	Agricultural Sample Survey of Tanzania Mainland 1986/87
BIS	Basic Industries Strategy
BNI	Basic Needs Income
ERP	Economic Recovery Program
ESAP	Economic and Social Action Program
EWCMB	Early Warning and Crop Monitoring Bureau
HBS	Household Budget Survey
MDB	Marketing Development Bureau
NAPB	National Agricultural Products Board
NESP	National Economic Survival Program
SAP	Structural Adjustment Program
TAG	Technical Advisory Group

FOREWORD

Work on this book started in early 1990 with the initiation of the collaborative research program concerning the impact of adjustment policies in households in Tanzania between Cornell University Food and Nutrition Policy Program (CFNPP) and the Economic Research Bureau (ERP) of the University of Dar es Salaam, and supported by the Africa Bureau of the U.S. Agency for International Development (USAID). The originally envisioned output was to include mostly descriptive and background information on the Tanzanian economy as a prerequisite to subsequent survey and model building work. Given, however, the massive early literature on Tanzania, the lack of recent analyses, and the considerable controversies concerning both the functioning of the economy as well as the need for and nature of adjustment, our interest quickly turned more analytical. The attempt was therefore made not only to give a background on the Tanzanian economy but also to analytically describe both the structure of households as well as the functioning of the true, as contrasted to the observed, economy.

The bulk of the work was completed in early 1991 and revised in late summer of 1991. It was subsequently revised in early 1992, taking into account comments and suggestions from several colleagues and external reviewers.

Among the authors, A. Sarris is responsible for Chapters 3, 4, and 6, and Rogier van den Brink for Chapter 5. The other chapters were written jointly.

Several people have contributed at various stages of the work. The authors would like to single out our Tanzanian collaborators, M.S.D. Bagachwa, A. Mbelle, R. Mabele, and A. Tibaijuka for various comments and suggestions; K. Budwar, E. Lugusha, L. Merid, A. Naho, E. Stephenson, and S. Zografakis for research assistance during the various stages of the research; and R. Christiansen, C. del Ninno, P. Fleuret, P. Pinstrup-Andersen, and two other anonymous reviewers for helpful suggestions for the revision. David Sahn was the director of the project under which this activity was a part, and is acknowledged for his overall support. The document was word processed by Elizabeth Vakalopoulou, typeset by Gaudencio Dizon, and produced by New York University Press.

Finally, we would like to thank our wives, Maria and Natasha, respectively, for their patience and support during the long period it has taken to complete this book.

ALEXANDER H. SARRiS
ROGIER VAN DEN BRINK

1

INTRODUCTION

The economic development of Tanzania, from independence in 1961 until now, has been characterized by a series of internal and external shocks that have tested the resilience of the economy, the stability of its institutions, and the tolerance and inventiveness of its people. Despite the fact that Tanzania is one of the world's poorest countries (the fourth-poorest, according to the 1990 World Bank Development Report), it has managed to weather all storms with a remarkable degree of political stability, and without extreme hardships such as the famines that hit other, more-developed countries.

The beginning of the decade of the eighties found the Tanzanian economy in deep economic crisis, resulting from a sequence of policy responses and a series of external shocks that, according to many observers, worsened an already critical situation. Recognizing the impossibility of dealing with the crisis alone, the government sought external assistance from multilateral donors, such as the International Monetary Fund (IMF). The conditions imposed by the IMF were at first strongly resisted on the grounds that they would undo all the social and distribution gains that had been achieved by Tanzania since independence. However, attempts by the government to implement its own stabilization and adjustment programs largely failed, with the result that in 1986 the government of Tanzania agreed to a three-year package of measures and policy reforms as a condition for multilateral and other donor assistance. The initial program has been succeeded by another program that started in 1989 and is still being implemented.

There are deep controversies surrounding the acceptance and implementation of externally or internally imposed policy reforms in Tanzania, which date from the end of the seventies. They concern the necessity of reforms, the type of policies adopted, the effectiveness of various measures in reviving the economy, and the impact of reforms on various segments of the population. The purpose of the present report is, first, to outline the main structural features of the Tanzanian economy, especially those relevant to the crisis, and second, to deal with the last of the above-mentioned aspects of the reform debate, especially the impact of previous policies and current stabilization and adjustment measures on the poorer segments of the Tanzanian population. Underlying all policy reform programs that are recommended as remedies to an economic crisis—which is usually manifested in a persistent, large balance-of-payments deficit—is the belief that the major reasons for the crisis lie with "wrong" policies previously adopted, whose modification will correct the fundamental structural disequilibria. Whether this will happen depends on the structure and response of the economy to various signals, on the degree of implementation of the stated reforms, and on the effectiveness of the new policies in changing the established structures of political and economic institutions. Much of the debate on the effectiveness and impact of adjustment programs—and Tanzania is no exception—has been driven by ideological biases rather than detailed analysis. Our effort in this report will be to contribute to the understanding of the functioning of the Tanzanian economy and its people during the crisis and under policy reforms, without invoking ideological arguments.

Our emphasis throughout will be on economic structure and behavior. Given the short period over which reforms have been in place in Tanzania, it is difficult to evaluate impacts, unless one understands how various parts of the economy are interrelated and function. It is in the same manner that we will approach understanding the impact on households. Another reason for our emphasis on economic and institutional structure concerns the difficulty of isolating effects of policy changes. Our effort will be to isolate external and internal causes of various economic changes, so as to pinpoint problems as well as positive aspects.

While the issue of the impact of adjustment programs on poorer sections of the population, in Africa and elsewhere, has received much political attention, especially after UNICEF's *Adjustment with a Human Face* (Cornia, Jolly, and Stewart 1987), there have been very few empirical studies examining the issue analytically. Recently, Sahn and Sarris (1991), in a comparative study of rural smallholders in five African countries, including Tanzania, showed that the economic signals after the onset of adjustment programs do not appear to have led to a deterioration of real rural smallholder incomes.

In the case of Tanzania, the only detailed study that has presented an examination of income trends over a period of almost two decades is the one by Bevan and his co-authors (1988), which is also reproduced in Bevan et al. (1989). That study shows that during the seventies and early eighties, rural and urban real incomes declined significantly. A recent study by Collier and Gunning (1989) showed that the adjustment efforts since 1984 have stopped the continuous earlier income decline, but as of 1989 no significant recovery in incomes is apparent. These conclusions seem to form the basis for current, informed opinion in Tanzania.

Our analysis in this report shows, to the contrary, that the earlier conclusion that serious income declines occurred throughout the seventies and early eighties must be questioned, and especially so as far as the rural, and even the urban, poor are concerned. There were indeed some real income declines, but these, it seems, were mostly concentrated among the urban middle class and not among the poor. Our analysis shows that during the period of adjustment, the rural and urban poor were hardly affected. The decline in urban, middle-class real incomes was stopped but not reversed. The only groups that seem to have suffered real income decline during the reform period are the rural middle-income and richer households, and the urban rich. These preliminary results (which need to be further substantiated by detailed empirical research involving the use of counterfactual models), have several implications for economic policy in Tanzania, which are explored in this report.

To arrive at our result, we employ a series of analyses that emphasize not only the structure and economic institutions of the economy, but also the observability of the economy in Tanzania. In fact, one of the major conclusions that emerge from the analysis is that official economic statistics have failed, at an increasing rate since the mid-1970s, to give an even moderately accurate picture of economic developments. In such a setting, turning points in the economy might be misjudged, and one has to rely on a very different set of data for analysis.

Our investigation starts in Chapter 2 with a quick overview of the structure of the economy and economic developments since independence, emphasizing the recent years. The years of crisis and concurrent economic events and politics are outlined as a background for the rest of the report.

In Chapter 3, we examine macroeconomic developments and policies and present an analysis of the size of the "second economy," the largely unobserved and uncontrolled, but apparently very substantial, part of the Tanzanian economy that we feel is the key to understanding the evolution of incomes. After an initial, descriptive review of macro developments and the reform program, the chapter estimates the size of the second economy and shows that the evolution of the total economy is different than what is apparent from the official statistics. In that chapter, we also analyze the various means of financing public expenditures, and we show that gradually, foreign sources ended up financing most of the domestic deficits.

In Chapter 4, we present a detailed structural profile of households in Tanzania, based on analysis of several household surveys. In that chapter, we also estimate poverty lines and the proportion of rural and urban poor in Tanzania. The results suggest a degree of poverty much larger than previously thought, but also a very equitable pattern of incomes. Tanzania, although it has some substantial income inequalities, appears to have been spared the enormous maldistribution of incomes observed in several other developing countries.

In Chapter 5, we present an analysis of developments in the agricultural sector, which is by far the most important economic sector in Tanzania. We discover that the trends in official production statistics must be seriously questioned and that more recent information seems to suggest that the official reports of growth in food production over the last decade are not warranted. Analysis of relative price trends suggests that the official, relative prices of food versus those of export products have not, on aggregate, changed very much over the last decade, while real official prices declined throughout the crisis, only to recover after the onset of adjustment reforms. Real prices in the open market, however, seem to be telling a different story; prices at least for food products, seem to have increased throughout the crisis, only to fall after the onset of reforms.

In Chapter 6, we present our analysis of household incomes. We first show that the alleged decline in household real income between the mid-1970s and mid-1980s is not supported by existing information. Then we develop a new methodology for analysis of household incomes based on an explicit recognition of the informal sector. We derive income and consumption patterns for typical members of six household income classes (poor, middle, and rich households in both rural and urban areas), and we show that the evolution of economic signals since the mid-1970s warrants the conclusions already mentioned. In the final chapter, we summarize and synthesize our conclusions and derive policy implications.

2

BACKGROUND

The purpose of this chapter is to describe the background against which recent developments must be examined. The first section gives a brief description of the resource characteristics of Tanzania. The next section reviews briefly the postindependence economic developments culminating in the recent adjustment efforts. The third section outlines the macroeconomic structure, while the fourth section briefly reviews the agricultural and industrial sectors.

POPULATION, NATURAL RESOURCES, AND AGROCLIMATIC ZONES

A low population density and a varied agricultural resource base give Tanzania a particularly robust agricultural sector. Its mineral resources include coal, iron ore deposits, phosphates, and smaller deposits of copper, lead, tin, nickel, and sulphur. Soda comes from Lake Natron, and salt can be obtained from certain springs and the sea. Gold and diamonds are present in significant quantities.

Tanzania has access to the Great Lakes region of East Africa (see Map 1). In the north, Lake Victoria borders both Uganda and Kenya. Lake Tanganyika in the west is the border with Zaire, and Lake Nyasa in the southwest borders with Malawi. These lakes, together with Tanzania's marine resources in the coastal areas, constitute major, but relatively undeveloped, fishery resources. Addition-

MAP 1
Map of Tanzania

Source: World Bank (1991).

ally, Tanzania's rivers have significant potential for hydroelectric power and irrigation.

Tanzania is a country of low population density. In 1988, 22.5 million people inhabited 881,289 square kilometers, which implies a density of about 25.5 persons per square kilometer. Relatively few towns exist, the major ones being Dar es Salaam, with approximately 1.4 million people, and Mwanza, with about 180,000 people. Only 5 percent of the total land area is cultivated, although nearly 90 percent of the country could at least theoretically support some type of farming (Land Resources Development Centre 1987). Large areas, however, are tsetse fly infested, which precludes their settlement by either people or animals. The incidence of the tsetse fly produces a typical pattern of population settlement characterized by pockets of densely populated, tsetse-free areas.

According to three demographic censuses (taken in 1967, 1978, and 1988, respectively) the population growth rate declined significantly, from 3.3 percent for the 1967–1978 period, to 2.8 percent during the 1978–1988 period. This trend has been accompanied by a slowing of the growth of the urban population, which grew at an average annual rate of 10.7 percent during 1967–1978 but at only 5.4 percent for the 1978–1988 period.

Tanzania has been described as the country with the most varied ecology of any in Africa, enabling a wide variety of agricultural activities to be undertaken. These range from highland tea and coffee production to arid-area nomadic pastoralism. Most of Tanzania's semiarid central zone is suited for extensive farming systems and livestock production, due to the high rainfall variability and fragile soils. Small-scale, rain-fed cultivation of cereals (sorghum and millet), tubers, and cotton is undertaken by farming communities that are often areas of locally high population densities due to the presence of the tsetse fly elsewhere. Livestock is produced by the nomadic Masai and a number of seminomadic groups who are responsible for most of the country's production.

A tropical forest cover is found along the coast and on Zanzibar. Here coconuts, cashew nuts, rubber, cocoa, cloves, sisal, various spices, and fruits are grown. Next to maize and rice, cassava is an important food crop. The main growing season is from March to July. The northern coastal area has a second, but short, rainy season in November-December. Soils are mainly sandy, except for the clayish bottomlands in the river valleys.

The western part of the country is dominated by a plateau about 1,000 meters high, which has an average rainfall of over 750 millimeters per year. The growing season is between November and April. It is here that the country's main potential for surplus food crop production can be realized. Maize, sorghum, millet, cassava, rice, cotton, and tobacco are the main crops grown. In some regions, the area under cultivation could be readily expanded. Oxen traction is widely practiced in the northern part of the region, where cotton and rice production dominate the cropping pattern. The region also includes large areas of forest reserves, and its lakes constitute important fishery resources.

The highland areas possess some agriculturally attractive features—high and generally reliable rainfall over a five-to-nine-month period, fertile volcanic soils, and a relatively cool climate. The soil types found in the highlands react relatively well to fertilizer application and permit intensive agricultural production systems. Fertilizer use is therefore widespread. Wheat, maize, cassava, sorghum, coffee, tea, potatoes, bananas, beans, and pyrethrum are some of the main crops grown in the highlands. Scope for the expansion of the cultivated area exists in the southern highlands only. The northern and western highlands are under considerable land pressure. The main farming systems are the banana-coffee intercrop system in the northern highlands and the pure-cropped maize system in the south.

The diversity of farming systems is illustrated in Table 1, which presents a selected number of zones and some main farm characteristics.

From this table it becomes clear that it is not possible to speak of a single, average Tanzanian farming system. Average farm size, for instance, varies from 0.78 hectare in Kagera to 4.35 hectares in Singida. Cropping patterns show equally marked differences across regions. First, the share of farm area devoted to export crops ranges from 80 percent in Kagera and 76 percent in the Coast regions to virtually nil in areas such as Iringa, Singida, Kondoa, and Mara. Note, however, that perennial export crops always allow for intercropping with food crops—coffee is nearly always intercropped with bananas, and cashew nuts are often intercropped with cassava. The shares devoted to annual export crops, which are more difficult to intercrop with food crops, are in general much lower—cotton is cultivated on 25 percent of total farm area in Mwanza, 13 percent in Shinyanga, and 6 percent in Morogoro.

Food crops cultivated center around maize mixed-cropping systems in most of the areas. Rice is particularly important in the Coast, Morogoro, Tanga, and Mwanza areas. The more drought resistant crops (sorghum and millet) are typically found in Morogoro, Shinyanga, Iringa, Ruvuma, Singida, Kondoa, and Mwanza.

The importance of cattle as a source of farm income for the mixed farm enterprise also varies quite prominently by region. Tabora, Iringa, and Singida record an average of more than five head of cattle per farm. In the Coast and Morogoro areas, no large livestock is reported. Many of the other areas have relatively low numbers of cattle kept on the farm. Off-farm income, as reported by this survey, varies from 12–13 percent of total income in Kilimanjaro, Ruvuma, and Singida, to 45–56 percent in Lushoto and Morogoro. Subsequent

TABLE 1

Tanzania: Selected Farming System.

Region	Average Farm Size (Hectares)	Export Crops	Share of Farm Area		Cattle (Head per Farm)	Off-Farm Income (Share of Total)
			Food Crops			
Arusha	1.00	Coffee/banana (0.56)	Maize/beans/vegetables (0.29)		n.a.	n.a
Coast	3.65	Cashew/coconut (0.76)	Rice/maize (0.15); cassava (0.06)		...	0.20
Iringa	2.32		Maize/beans/vegetables (0.52); maize/millet (0.36)		7.1	0.27
Kagera	0.78	Coffee/banana (0.80)	Roots/pulses (0.17)		2.0	n.a.
Kilimanjaro	1.18	Coffee/banana (0.66)	Maize/beans (0.31)		1.5	0.12
Kondoa	2.88		Maize/millet (0.29); maize/sorghum/millet (0.20); maize (0.16)		n.a.	n.a.
Mara	1.85		Cereals/pulses (0.51); sweet potatoes (0.43)		2.9	n.a.
Mbeya	1.68	Coffee/banana (0.18)	Maize (0.40)		0.7	0.22
Morogoro	0.99	Cotton (0.06)	Maize (0.39); rice (0.22); sorghum 0.14)		...	0.45
Mtwara	1.38	Cashew nuts (0.29)	Cereals/pulses (0.31); pulses/roots (0.23); cereals (0.17)		n.a	n.a.
Ruvuma	3.24	Tobacco (0.05)	Maize/beans/cassava (0.24); maize (0.23); maize/millet (0.20)		1.3	0.12
Shinyanga	2.66	Cotton (0.13)	Maize (0.37); maize/sorghum (0.14)		1.2	0.28
Singida	4.35		Millet/maize/sorghum (0.73); maize/millet/groundnuts/(0.08); pulses (0.17)		5.7	0.13
Tabora	1.29	Tobacco (0.06)	Maize/groundnuts/cassava (0.50); maize (0.14)		6.2	0.29
Tanga	1.24	Cashews/coconut/cassava (0.46)	Maize, rice, maize/cassava (0.50)		n.a.	n.a.

Source: FAO/IBRD Cooperative Research Project (1975).
Notes: n.a. denotes data not available; ... denotes less than 0.05.

surveys (Collier et al. 1986) attest to this wide-ranging diversity (Tanzania, Agricultural Sample Survey 1989).

POSTINDEPENDENCE ECONOMIC DEVELOPMENTS

At independence in 1961, Tanzania inherited an economic system based on private enterprise under some government regulation. The country was mainly agricultural—producing food for domestic consumption, and sisal, coffee, cotton, and a few other, minor crops for export. Although sisal production was concentrated on European-owned plantations, most of the agricultural products were produced by African farms. Industry was undeveloped, with cotton ginning the major activity. The government guaranteed prices on major marketable crops, and parastatals were involved in export-crop marketing. In the first three years after independence, no major changes were made in the system, and policy was guided by a three-year plan that had been developed before independence.

The first five-year plan, 1964–1969, adopted in 1964, did not change the basic structure of the free-enterprise economy, although the state was supposed to have a more direct role in development. Agriculture was to be the leading sector, evolving by "improvement"—namely, by promoting government-controlled extension, marketing, and credit—and by "transformation"—trying out some pilot, large-scale village settlement schemes designed to promote modern, capital-intensive cultivation methods. The internal demand generated by agricultural growth, it was hoped, would facilitate expansion of import-substituting manufacturing, and some import restrictions were imposed. The plan also emphasized Africanization, by promoting investments in education, and economic independence, by cutting the rigid link of the money supply to the sterling balance and establishing the Central Bank (1966).

The country's economic performance in these early, postindependence years was quite adequate, with an average annual Gross Domestic Product (GDP) growth of more than 6 percent and agricultural growth of about 4 percent. Exports grew rapidly, at about 8 percent annually, and manufacturing also expanded very fast. No major institutional changes occurred until 1967, and the pre-independence, farmer-controlled cooperative movement in agriculture continued to evolve (Coulson 1982).

The period 1967–1973 produced drastic change in economic and social policy in Tanzania. The Arusha declaration on socialism and self-reliance, in February 1967, established as national goals the creation of a socialist state and self-reliance in national development. Socialism was viewed as necessary for the achievement of economic justice and equality. It was deemed important that the state be responsible for meeting basic needs such as health, education, and nutrition. To promote these goals, responsibility for control and expansion of economic and social assets and activities was to be transferred to the state.

Following the declaration, all major firms in production, marketing, distribution, and finance were nationalized. A large number of parastatals were created. Traditional agricultural cooperatives, which had been encouraged since independence, were given rights to enable them to replace private traders. However, the cooperatives were drawn under state control, and in 1975, they were replaced by crop-marketing parastatals. In 1967, the State Trading Corporation was created to monopolize international commerce, and later in the 1970s, private village shops were closed, to be replaced by communal ones.

In rural areas, *ujamaa* (familyhood) villages were promoted as the basic economic and social unit. The idea of these villages was that scattered rural households would be brought closer together, so that social services could be made available, communal activities could be promoted, and farmers would become more socially, politically, and economically active. These ideas also motivated wider national policy. It was, however, the slow pace of voluntary villagization, that by 1973 led to compulsory villagization, and over the next three years large numbers of rural households were forced to relocate in villages. Those villages were not just the physical locations of households. They acquired legal status, as incorporated entities, and were governed by elected councils along with government-appointed civil servants. As legal entities they could manage local trading stores and communal farms.

During the period 1967–1973, decentralization of public administration took place. Responsibility for planning and running public services was given to the regions, and civil servants were transferred from central headquarters to the regions. Export crops were encouraged through credit facilities and projects, and several state farms were established.

Economic performance slowed during this period. According to the best available figures, GDP growth slowed to about 3 percent annually, less than half its pre-1967 rate. Manufacturing grew at 7.6 percent annually, compared with 13.2 percent between 1964 and 1967. Agriculture grew only in line with population growth, at 2.6 percent, for a stagnant per capita output (Stewart 1986), but it continued to provide the subsistence needs of the country. Investment rose quite fast, reaching about 20 percent of GDP by 1973. Public investment, mainly by parastatals, grew to 66 percent of total gross fixed capital formation by 1973. The volume of exports grew by an average of only 1.1 percent annually, while imports increased substantially, at 7.1 percent annually. The result was that by 1970 a previously balanced external trade account showed, for the first time, a significant deficit. By 1973, the external trade deficit had reached 35 percent of total export earnings, or almost 7 percent of GDP. However, the external deficit was easily financed by long-term capital inflows, and the overall current and capital account balances remained positive. During the period, public spending grew by about 16 percent annually, and revenue grew similarly at 15.2 percent, both at rates higher than that of nominal GDP, which grew by 10.7 percent annually. The result was that by 1973 public expenditure (recurrent and development) accounted for 23 percent of GDP, compared with 18 percent in 1968. Of total public expenditures during the period, about 30 percent, on average, was spent for basic needs (education, health, housing, water and electricity, and social security). During the period the public sector experienced small deficits, averaging about 4–5 percent of GDP, which were financed initially by domestic borrowing. However, by 1973 foreign borrowing made up more than half of the financing of the government deficit. Inflation during this period, as measured by the National Consumer Price Index (NCPI) averaged a meager 6.6 percent annually.

The year 1974 marked the first of a series of crises that were to shock the Tanzanian economy throughout the rest of the decade. Year 1973/74 brought drought and a major drop in domestic food supplies, necessitating cereal imports. The first oil shock, in 1973, with the quadrupling of world oil prices, necessitated sharp increases in import expenditures. The government responded by trying to curtail consumer good imports and drawing on the first of the two tranches of the IMF quota. It also sharply increased its domestic borrowing. Net claims of the domestic banking system on government increased by 137 percent in 1974, compared with an average annual growth of 29 percent in the three years prior to 1974. As a consequence, the money supply increased by 22 percent, and inflation, as measured by the NCPI, jumped to 19.5 percent in 1974, compared with an annual average of 6.5 percent for the four years before that.

Import expenditures in 1974, despite the government's pledge to reduce them, increased by 53.5 percent over 1973, while export earnings increased by only 12.6 percent. The current account deficit almost tripled, from 755 million Tanzanian shillings (Tsh) in 1973 to 2,037 million Tsh in 1974. Cereal imports accounted for 22.1 percent of total imports in 1974.

The government's response to this first crisis was to adopt a stabilization policy package that included the following measures (Weaver and Anderson 1981):

1. Major increases in producer food crop prices
2. A 40 percent increase in the minimum wage, and progressively smaller wage increases for higher-echelon civil servants
3. Sharp increases in the retail prices of basic foods
4. Price increases in the main consumer products to cover costs

5. Credit restrictions
6. Import allocation to essential goods
7. Maintenance of public service levels and expansion of education, extension, and rural health programs
8. Moderate curtailment of public infrastructure projects
9. Mobilization of external finance to cover external deficits
10. Tax increases

Good weather returned in the 1974/75 year, but cereal imports continued at a high level in 1975 because of a continued shortfall in domestic marketed supplies. Export earnings were slightly lower in 1975, but import expenditures increased by 5 percent. The government increased long-term external borrowing and also received help from the IMF oil facility and the IMF compensatory finance facility, both relatively low conditionality loans. Nevertheless, public expenditures sharply increased, by 46 percent, although revenues increased by only 31 percent. Financing for the sharply increased domestic deficit (1,862.5 million Tsh in 1975 vs. 851 million Tsh in 1974) came from a 99 percent increase in domestic borrowing and a 169 percent increase in foreign borrowing. Inflation continued at a 26 percent pace in 1975, and in October 1975 the government devalued the shilling by 11 percent. During 1974 and 1975, besides the aid from the IMF, the government received program loans from the World Bank and external aid from a variety of other donors who had been supportive of the government during the first decade of independence. In the 1970s the major bilateral donors were the Scandinavian countries (Sweden, Norway, Denmark, and Finland), the Federal Republic of Germany, and the Netherlands.

In the years 1976 and 1977, the external constraint eased significantly, as world price increases for coffee and tea led to sharp increases in export earnings, and the weather was normal in Tanzania. Those factors, coupled with producer food price increases, brought greater supplies of domestic cereals onto official markets and reduced the need for cereal imports. Import expenditures in 1976 came down by 22 percent, while export earnings increased by 49 percent, leading to an almost-balanced trade account. The favorable export situation continued in 1977, but imports again sharply increased. Because of the continued inflow of long-term capital, however, the external account was quite healthy, and in fact, by the end of 1977, the government had accumulated large foreign reserves.

Major institutional policy changes during the period included the abolition of village primary cooperatives, which until that time had been responsible for collecting and delivering food and export crops to the crop parastatals, and their replacement by parastatal crop authorities. Another major initiative was the implementation of the Basic Industries Strategy (BIS), which sought to foster

import substitution and self-reliance by building capacity in several key industries, such as steel. In 1977, the breakup of the East African Community (Kenya,
Tanzania, and Zambia) added further impetus to a policy of self-reliance that
necessitated heavy investment in infrastructure, such as transportation and
communications.

In 1978, at the recommendation of the IMF and the World Bank the government used much of its accumulated foreign exchange reserves to liberalize
imports, which indeed soared by 43 percent from their already high 1977 level.
Exports, however, fell by 18 percent, as the coffee crisis eased and world prices
declined. The result was a sharply increased trade deficit that depleted foreign
exchange reserves, and external accounts that could not be balanced by capital
inflows. Many of the official loans were transformed into grants in 1978. The
situation became much worse in 1979. Due to the war with Uganda, which started
at the end of 1978 and lasted for most of 1979, the government had to import
substantial amounts of arms and war-related supplies that are estimated to have
cost about US$ 300 million, equivalent to more than half of Tanzania's 1977
export earnings.

In early 1979, the government again resorted to the IMF and drew on its first
tranche for balance-of-payment support. It also appealed for external aid, which
was not easily forthcoming this time in the aftermath of the war. It was at this
stage that more credit was sought from the IMF, and for the first time, major
internal controversies arose regarding specific policy reforms that the IMF requested (Biermann and Campbell 1989). The opposition stemmed from anxiety
about the impact of devaluation, requested cuts in social services, and about
external examination into some types of personal appropriation expenditure.
Negotiations broke off in November 1979. In that year the government expanded
the money supply (by 47 percent), as public expenditure rose by 34 percent and
revenues declined.

Negotiations with the IMF resumed in early 1980, at the time that the second
oil shock of 1979 started taking its toll. Despite its hard conditions, the IMF loan
was the only alternative, since 1980 official marketings of food were poor, and
significant cereal imports had to be obtained. The agreement was not conditional
on a devaluation, however, and that made it politically more palatable. The Fund
agreement released other external funds from the World Bank and elsewhere.
But by December 1980, Tanzania failed to comply with the limitations on public
borrowing and imports, and the IMF agreement was suspended, cutting off
Tanzania from other sources of external finance.

The foreign exchange crisis, which became more acute in 1981, meant that
the government had no other way but to cut imports, which it did, but not until
1982. That action intensified shortages of consumer goods and at the same time

curtailed domestic production of substitutes that relied on imported intermediate inputs. Large excess demand forced many Tanzanians into the parallel markets, where prices of scarce goods soared. Simultaneously, the supply of export crops and food crops to the official parastatals declined, worsening the foreign exchange shortage. The government obtained external commercial credits at high interest rates and quickly accumulated substantial arrears. It used inflationary financing to keep up recurrent public expenditures.

The seriousness of the situation led, in 1981, to the first attempt at internal adjustment, the National Economic Survival Program (NESP). The basic thrust of the NESP was redistributionary. It entailed a cut in salaries and social services, an increase in taxes for salaried workers, and an increase in official producer prices. Prices did not, however, reach the levels of those in the parallel market, and marketed production did not increase. Inflation rose strongly due to monetary expansion.

The short-lived NESP gave rise in 1982 to a Structural Adjustment Program (SAP). This program attempted to implement the recommendations of an impartial technical advisory group of experts funded by the World Bank. The aims of the program were to limit the public deficit by cutting recurrent expenditures, without cutting social and economic services, and to implement efficiency- and productivity-enhancing measures for parastatals, while maintaining employment. Simultaneously the government undertook some small devaluations (10 percent in March 1982; 20 percent in June 1983) but kept tight import controls.

The government anticipated increased IMF and World Bank financing with its program, but this did not come because some of the preconditions for IMF agreement were not met. In the absence of an IMF agreement, most bilateral donors, with the exception of the Scandinavian countries, curtailed aid, and that made the situation worse.

In 1983 and 1984, the budgets were based on the deflationary measures that the IMF had demanded during earlier negotiations. Fundamental changes in orientation also took place in 1984, with the liberalization of domestic food markets and the abandonment of state monopolies and marketing boards. In June 1983, a further devaluation of 23 percent was announced, but that was still much lower than demanded by the IMF, which regarded external trade as the key growth constraint, while the government regarded domestic demand as the constraint. In June 1984, food subsidies were abolished. But although the measures were steps in the right direction, they did not seem to alter any of the fundamental problems; extensive shortages and parallel markets prevailed. An official crackdown on economic saboteurs and racketeers in 1983 only worsened the situation.

The crisis and the lack of foreign exchange finally forced the government to abandon its efforts to deal with the crisis alone, and it again started discussions with the IMF. In August 1986, an agreement was reached based on the adoption of a three-year Economic Recovery Program (ERP), which included several of the earlier IMF conditions, the main elements of which were the following (World Bank 1987a):

1. Trade policies

(a) Exchange rate devaluation, with the goal of an equilibrium rate by 1988

(b) An improved foreign exchange allocation system

(c) Tariff reform

(d) Expansion of the "own funds" import scheme first established in 1984

(e) Improvements in the export retention scheme through expansion of the list of goods allowed to be imported and the narrowing of differentials between retention rates

(f) Aid coordination

2. Fiscal and monetary policies

(a) Expenditure ceilings

(b) Parastatal reforms, such as subsidy reduction and commercial orientation

(c) Credit ceilings

(d) Interest rate adjustments toward a positive real rate

3. Price policies

(a) Reduction of the number items under price control

(b) Large price increases for items controlled

4. Agricultural policies

(a) Producer price increases for export crops, aiming at prices close to 60–70 percent of f.o.b. levels

(b) Marketing reforms, such as food trade liberalization through abandonment of the parastatal monopoly and allowing cooperative unions and large producers to participate in export marketing

(c) Liberalization of input supply and distribution; cooperatives and private organizations to be allowed to carry out these functions

Adoption of the program and agreement with the IMF led to substantial inflows of financing from the World Bank and other donors. The main reforms undertaken under the ERP were (1) a very large exchange rate devaluation (from 17 Tsh/US\$ in early 1986 to 190 Tsh/US\$ in March 1990); (2) establishment of an Open General Licensing Facility (OGL) for foreign exchange allocation;

(3) positive real interest rates; (4) removal of price controls (reducing from 400 to 12 the number of categories of goods controlled); (5) real increases in official producer prices for export crops; (6) agricultural marketing reforms; and (7) establishment of fiscal and monetary targets.

In 1989, the government adopted a new, three-year Economic and Social Action Program (ESAP) that was to run until 1992, and which stresses the social dimensions of adjustment and poverty alleviation, while continuing the pace of economic reforms. The main elements of this program are (1) continued exchange rate adjustment; (2) continued trade policy reforms; (3) public sector management reform, including parastatal reform; (4) financial sector restructuring; (5) reform of agricultural pricing and marketing; (6) industrial restructuring; (7) rehabilitation of infrastructure; (8) rehabilitation of social service delivery capacity; and (9) alleviating impact of environmental degradation. Clearly the government has made substantial changes since the late 1970s and early 1980s, when it strongly resisted reforms implemented under the ERP and envisioned under ESAP.

GENERAL STRUCTURE OF THE MACROECONOMY

According to the latest official figures, the Gross Domestic Product (GDP) at factor cost of Tanzania mainland in 1989 stood at 351.2 billion Tsh. With a mainland population estimated by the 1988 census at 22.5 million people, the per capita GDP in the same year (assuming 2.8 percent population growth) was 15,184 Tsh, or, at the average official exchange rate for the year of 143.38 Tsh/US$, it was equal to US$ 105.90. This would put Tanzania among the poorest countries in the world. In fact, the 1990 World Bank Development Report classifies Tanzania as the world's fourth-poorest country. By comparison, and again using official figures, the current-price GDP in 1978 was 28.58 billion Tsh, and the per capita GDP was 1,678 Tsh. At the then official exchange rate of 7.71 Tsh/US$, that translates to US$ 217.60. This apparent, enormous decline in per capita income and its causes will be one of the objects of our investigation.

Before we proceed, a major caveat is in order. The quality of national accounts statistics in Tanzania appears to have deteriorated during the last decade. In Chapter 5, we present ample evidence to support the view that official statistics are seriously flawed, and hence any conclusions based on them must be viewed as tentative.

In 1988 and 1989, agriculture accounted for 46.6 percent of GDP in constant prices, but for 60 percent of GDP in current prices. Nonagricultural-goods-producing sectors (manufacturing, mining and quarrying, electricity, water, and construction) accounted for 13.4 percent of GDP in constant prices, but only 7.8 percent in current prices. The remaining sectors, comprising private and public services (trade, transport, communications, finance, insurance, real estate, public administration, and other services), accounted for the remaining 40 percent of GDP in constant prices, but only 24.1 percent in current prices. Agriculture has grown in importance in the recent period, while public administration, a sector that had grown substantially in the 1970s, seems to have declined in importance under the economic pressures of the 1980s.

Table 2 exhibits aggregate and sectoral average annual growth rates over the period 1966 to 1989. During the period 1976–1989, the aggregate GDP in real terms grew by 2.1 percent annually, with the most recent four-year period exhibiting the fastest growth, and the five-year period 1980–1985 the smallest, compared with an average growth rate of 3.8 percent for the ten-year period before 1976. Although national accounts data before and after 1976 are not comparable because of a major revision in methods and coverage based on primary 1976 information, it appears from these official statistics that the

TABLE 2

Tanzania: Average Annual Growth Rate of GDP by Sector (percentages).

Economic Activity	1966– 1971	1971– 1976	1976– 1980	1980– 1985	1985– 1989	1976– 1989
Agriculture, forestry, fishing and hunting	1.4	3.7	1.0	3.0	4.8	2.9
Mining and quarrying	0.1	−7.1	−2.5	−1.5	−5.5	−3.3
Manufacturing	8.4	6.5	−1.1	−4.9	2.6	1.5
Electricity and water	9.4	7.8	16.4	2.9	6.3	7.9
Construction	12.2	−1.0	1.8	−5.9	8.1	−0.6
Trade, hotels, and restaurants	3.4	2.4	0.0	−1.3	6.1	1.4
Transportation and communication	11.1	4.9	2.1	−3.4	3.4	0.2
Finance, insurance, real estate, and business services	5.4	3.7	5.1	4.2	4.5	4.6
Public administration and other services	6.8	13.5	8.3	2.6	1.2	3.0
Total industries	4.0	4.3	2.1	0.9	3.9	2.2
GDP at factor cost	3.8	4.3	2.0	0.7	3.9	2.1

Sources: Tanzania Bureau of Statistics (1987); TET (1989, 1990).
Notes: Data for 1966–1975 calculated from Tanzania, Bureau of Statistics (1987)l; 1976–1988 calculated from information in TET (October 1989, January 1990).

post-1976 period has been one of more-or-less continuous crisis. Public administration was the fastest growing sector throughout the 1970s, while construction has been the fastest growing sector since 1985. The overall annual growth rate of official GDP in the 13 years since 1976 (2.1 percent) has been smaller than the 1978–1988 (intercensal) annual population growth rate, which was 2.8 percent.

The major factor affecting the economy in the 1970s and 1980s has been the adverse external position. Although during the 1960s and mid-1970s the external accounts were in balance, with exports closely tracking imports, an external imbalance started in 1978, which grew throughout the next decade and continues today. In 1976, the deficit in the trade balance was 2.2 percent of GNP. In 1978, it jumped to 15.2 percent of GNP. During the crisis period 1980–1984, it declined to about 8 percent of GNP, but by 1988 it had surged to 26 percent of GNP. Another significant aspect of Tanzania's development has been the consistently large share of GDP (around 20 percent) that is absorbed by fixed capital formation, excepting the period 1983–1985. A large proportion of that has been financed by aid from various donors.

In the external accounts, merchandise exports comprised about 60 percent of receipts from exports of goods and services until 1984. Merchandise imports constituted an even larger proportion of imports of goods and services, larger than 90 percent. A sizable proportion of total external receipts all through the period, especially after 1985, is accounted for by current transfers from abroad. Before 1985, these were mainly official. Since 1985, however, the share of transfers in external receipts has increased substantially accounting for 57 percent and 60 percent of total export receipts in 1987 and 1988. This compares with a range of 20–25 percent in the period before 1985. The rise reflects increasing imports under own-funds since 1984, for which a balancing credit item is added in the external inflows category under transfers.

In the pre-1985 period, most of the financing of the current account deficit was through capital transfers. Since 1985, however, a significant amount has been financed by net external borrowing. This is bound to create serious problems of debt servicing. In fact, since 1984 the outflows on the capital account of the balance of payments have been close to or larger than inflows, although in the pre-1984 period the inflows were substantially higher.

Tanzania's six top export earners are agricultural primary products—coffee, cotton, sisal, tea, tobacco, and cashew nuts. Together they account for about 60 percent of total export earnings. Since the mid-seventies, the volumes of all six have declined significantly, with declines ranging from 10 percent (coffee) to as much as 80 percent (sisal).

The bulk of imported items consists of capital and intermediate goods, with consumer goods accounting for only about 20 percent of total imports. Food imports account for 40–60 percent of consumer imports. Very few imports of nonessential, consumer-incentive goods seem to have been officially recorded before 1988.

Table 3 indicates Laspeyres volume indices for exports and imports, with base weights for the year 1976. It is quite clear from the table that compared with the early and late 1970s, the decade of the 1980s saw a significant reduction in the officially recorded quantity of exports. The reduction affected all export categories. A slightly different pattern seems to have been followed by imports. There seems to have been a massive decline in the early 1980s, particularly of capital and consumer goods. Imports of intermediate goods (among which oil products feature prominently) increased substantially until 1981 and then declined precipitously until 1986. It was only in 1988 that imports of these goods increased in value to a level similar to that of 1980. The trends obvious in Table 3 do not change significantly if one changes the base year for the calculations of the index weights.

In Table 4 we exhibit unit value indices for exports and imports and the barter and income terms of trade from 1974 to 1986. With the exception of 1977, which was the year of the world coffee boom, the barter terms of trade (defined as the ratio of the unit value of exports to the unit value of imports) seem to have declined, despite the fact that oil prices have declined since the second oil shock of 1979. Given the decline in the volume of exports evident in Table 3, it is only natural that the income terms of trade (defined as the ratio of the value of exports divided by the unit import value) would exhibit an even steeper decline; this is evident from the final row of Table 4.

In 1987, 55 percent of all exports were destined for western Europe, a larger share than in 1980 (48 percent). Germany, UK, Netherlands, Italy, and Finland currently absorb the bulk of exports to western Europe. Countries in Asia and Oceania absorb another 25 percent of Tanzania's exports, with India, Japan, Singapore, Taiwan, and Hong Kong as the largest markets. Another 12 percent of exports go to African countries, with Kenya and Algeria accounting in 1987 for about half of that. The United States accounts for a meager 2 percent of Tanzania's exports, a share that is half of what it was in the early 1980s. The geographical pattern of imports resembles that of exports, with 57 percent originating in western Europe, 19 percent in Asia and Oceania, 12 percent in the Middle East (largely oil products), and a meager 5 percent from the United States.

The public sector is a dominant aspect of the Tanzanian economy, accounting for a large portion of the monetary economy. In the early years after independence the public sector was kept small, and the private sector functioned much as it did before independence. In 1967, with the Arusha declaration, the public sector started becoming heavily involved in all aspects of the Tanzanian econ-

TABLE 3

Tanzania: Laspeyres Volume Indices for Domestic Exports and Direct Imports, 1974–1986 (1976=100).

	1974	1975	1976	1977	1978	1979	1980	1981	1982	1983	1984	1985	1986
Exports (all)	86.18	90.13	100.00	80.50	73.17	76.15	73.22	69.45	68.97	55.46	58.00	58.95	56.23
Food, drink, and tobacco	75.71	93.72	100.00	81.81	74.81	78.81	75.91	72.70	74.13	56.54	64.24	70.70	66.27
Raw materials, including fuel	99.76	90.96	100.00	73.48	73.47	68.38	62.66	67.26	62.24	59.02	47.21	38.74	39.10
Manufactured products	81.81	75.79	100.00	91.92	64.97	80.52	84.69	59.02	62.62	40.74	58.44	55.83	36.16
Imports (all)	132.82	101.73	100.00	88.82	113.39	85.96	83.64	77.73	58.19	46.83	71.08	72.87	66.42
Capital goods	249.41	158.08	100.00	91.30	76.91	52.78	84.98	66.20	62.94	65.16	100.83	116.53	105.30
Intermediate goods	90.60	81.65	100.00	88.97	158.45	140.94	126.68	181.61	63.30	53.84	77.18	88.36	72.14
Consumer goods	130.60	87.71	100.00	87.57	119.47	81.88	72.84	57.71	55.26	37.28	59.85	49.85	46.47

Source: Tanzania, Bureau of Statistics, "Foreign Trade Statistics, 1987" (March 1989).

TABLE 4

Tanzania: Laspeyres Unit Value Indices for Domestic Exports and Imports by Commodity Group (1976=100).

	1974	1975	1976	1977	1978	1979	1980	1981	1982	1983	1984	1985	1986
Exports (all)	76.44	73.68	100.00	139.02	120.64	135.29	159.00	168.61	150.21	188.53	256.35	245.70	457.14
Food, drink, and tobacco	58.10	63.54	100.00	151.62	123.44	127.03	141.98	159.62	139.59	173.54	236.29	228.88	498.67
Raw materials, including fuel	104.29	81.54	100.00	121.18	99.56	130.47	166.00	176.07	163.70	204.71	291.79	267.86	333.80
Manufactured products	109.29	113.92	100.00	113.10	166.01	201.77	245.25	202.95	174.68	236.87	277.25	286.92	572.75
Imports (all)	78.44	99.28	100.00	120.21	128.29	177.49	234.60	252.50	331.09	326.59	335.07	431.56	761.50
Capital goods	66.87	109.26	100.00	131.81	194.24	255.79	359.88	390.21	458.99	401.22	306.13	419.11	685.23
Intermediate goods	73.07	91.75	100.00	126.35	117.11	144.65	140.66	126.08	289.93	221.15	241.09	336.04	748.52
Consumer goods	86.27	97.80	100.00	109.14	95.23	150.14	215.14	246.11	276.80	337.32	405.75	493.37	809.78
Barter terms of trade	97.45	74.21	100.00	115.65	94.04	76.22	67.77	66.78	45.37	57.73	76.51	56.23	60.03
Income terms of trade	87.60	62.50	100.00	91.25	69.82	60.34	49.41	45.96	30.68	31.62	44.37	34.56	35.32

Source: Tanzania, Bureau of Statistics, "Foreign Trade Statistics, 1987" (March 1989).

omy. Through nationalization, the state acquired control of a significant proportion of the productive assets of the nonagricultural sector, as well as the large-scale agricultural sector. In subsequent years, parastatals proliferated to the point that by the mid-1980s there were 425 of them in Tanzania, a number comparable only to countries such as Brazil and Mexico with GDPs 50 and 35 times, respectively, that of Tanzania (World Bank 1988).

Table 5 presents a summary of central government revenues and expenditure for the period 1975–1976 to the most recent available year. It can be noticed that ever since 1976 there has been a public-sector deficit, amounting to as much as 14.5 percent, and never less than 7.5 percent, of GDP at market prices. In the composition of public expenditure, current expenditure has been kept quite high, while development expenditure since 1982 has declined to about half of its pre-1980 share of GDP. A large share of total public expenditures is for internal transfers, such as interest on public debt and subsidies to parastatals.

Table 6 exhibits the composition of public revenues and expenditure from 1975–1976 to 1986–1987. Trade taxes (import and export duties) constitute a small portion of total public revenue, declining from a high of about 21 percent in 1978–1979 to only 6 percent of revenues in 1982–1983, to recover to 13 percent in 1986–1987 and an estimated 15 percent in 1988–1989. It is quite noticeable that in contrast to many primary exporting countries, export tax revenues since 1980 are almost negligible. However, export producers are heavily taxed implicitly, as will be seen later, with the implicit revenue being largely absorbed as parastatal marketing costs. The bulk of public revenue comes from consumption and excise taxes, as well as personal and income taxes.

Turning to the composition of public expenditure, the most noticeable trends in the eighties are the increase in the share of general public services (mainly administration), the sharp decline in the shares of education, health, and economic services to about half their 1975–1976 shares, and the quadrupling of the share of servicing the public debt.

The importance of the public sector is underestimated by the data in Table 5. Parastatals production accounted for about 13 percent of GDP by 1985, a share that had grown rapidly from 7 percent in 1967 and 9 percent in 1972. In manufacturing, parastatals accounted for about 47 percent of value added and 47 percent of wage employment. In all sectors except agriculture, parastatals account for more than 20 percent of sector value added and an equal or larger share of wage employment. When that is added to the 13 percent share of public administration in the GDP, we obtain a combined share of the public sector in reported GDP of about 26 percent.

The importance of the public sector is reflected in the structure of formal wage employment. "Formal employment" refers to people working in formal estab-

TABLE 5

Tanzania: Summary of Central Government Operation, 1976–1987.

	1976	1977	1978	1979	1980	1981	1982	1983	1984	1985	1986	1987
Percent of GDP at market prices												
Current revenue	18.53	19.41	19.34	19.01	18.86	18.64	18.97	19.70	18.97	16.12	15.98	18.05
Current expenditure	18.32	18.38	19.94	20.18	20.12	22.98	23.27	20.80	20.61	19.79	21.36	22.57
Surplus/(deficit)	0.21	1.03	(0.60)	(1.17)	(1.26)	(4.34)	(4.30)	(1.10)	(1.64)	(3.68)	(5.39)	(5.55)
Development expenditure	11.26	11.39	12.56	13.69	11.80	10.14	8.22	6.45	6.00	4.88	5.45	6.38
Total surplus/(deficit)	(11.05)	(10.36)	(13.16)	(14.86)	(13.06)	(14.48)	(12.52)	(7.54)	(7.64)	(8.55)	(10.78)	(11.93)

Sources: World Bank, "Tanzania Public Expenditure Review," Report No. 7559-TA (May 22, 1989); and authors' computations.

Note: GDP data are reported in calendar year while public expenditure data are in fiscal years. To compute the ratios to GDP indicated in the table for each calendar year, the average of the two adjacent fiscal years was used in the numerator of the relevant fractions.

TABLE 6

Tanzania: Composition of Revenue and Expenditure, 1975/1976/–1986/1987 (as percentage of total revenue and percentage of public expenditure).

	1975–1976	1976–1977	1977–1978	1978–1979	1979–1980	1980–1981	1981–1982	1982–1983	1983–1984	1984–1985	1985–1986	1986–1987
Revenues												
Import duties	11.7	6.2	10.1	13.9	11.0	7.7	6.9	5.9	6.2	8.4	7.5	13.0
Export duties	4.1	16.1	8.9	7.0	6.3	2.5	0.2	0.1	0.1	0.1	0.0	0.0
Consumption and excise duties	42.4	33.6	36.4	40.6	40.2	51.3	52.5	49.5	51.6	55.9	52.1	53.4
Income and personal taxes	28.4	26.8	23.1	29.5	33.0	32.2	33.2	30.8	26.5	25.8	30.9	23.0
Other taxes and income sources	13.4	17.2	21.6	9.0	6.2	7.3	13.7	15.6	15.6	9.9	9.5	10.6
Expenditures												
General public service	15.8	17.4	16.0	16.0	14.7	16.4	17.9	17.1	22.0	29.9	28.9	25.5
Defense	12.2	12.3	13.5	24.6	7.7	11.0	12.5	13.3	12.8	13.9	10.4	14.6
Education	14.1	13.6	13.3	11.3	11.2	11.8	12.5	13.2	11.7	7.3	7.3	6.4
Health	7.1	7.1	6.7	5.3	5.0	5.4	5.4	5.1	5.5	5.0	4.3	3.7
Social security and welfare	0.4	0.2	0.2	0.3	0.4	0.3	0.3	0.3	0.3	0.5	0.2	0.3
Housing and community amenities	1.8	1.2	0.9	0.8	1.0	1.2	1.0	1.1	1.0	1.0	0.6	0.4
Other community social services	2.4	2.3	1.7	1.8	1.9	2.1	2.1	2.0	2.0	2.2	0.5	0.5
Economic services	36.9	38.1	34.1	35.1	36.1	34.8	29.8	27.0	26.0	24.2	22.8	16.5
Other purposes	9.2	7.9	13.6	4.8	22.0	16.9	18.5	21.0	18.8	16.1	25.0	32.1
Public debt	7.3	5.9	7.0	3.9	7.5	11.4	17.8	20.2	18.1	15.4	24.2	31.4

Sources: World Bank, "Tanzania Public Expenditure Review," Report No. 7559-TA (May 22, 1989).

lishments, and hence does not count smallholder agriculture or small-scale, unincorporated, "informal" sector activities, which account for the great bulk of employment in the country. In 1965, government employment accounted for 27 percent of the total formal wage employment of about 250,000, and parastatals for 5 percent, for a combined total of 32 percent. In 1970, the joint share rose to 59 percent (out of a total of 376,000); in 1976 to 66 percent (out of a total of 481,000); and in 1984 it stood at a dominating 77 percent (of a total of 633,000). Almost all the growth in formal employment in the country since 1970 occurred in the public sector, with the number employed in government and parastatals more than doubling over the period, while formal employment in the private sector grew very little. Of the total of 622,000 formal-sector employees in 1981, 120,000 were listed by the Bureau of Statistics as casual. Agriculture (plantations and large state and private farms), occupied 119,000 employees, industry 135,000, construction 46,000, transportation 55,000, and all the other services remaining 266,000.

The formal financial sector in Tanzania is not large. Apart from the Bank of Tanzania, which is the central bank, the commercial banking system is composed of one major mainland bank (the National Bank of Commerce) and a few smaller, specialized ones (Cooperative Rural Development Bank, Tanzania Investment Bank, Tanzania Housing Bank, Tanganyika Post Office Savings Bank, Tanganyika Development Finance Company Ltd.). The major function of the banking sector has been to lend to parastatals and to the government, with very little lending extended to the private sector. The bulk of the lending that is reported as going to the private sector in fact goes to cooperatives. So almost all bank lending in Tanzania is directed to the public sector. This has consequences for the causes of inflation, as will be seen later.

3

MACROECONOMIC POLICY AND PERFORMANCE

To understand the nature of current adjustment efforts in Tanzania, it is necessary to review analytically the evolution of macroeconomic and other key policies and government responses over the last two decades. There are four periods that seem to characterize economic developments and policies in Tanzania. The first covers the period from independence in 1961 to the Arusha declaration in 1967. The second extends from 1967 to 1973. The third covers the period from 1974 to 1982, and the final one concerns the recent years, from 1982 to now. The last period could be further subdivided into 1982–1985, when Tanzania attempted to adjust without external help, and the period after 1986, since the agreement with the IMF. Each subperiod is characterized by a different set of policies and external influences and hence must be examined separately. Given our interest in structural adjustment and the recovery, our natural focus will be on the last two of the four periods mentioned, particularly the most recent, since the earlier ones have been covered extensively in other literature. Our effort will be to understand the extent to which economic performance has been related to policies and external shocks and how the government and the economy of Tanzania have responded.

Our analysis in this chapter starts with a review of debate on the origins and causes of the economic crisis. The second section reviews recent macroeconomic developments and existing interpretations of the trends. The third section reviews the debate concerning devaluation, the policy that has been the source of the most controversy in the context of stabilization and adjustment. In the subsequent section we examine the financing of the domestic and external deficit. In the final section we make new estimates of the unobserved, "second" economy in Tanzania and provide a picture of the total economy, observed and unobserved.

INTERPRETATION OF THE CRISIS AND THE ADJUSTMENT DEBATE

There has been wide debate concerning both the causes of the crisis in Tanzania and the appropriate responses. In this section we shall review some of the major arguments, providing wherever possible some new elements.

Our earlier review of the structure of the economy and the evolution of policy from independence until the late 1970s shows a continuing effort by the government to control the economic forces and processes in the country through direct control of all spheres of economic activity. The underlying rationale for this attitude was that the best way to achieve a fast pace of economic and social development was to rely on a top-down system of economic and social control and modernization through adoption of foreign technology. These attitudes were manifested in the nationalization of private firms, the abolition of producer cooperatives, the villagization campaign, the substitution of state production and marketing of both agricultural and nonagricultural products, and the adoption of the largely foreign-exchange-intensive Basic Industries Strategy. The result of these policies, by the late 1970s, was an economic structure in which activity was supply constrained and depended quite heavily on imports for its proper performance. Despite efforts at diversification, agriculture and even up to the present, remains dominant as a generator of income and, more crucially, foreign exchange.

Ndulu (1988) has aptly summarized the main macro features of the Tanzanian economy. Besides the overwhelming importance of agriculture and the supply-constrained, import-dependent nature of production, the links among the fiscal deficit, the balance of payments, and the money supply process are key. While in the late 1960s and early 1970s, the monetary base was backed mainly by foreign asset holdings, by the late 1970s, almost 90 percent of the expansion of the monetary base was due to net claims on government. This latter development was the result of high domestic credit demand from the public sector, including the parastatals. In 1978, the 1965 Bank of Tanzania Act was amended to lift the limit on government borrowing, which had been 25 percent of recurrent revenue. This amendment allowed sharp and inflationary increases in the monetary base, in order to accommodate the mounting deficits.

The final major feature identified by Ndulu is the contrast between the flex-price nature of the food markets, and the fix-price nature of many of the nonfood markets, especially those for domestic manufactures and services. Prices in the latter sectors were largely administered and insulated from world market developments.

In terms of political economy, besides the ruling party (CCM) and the government, Ndulu identifies three major interest groups, namely, the largely urban-based wage/salary earners, including government employees; the commercial entrepreneurs; and the rural peasantry. Policy in the 1960s and 1970s, while emphasizing modern, urban-centered development, tried explicitly to benefit the peasants through provision of social services at the expense of commercial entrepreneurs. During the late 1970s, however, budgetary pressures led to formal-sector wage restraints and sharp declines in the real incomes of urban wage earners, while peasants were better insulated through the growth of parallel markets. The commercial entrepreneurs, mostly traders, gained significantly, however, as the erosion of government controls led to massive parallel and black markets (some legal, but mostly not) both domestic and external.

Bienenfeld (1989) has summarized the process that led to the crisis of the early 1980s as the gradual construction of a geographically dispersed, import-intensive, urbanized economy, critically dependent on expanding agricultural surpluses to feed the urban population and earn foreign exchange. The crisis arose because the agricultural surplus did not grow fast enough.

There has been wide debate concerning the causes of the crisis that led to the first IMF negotiations in 1979–1980 and subsequent adjustment efforts. There are those that argue that the major causes were mainly external, such as the oil shocks, the drought, and the Uganda war (Green, Rwegasira, and van Arkadie 1980), while others suggest that the causes were mostly internal and due to economic mismanagement (Sharpley 1985; Lofchie 1989).

In Table 7, we display the Tanzanian balance of payments in U.S. dollars for 1970–1988 as reported by the IMF. The number that gives a clear picture of the evolution of the crisis is the basic balance, that is, the sum of the balance of trade in goods and services and net long-term capital inflows. It can be clearly seen from Table 7 that 1974 and 1978 produced the first major external crises.

The 1974 crisis appears to have been caused by a sudden, 50 percent increase in import expenditures (in U.S. dollars), while exports increased by only 10 percent. In the subsequent three years, 1975–1977, export earnings increased due to the coffee boom, and import expenditure declined. In 1978, a sharp drop in merchandise export earnings, simultaneous with a 53 percent increase in import expenditure, created the new crisis. While the high import expenditures in 1978 and 1979 can be rationalized in terms of the spending of foreign exchange

TABLE 7

Tanzania: Balance of Payments, 1970–1988.

	1970	1971	1972	1973	1974	1975	1976	1977	1978	1979
1. Exports of goods and services	321.8	349.7	411.7	455.8	488.4	391.3	633.2	656.4	625.2	697.2
2. Total transfers	12.8	5.8	-4.1	4.9	49.2	102.3	54.6	114.7	164.0	174.8
Private unrequited transfers (net)	11.1	3.5	-14.5	-14.4	-11.4	11.5	11.5	19.4	23.1	29.5
Official unrequited transfers (net)	1.7	2.3	10.4	19.3	60.6	90.8	43.1	95.3	140.9	145.3
3. Imports of goods and services	-370.2	-455.2	-473.3	-568.2	-822.9	-823.6	-722.3	-843.5	-1,262.6	-1,218.5
4. Current account surplus (1+2+3)	-35.6	-99.7	-65.7	-107.5	-285.3	-330.0	-34.5	-72.4	-473.4	-346.5
5. Long-term capital inflows (net)	71.6	137.7	108.3	155.3	117.6	170.5	102.4	100.7	136.0	225.4
6. Basic balance (4+5)	36.0	38.0	42.6	47.8	-167.7	-159.5	67.9	28.3	-337.4	-121.1
7. Short-term capital inflows (net)	-7.8	-37.7	-8.0	-18.0	-4.6	11.3	-18.4	20.9	60.7	-75.1
8. Exceptional financing					7.1	35.9	0.8	21.6	63.5	98.9

	1980	1981	1982	1983	1984	1985	1986	1987	1988
1. Exports of goods and services	686.7	884.8	530.2	486.3	480.3	432.8	456.6	447.1	499.4
2. Total transfers	128.7	130.3	119.2	103.4	158.6	456.3	474.1	707.0	722.0
Private unrequited transfers (net)	21.8	22.6	25.4	18.8	62.1	233.3	250.6	230.0	232.0
Official unrequited transfers (net)	106.9	107.7	93.8	84.6	96.5	223.0	223.5	477.0	490.0
3. Imports of goods and services	-1,249.0	-1,187.0	-1,030.4	-785.7	-853.4	-1,036.5	-1,105.0	-1,419.4	-1,479.8
4. Current account surplus (1+2+3)	-433.6	-171.9	-381.0	-196.0	-214.5	-147.4	-174.3	-265.3	-258.4
5. Long-term capital inflows (net)	166.3	204.5	167.9	177.7	89.7	-39.5	-24.7	-36.5	31.8
6. Basic balance (4+5)	-267.3	32.6	-213.1	-18.3	-124.8	-186.9	-199.0	-301.8	-226.6
7. Short-term capital inflows (net)	-85.8	57.0	157.6	-136.6	-108.1	-410.9	895.6	4.4	-5.9
8. Exceptional financing	270.1	89.1	45.6	321.3	305.8	469.4	-657.3	124.2	163.9

Source: IMF International Financial Statistics (various issues). Inflows are described by positive numbers, while outflows by negative.

reserves accumulated in 1977, the Uganda war, and the 1979 oil price hike, it is hard to see why import expenditure stayed at a continued high level until 1981. In fact, apart from a small decline in 1981, it was not until 1982 that import expenditures were seriously curtailed. Meanwhile export earnings seemed to be doing quite well until 1981, but from 1982 on, they took a sharp dive from which they have not as yet recovered. When we examine the volume and value indices of merchandise trade exhibited earlier in Tables 3 and 4, it can be seen that although the barter terms of trade have turned against Tanzania between the "non-crisis," "non-boom" year 1975 and the early 1980s, it was the decline in the volume of exports that seems to have been a key element in the decline in export earnings.

The well-documented decline in total and certainly per capita, export crop production contemporaneous with an increase in total food crop production (see Chapter 5) have been rationalized by several analysts (Odegaard 1985; Ellis 1982) in terms of declining official producer prices for export crops, both in real terms and relative to those of food crops (especially in the parallel, uncontrolled markets), the declining efficiency and resultant rising marketing margins of the official marketing system, which resulted in large transfers from peasants to the state (Ellis 1983), and by the unavailability of incentive consumer goods in rural areas due to official rationing (Bevan 1989).

The response of the government of Tanzania to the major shocks of 1978 and 1979 was slow in coming. Current spending continued at a rapid pace. While during the period 1976/77 to 1979/80 current expenditures grew by an average of 13.9 percent annually, in the next three years they grew by an average of 23.7 percent annually, despite the foreign exchange crisis and the fact that recurrent revenues grew by only 18.7 percent annually. Development expenditures also continued at a high rate as a share of GDP, and it was only in 1982 that they were severely curtailed. Thus the current deficit grew from a small 1.2 percent of GDP in 1979 to 4.3 percent of GDP in 1982. The total government deficit, which reached a high of 14.9 percent of GDP during the crisis year 1979, declined only marginally to 12.5 percent by 1982 and was not seriously cut until 1983. The portion of the fiscal deficit that was financed through bank borrowing increased from 8 percent in 1977–1978 to 50 percent in 1979–1980. The net claims of the banking system on the government grew by an average 19.5 percent annually between 1976 and 1978. They jumped by 73 percent in 1979 and by an average of close to 30 percent annually for the next three years. It thus appears that the government attempted to keep up demand in the face of a supply shock.

The result was a sharp increase in inflation. As measured by the National Consumer Price Index (NCPI), prices that had increased by 6.9, 11.6, 6.6, and 12.9 percent in 1976, 1977, 1978, and 1979, respectively, jumped by 30.3 percent in 1980 and kept growing at a rate higher than 25 percent for the next several years. At the same time, the exchange rate kept appreciating because the government steadfastly refused to make more than token adjustments in the nominal exchange rate. The result was a sharp increase in the parallel market premium on foreign exchange and hence further evasion of the official markets.

In Table 8 we exhibit the official and parallel market exchange rates, as well as estimates of the real exchange rate (column 9) computed by a simplification of the IMF method, as explained in Appendix A. It is evident from that table that the parallel market premium (column 6)—that is, the percent by which the parallel market rate exceeds the official rate—jumped to more than 150 percent in 1980 and continued at levels above 200 percent until 1987. The computations of the real exchange rate (column 9) show a significant appreciation of the Tanzanian shilling starting in 1981 and continuing until 1986, the first year of the ERP.

It thus appears that while external shocks were instrumental in initiating the crisis, it was largely weak internal adjustment efforts, coupled perhaps with optimism concerning the continuation of foreign capital and aid inflows, that eventually led to an uncontrollable situation. Underlying causes were the structural weaknesses of the economy—reliance on agricultural exports for foreign exchange generation, import dependence by the industrial sector, and the inefficiencies of the parastatal marketing sector.

MACROECONOMIC PERFORMANCE UNDER ADJUSTMENT

The history of adjustment efforts in Tanzania over the past decade reveals strong efforts at expenditure control, but consistently excessive optimism in economic targets. Ndulu (1988) presented tables contrasting SAP targets and the actual performance of several macro indicators over the years of the first adjustment effort, 1982–1985. In terms of fiscal targets, performance during that period was better than planned. However, increases in external resources, in export earnings as well as external loans and grants, fell far short of what was expected. The serious external gap that resulted pushed the government to resort to inflationary domestic finance, and money supply grew faster than planned in all but the first year of the SAP.

The targets set for the 1986/87 to 1988/89 ERP were quite ambitious: an average rate of economic growth of 4–5 percent annually, a progressive reduction in the rate of inflation to less than 10 percent in 1988/89 from over 30 percent in 1985, improvements in the external position through faster export growth, increases in utilization rates in manufacturing from 20–30 percent in 1985 to 60–70 percent by 1989, and increases in export earnings of 16 percent annually.

TABLE 8

Tanzania: Official Parallel and Real Exchange Rates, 1965–1989 (Tsh/US$).

	Official Rate End of Period (1)	Official Rate Period Average (2)	Parallel Rate End of Period (3)	Parallel Rate Period Average (4)	Ratio (3)/(1) End of Period (5)	Ratio (4)/(2) Period Average (6)	Real Exchange Rate[a] vis-à-vis $ (index 1969=100) (7)	Other Currency Correct. Factor (index 1969=100) (8)	Real Exchange Rate[a] (Index 1969=100) (7)x(8) (9)	Nominal Equivalent Exchange Rate (Tsh/US$) (10)	Ratio (10)/(2) Period Average (11)	Ratio (10)/(4) Period Average (12)
1965	7.143	7.143	8.52	n.a.	1.193	n.a.	143.21	1.04	149.41	4.78	0.67	n.a.
1966	7.143	7.143	8.64	8.80	1.210	1.232	134.77	1.05	141.65	5.04	0.71	0.57
1967	7.143	7.143	8.68	8.70	1.215	1.218	122.38	1.00	122.30	5.84	0.82	0.67
1968	7.143	7.143	8.25	8.50	1.155	1.190	110.51	0.99	109.93	6.50	0.91	0.76
1969	7.143	7.143	9.10	8.70	1.274	1.218	100.00	1.00	99.99	7.14	1.00	0.82
1970	7.143	7.143	10.45	10.10	1.463	1.414	102.92	1.00	102.93	6.94	0.97	0.69
1971	7.143	7.143	15.00	11.60	2.100	1.624	101.56	1.11	112.91	6.33	0.89	0.55
1972	7.143	7.143	15.40	15.20	2.156	2.128	97.38	1.13	109.79	6.51	0.91	0.43
1973	6.900	7.021	13.45	14.53	1.949	2.070	90.99	1.22	111.26	6.20	0.88	0.43
1974	7.143	7.135	14.00	13.46	1.960	1.886	87.05	1.29	112.28	6.36	0.89	0.47
1975	8.264	7.367	25.00	20.58	3.025	2.794	87.31	1.25	109.24	7.56	1.03	0.37
1976	8.324	8.377	20.40	21.93	2.451	2.618	87.27	1.27	111.10	7.49	0.89	0.34
1977	7.960	8.289	15.05	21.47	1.891	2.590	79.50	1.47	116.67	6.82	0.82	0.32
1978	7.415	7.712	11.75	13.07	1.585	1.695	71.34	1.63	116.31	6.38	0.83	0.49
1979	8.221	8.217	13.50	11.98	1.642	1.458	77.41	1.57	121.50	6.77	0.82	0.57
1980	8.182	8.197	26.50	21.02	3.239	2.564	67.21	1.57	105.59	7.75	0.95	0.37
1981	8.322	8.284	24.35	26.57	2.926	3.207	60.15	1.33	80.21	10.38	1.25	0.39
1982	9.567	9.283	29.15	32.60	3.047	3.512	56.82	1.22	69.15	13.83	1.49	0.42

(Table continues on the following page.)

TABLE 8
(continued)

	Official Rate End of Period (1)	Official Rate Average Period (2)	Parallel Rate End of Period (3)	Parallel Rate Period Average (4)	Ratio (3)/(1) End of Period (5)	Ratio (4)/(2) Period Average (6)	Real Exchange Rate[a] vis-à-vis $ (index 1969=100) (7)	Other Currency Correct. Factor (index 1969=100) (8)	Real Exchange Rate[a] (Index 1969=100) (7)x(8) (9)	Nominal Equivalent Exchange Rate (Tsh/US$) (10)	Ratio (10)/(2) Average Period (11)	Ratio (10)/(4) Period Average (12)
1983	12.457	11.143	50.00	39.62	4.014	3.556	60.16	1.13	67.87	18.35	1.65	0.46
1984	18.105	15.292	70.00	57.08	3.866	3.733	67.38	0.98	66.06	27.41	1.79	0.48
1985	16.499	17.472	150.00	100.80	9.091	5.769	47.42	1.20	57.08	28.90	1.65	0.29
1986	51.719	32.698	180.00	165.00	3.480	5.046	114.39	1.40	160.07	32.31	0.99	0.20
1987	83.717	64.260	190.00	180.00	2.270	2.801	147.76	1.69	250.39	33.43	0.52	0.19
1988	125.000	99.292	230.00	210.00	1.840	2.115	174.84	1.58	276.43	45.22	0.46	0.22
1989	192.300	143.377	300.00	250.00	1.560	1.744	227.29	1.48	337.01	57.06	0.40	0.23

Sources: P. P. Cowitt (ed.), World Currency Yearbook, International Currency Analysis (Brooklyn, N.Y., 1985); Pick's Currency Yearbook (Pick Publishing Corp, N.Y. various issues); IMF International Financial Statistics (various issues); Bagachwa et al., 1990, "Tanzania: A Study of Non-Traditional Exports," University of Dar es Salaam, January, and authors' computations.
[a] A decline implies appreciation.

In terms of official GDP growth, the performance since 1985 has been one of revival, with agriculture leading the way. Table 2 exhibits growth rates of real GDP in the various sectors from which it is clear that since 1985 all sectors, with the exception of mining and quarrying, have improved on their 1980–1985 performance. For 1989, first estimates indicated a real GDP growth rate of 4.4 percent, with all sectors growing, agriculture growing at 4.6 percent, and manufacturing at 5.1 percent. Despite this growth, however, in 1989 only agriculture, electricity and water, commerce, finance, and public administration achieved real product levels higher than those of 1980.

On the external account front, as can be seen from Table 7, the target of 16 percent growth in export earnings was not attained. Total export earnings from the six major agricultural exports were at their lowest level of the decade in 1989, at US$ 180.4 million, after a brief revival in 1986 due to a small coffee boom, compared with US$ 264 million in 1980 and US$ 196.1 million in 1985, at the depth of the crisis. Among the major export crops, only cotton appears to have exhibited a strong export volume increase, with the other crops not showing increasing trends. This outcome might be related to the fact that very little price marketing liberalization in agricultural exports took place until 1990. Nontraditional exports, however, especially manufactured products, have staged a strong recovery. From a continuous decline between 1980 and 1985, from US$ 241.5 million to US$ 90.5 million, this category has recovered to US$ 214.8 million in 1989. This recovery was no doubt aided by the generous export retention scheme instituted under the ERP. Imports, on the other hand, surpassed their 1980 level in 1982, and because of donor support as well as the own-fund import scheme, they have stayed quite close to their targeted levels.

On the inflation front, performance has not lived up to the targets. The changes in the NCPI for the years 1986, 1987, 1988, and 1989 were 32.4, 30.0, 31.2, and 25.9 percent, respectively. This is no different from the performance during 1980–1985, when annual inflation ranged between 26 and 36 percent.

The ambitious targets for industrial production also did not materialize. The doubling or tripling of capacity utilization envisioned in 1986 implied a corresponding increase in output. But of 31 industries whose output for the period 1980–1988 is reported in the 1989 Bank of Tanzania's *Economic and Operations Report*, only 15 exhibited an increase in production between 1985 and 1988, and of these only 10 experienced a total increase of more than 50 percent over the three-year period, despite the fact that the bulk of imports during that time were intermediate goods and machinery.

In Table 9 we summarize some of the recent sectoral and macro developments. The significant growth in real GDP observed since 1983 is due mostly to the growth in agricultural production, as has already been mentioned, while manu-

TABLE 9

Tanzania: Recent Macroeconomic Developments.

	1976	1977	1978	1979	1980	1981	1982
GDP real index	100.0	100.4	102.5	105.5	108.2	107.6	108.3
GDP agriculture total index	100.0	101.1	99.5	100.2	104.1	105.1	106.6
GDP manufacturing real index	100.0	94.0	97.1	100.4	95.4	84.7	82.0
GDP construction real index	100.0	103.5	88.6	99.4	105.4	100.7	105.2
GDP trade real index	100.0	98.0	98.5	100.0	100.0	96.0	94.0
GDP public administration real index	100.0	106.6	128.0	139.0	136.1	151.6	151.8
Gross fixed capital formation real index	100.0	110.9	110.7	124.1	108.8	112.5	117.3
GFCF public real index	100.0	114.0	104.2	110.9	107.2	108.0	112.9
GFCF private real index	100.0	106.7	119.4	141.7	111.0	118.7	123.2
GFCF buildings real index	100.0	115.3	102.0	117.1	119.1	141.2	125.3
GFCF other works real index	100.0	96.7	79.7	88.5	97.0	76.2	91.8
GFCF machinery and equipment real index	100.0	118.1	133.3	148.9	112.4	124.7	130.3
GDP deflators (1976=100)							
GDP at factor cost total	100.0	118.2	128.7	141.4	159.9	188.4	224.2
Agriculture	100.0	121.7	139.0	162.5	176.6	213.8	274.4
Manufacturing	100.0	124.5	141.4	137.1	152.7	189.0	189.3
Construction	100.0	121.4	134.4	139.8	160.7	181.4	200.3
Trade	100.0	122.5	139.0	153.0	166.0	201.1	255.4
Public administration	100.0	104.0	95.9	102.7	124.2	133.3	153.2
Terms of trade (TOT) agriculture/manufacturing	100.0	97.7	98.3	118.5	115.7	113.2	145.0
TOT agriculture/construction	100.0	100.2	103.4	116.2	109.9	117.9	137.0
TOT agriculture/trade	100.0	99.3	100.0	106.2	106.4	106.4	107.4
TOT manufacturing/construction	100.0	102.5	105.2	98.1	95.0	104.2	94.5
Per capita real currency holdings in 1976 Tsh	144.7	144.3	160.5	192.4	185.8	181.4	165.2
Index of real per capita currency holdings	100.0	99.7	110.9	133.0	128.4	125.3	114.1
Currency/dem deposit ratio (percent)	63.5	59.4	74.5	63.6	64.8	75.3	77.3
Currency/TOT deposit ratio (percent)	42.5	39.9	45.0	41.6	42.7	47.0	47.7

	1983	1984	1985	1986	1987	1988	1989
GDP real index	105.7	109.3	112.1	115.5	120.0	124.9	130.6
GDP agriculture total index	109.6	114.0	120.8	127.8	133.4	139.4	145.7
GDP manufacturing real index	74.8	76.8	73.8	70.8	73.8	77.8	81.8
GDP construction real index	62.1	74.7	68.0	79.8	81.6	85.6	92.9
GDP trade real index	92.0	93.0	93.8	104.2	109.6	114.0	119.0
GDP public administration real index	151.3	151.5	154.4	137.7	138.5	142.7	147.0
Gross fixed capital formation real index	78.3	114.2	140.0	135.8	134.3	129.8	
GFCF public real index	66.0	76.5	98.1	94.1	66.6	60.7	
GFCF private real index	95.0	164.8	196.0	191.9	225.1	222.4	
GFCF buildings real index	84.3	98.8	95.7	105.3	137.9	126.4	
GFCF other works real index	45.8	52.2	48.8	62.3	49.2	78.6	
GFCF machinery and equipment real index	96.5	158.6	213.3	193.1	186.2	163.0	
GDP deflators (1976=100)							
GDP at factor cost total	273.6	330.3	445.2	563.0	743.0	967.7	1,242.0
Agriculture	330.2	400.5	560.2	728.2	1002.3	1,413.7	1,571.0
Manufacturing	231.5	274.8	321.2	429.5	712.9	1,118.1	1,320.3
Construction	228.1	251.7	342.9	444.1	480.9	601.1	719.0
Trade	311.9	395.7	533.2	658.4	834.3	1,353.5	1,585.9
Public administration	208.1	242.7	296.9	314.4	398.0	481.2	651.9
Terms of trade (TOT) agriculture/manufacturing	142.6	145.8	174.4	169.5	140.6	126.4	119.0
TOT agriculture/construction	144.8	159.1	163.3	164.0	208.4	235.2	218.5
TOT agriculture/trade	105.9	101.2	105.0	110.6	120.1	104.4	99.1
TOT manufacturing/construction	101.5	109.2	93.7	96.7	148.2	186.0	183.6
Per capita real currency holdings in 1976 Tsh	129.6	118.4	104.9	110.9	111.2	106.5	
Index of real per capita currency holdings	89.6	81.8	72.5	76.6	76.9	73.6	
Currency/dem deposit ratio (percent)	66.2	104.1	101.3	104.6	108.7	94.1	
Currency/TOT deposit ratio (percent)	39.1	53.0	48.5	57.1	58.6	54.6	

Source: Computed from the national accounts and Bank of Tanzania yearbooks.

facturing output has stagnated. The output of the trade sector has not kept up with that of agriculture, while the output of public administration, after a brief decline in the first two years after the onset of the ERP, grew in 1989 at a rate close to its pre-ERP level.

The most interesting development seems to be occurring in gross fixed capital formation (GFCF). The private sector GFCF has grown very fast since 1983, while public sector GFCF declined and remained stagnant at its already low, pre-ERP levels.

Examining the implicit deflators for the various sectors, it can be noticed that the deflator for agriculture has grown faster than all others, except the one for trade. Notice the very small rise in the deflator for public administration, which reflects the small rise in public sector wages in the face of inflation.

In terms of relative prices (see Figure 1), it can be clearly seen that the terms of trade of agriculture after 1983 (remember, these are official prices) initially grew vis-à-vis manufacturing, but since 1986, they have declined. The terms of trade of agriculture relative to construction, a largely nontraded activity, have

FIGURE 1
Internal Terms of Trade.

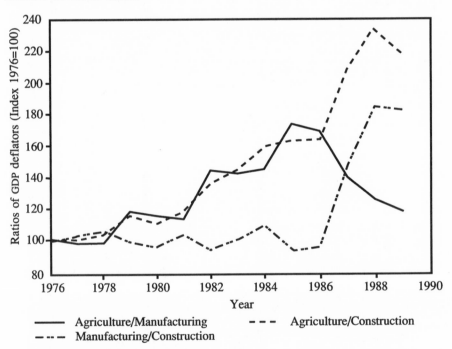

Source: Computed by authors.

increased substantially. This also obtains for the terms of trade between manufacturing (which is largely an import substitute) and construction. It is not clear to what extent these trends are influenced by the use of official prices in the national account statistics.

In the last rows of Table 9, the developments in real per capita currency holding are examined. After an initial rise between 1978 and 1981, holdings declined significantly until 1985, to levels much below those of 1976–1977, and have remained relatively constant since then. The decline of per capita real cash balances cannot be attributed to the expanded use of demand or time deposits. In fact, as shown by the last two rows in Table 9, the ratio of currency held outside the banks to demand or total deposits between 1982 and 1985 increased rather than declined, which would be compatible with a substitution toward bank deposits during the years 1982–1985. This indicates the preference of the private sector for cash.

Collier and Gunning (1989) used the developments in currency holdings as a key indicator supporting their theory of income decline and peasant supply response under rationing and shortages during the period 1980–1985.

In Figure 2 we exhibit the indices of real per capita currency and M_2 holdings in Tanzania from 1967 to 1989 (deflated by the NCPI). It is clear first that currency and M_2 moved in unison throughout the period, especially during 1975–1985. Also notice that there are two peaks in real currency holdings per capita, in 1972 and 1979, the latter lasting until 1981. Finally, notice that real per capita currency holdings in the post-SAP period, 1986–1988, are similar to those held during the "normal" period 1968–1969.

According to Collier and Gunning, the increase in cash holdings in the years 1978–1981 was due to shortages of consumer goods that made their availability random, which required consumers to hold more cash so as to be ready to buy when goods became available. After 1981, shortages became so endemic that cash needs declined and producers, especially peasants, reduced their marketed supply. This presumably was associated also with a decline in their real incomes. After 1985, liberalization of marketing and improved availability of consumer goods led to positive supply response, but real cash needs did not increase significantly as consumer goods were now more readily available and precautionary demand for cash declined.

Collier and Gunning used the apparent decline in real per capita currency holdings between 1982 and 1985 as further evidence that total real income declined during the period. Our analysis of second economy GDP, later in this chapter, however, suggests that apart from 1979, 1982, and 1983 (as well as 1986, which is a post-SAP year), real GDP grew. Between 1977 and 1985 official GDP grew annually at an average rate of 1.4 percent, while total GDP

FIGURE 2

Real per Capita Currency and M_2 Holdings.

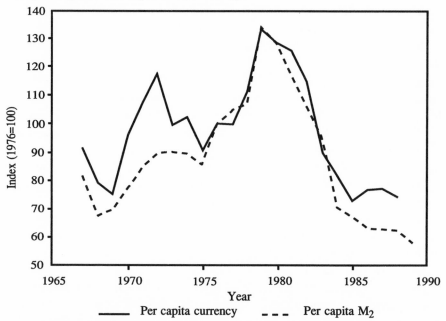

Source: Computed by authors.

(official and second-economy) seems to have grown somewhat faster, at 2.1 percent annually.

The apparent decline in real per capita currency holdings during the 1982–1985 period could have occurred because of an increase in expected inflation, in addition to the shortages that were investigated by Collier and Gunning. In Figure 3, we plot the year-to-year percentage changes in the parallel exchange rate and the NCPI. It can be noticed that during the period 1980–1985 both the rate of inflation, as measured by the rate of change of the NCPI, and the rate of change of the parallel exchange rate were at higher average levels than during any previous four- or five-year period. This, of course, on the basis of traditional theory, should have led to a decrease in real per capita cash holdings, and indeed this appears to have happened.

After 1985 the rate of inflation did not change much from the crisis period, so that this factor is not expected to have led to a change in real per capita cash holdings. To the extent that both official and as total real GDP have increased at rates higher than population growth, the demand for real cash balances should have increased somewhat. The lack of a perceptible increase has been attributed by Collier and Gunning to improved consumer good availability.

FIGURE 3
Yearly Changes in NCPI and the Parallel Exchange Rate.

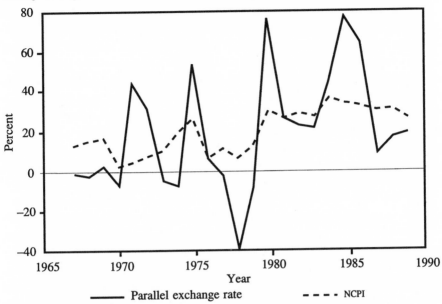

Source: Computed by authors.

THE DEVALUATION DEBATE IN THE CONTEXT OF ADJUSTMENT

One of the subjects of major debate in Tanzania in the early and mid-1980s was over currency depreciation as a tool of balance-of-payments adjustment. In fact, it was mostly over the reluctance of the government to devalue that negotiations with the IMF broke off several times. There is extensive literature on the reasons for the government of Tanzania's resistance to devaluation, even though it had accepted several other orthodox stabilization measures (e.g., van Arkadie 1983; Jamal 1986; Loxley 1989; Ndulu 1988; Singh 1986). In fact, almost all the measures recommended in the report of the mostly neutral Tanzania Advisory Group (TAG) were implemented in the first Structural Adjustment Program, except the suggestion of a mild devaluation.

The basic arguments of those opposing devaluation were that devaluation would not lead to an improvement in the balance of payments, that it would generate inflation and hence tension over income shares, and that it would not lead to an improvement in the real exchange rate (the ratio of traded to nontraded goods prices) because of inflation, thus necessitating further devaluations and an inflationary spiral.

The reason that the critics thought devaluation would not improve the balance of payments was elasticity pessimism. Supply response of export crops to price increases was thought to be very small, given that many such crops were perennial ones. Smuggling would not decline, according to the critics, because the main motivation for smuggling was the exchange with consumer and luxury goods not available in Tanzania and capital flight. On the demand side, most of the rationed imports were intermediate and capital goods, and they were already quite compressed. Hence very little reduction of imports was possible. Inflation was seen as inevitable, as those whose incomes would be most affected (mainly urban salary earners) would resist and demand wage adjustments, thus creating an inflationary spiral and frustrating efforts to change relative prices. The conflicting claims on income could generate a contraction along the lines of the well-known argument by Krugman and Taylor (1978).

The basic counterproposal put forth by critics of devaluation was that, given the severe foreign exchange constraint, an initial injection of foreign exchange was a prerequisite for any recovery. Such an increase in foreign exchange inflows would improve the availability of incentive consumer goods and motivate export crop supply response in addition to mobilizing idle domestic manufacturing capacity. This was also one of the suggestions of the TAG. However, the TAG believed that the currency had become so overvalued that some devaluation was necessary. Our calculations shown in Table 8 indeed indicate that devaluation of the order of 25–50 percent was necessary in 1981–1982. The TAG believed that the arguments of the devaluation critics were exaggerated. The inflationary impact would not be that severe because official price controls had already broken down, and most prices, especially those of food, followed parallel market rates. Furthermore, the strength of urban workers was overestimated, and those favoring devaluation argued was that lower-paid workers could be protected by increases in the minimum wage.

Perusing the debate, it appears that what led to the acrimonious arguments between the government and the IMF was not so much the principle of devaluation as the magnitude and pace of devaluation and adjustment. The IMF argued for a shock treatment, with more than 100 percent devaluation, abolition of the subsidy on *sembe* (maize flour, an urban staple) and hence a sevenfold increase in its price, substantial increases in producer prices of export crops, and liberalization of all price controls. Apart from the speed of adjustment, the other major concern of the Tanzanian government was about equitable sharing of the burden of adjustment, something the IMF was not so concerned with.

The evidence on the pace of devaluation to some extent bears out the criticisms of a sudden devaluation. Jamal (1986) computed the parity exchange rates (in Tsh/US$) that would have been required in the period 1979–1984 to restore real farm prices to 1972–1973 levels under the assumptions of maintaining or abolishing farm input subsidies. We exhibit his estimates in Table 10 and contrast them with our own calculations of the nominal equivalent exchange rate from Table 8, column 11, which is computed as the rate that would have maintained a constant real exchange rate (based on relative CPIs, as explained in Appendix B) at the 1969 level. It can be seen that under any of the scenarios suggested, the required devaluation is nowhere near the nearly 100 percent required by the IMF in 1980–1981. It appears that the principal frame of reference for the IMF must have been the parallel market rate, which was indeed more than 100 percent above the official rate throughout the period 1980–1984. To argue in those terms, however, presupposes an understanding of the behavior of the parallel economy, a topic which we examine later in this chapter.

FINANCING OF PUBLIC AND EXTERNAL DEFICITS AND MONETARY ADJUSTMENTS

One of the major objects of reform under the SAP and the ERP has been the public budget. The fiscal deficit—that is, the amount that requires financing—has increased slightly as a share of GDP since 1985, but it has stayed much below the very high levels of the late 1970s and early 1980s.

Table 11 presents the public financing requirements on a fiscal year basis from 1976 to 1989 and the methods of financing them. Throughout the period, the

TABLE 10

Tanzania: Estimates of Parity Exchange Rates, 1979–1984 (Tsh/US$).

| | *Official Nominal Exchange Rate*[a] *(period average)* (1) | *Exchange Rate to Restore Real Farm Prices to 1972–1973 Levels*[b] | | *Nominal Equivalent Exchange Rate*[a] (4) |
		With Subsidy (2)	*Without Subsidy* (3)	
1979	8.217	8.24	8.24	6.77
1980	8.197	8.24	8.24	7.75
1981	8.284	n.a.	n.a.	10.38
1982	9.283	13.23	14.10	13.83
1983	11.143	13.23	14.10	18.35
1984	15.292	15.51	17.00	27.41

[a] Derived from Table 8.

[b] Derived from Jamal (1986), Table 2.

TABLE 11

Tanzania: Financing of Public Deficit.

Fiscal Year	Public Financing Requirements (1)	Foreign Grants and Loans (2)	Import Support and Counterpart Funds (3)	Domestic Borrowing (4)	Nonbank Borrowing (5)	(2)/(1) (6)	(3)/(1) (7)	(2+3)/(1) (8)	(4)/(1) (9)	(4−5)/(1) (10)
			(million Tsh)					(percentages)		
1976	2,461	1,033	0	1,422	n.a.	41.97	0.00	41.97	57.78	n.a.
1977	1,604	1,402	0	202	n.a.	87.41	0.00	87.41	12.59	n.a.
1978	2,836	1,529	0	1,320	n.a.	53.91	0.00	53.91	46.54	n.a.
1979	3,891	1,930	0	1,940	n.a.	49.60	0.00	49.60	49.86	n.a.
1980	6,668	2,268	802	3,511	1,374	34.01	12.03	46.04	52.65	n.a.
1981	6,380	1,845	875	3,686	1,374	28.92	13.71	42.63	57.77	36.24
1982	4,018	1,838	1,022	1,112	−1,499	45.74	25.44	71.18	27.68	64.98
1983	4,837	1,858	751	2,215	−1,231	38.41	15.53	53.94	45.79	71.24
1984	7,995	1,895	611	5,486	1,913	23.70	7.64	31.34	68.62	44.69
1985	7,931	2,658	1,236	4,016	2,144	33.51	15.58	49.10	50.64	23.60
1986	9,709	2,045	1,489	6,182	1,257	21.06	15.34	36.40	63.67	50.73
1987	18,712	6,235	8,001	4,514	2,858	33.32	42.76	76.08	24.12	8.85
1988	27,719	9,881	12,909	4,938	2,355	35.65	46.57	82.22	17.81	9.32
1989	29,739	10,619	20,889	−1,774	2,686	35.71	70.24	105.95	−5.97	−15.00

Source: Computed from data in Bank of Tanzania Economic and Operations Report, June 1989 and June 1982.
Note: A year refers to a fiscal year starting the previous year (e.g., 1986 is the 1985/86 fiscal year).

major source of finance has been foreign grants and loans, as well as import support and counterpart funds (columns 2, 3, and 8). During the crisis years 1980–1986, this share declined considerably, and the main method of finance became domestic borrowing (see columns 8 and 9), with bank borrowing becoming quite important (see column 10). Since 1986, bank borrowing (that is, financing through money creation) appears to have declined dramatically, and in fact, it appears that in 1988/89 some of the public debt held by banks was redeemed.

If this picture truly reflected the mode of financing, then the money supply (M_1 or M_2) should not have expanded very much since 1986, in accordance with the ERP guidelines. However, as shown in Table 12, the volume of currency in circulation and the money supply have grown by very large amounts since 1986, much larger than what is justified by reported domestic bank borrowing.

The explanation of this apparent paradox, as Collier and Gunning (1991) have argued, is that in Tanzania there is no commercial banking system in the traditional sense. The main function of the existing commercial banking system, which is basically composed of only one bank, the National Bank of Commerce (NBC), is to extend loans to the parastatals. In fact, 70–90 percent of all lending is to official entities. A large part of that is to cover current parastatal deficits, especially those of official agricultural marketing authorities, the chief being the National Milling Corporation (NMC), and cannot be repaid. Such lending should, therefore, be treated very much like money creation.

TABLE 12

Tanzania: Changes in Monetary Aggregates during the ERP (absolute changes from previous year).

	Change in Currency in Circulation		Change in Money Supply (M2)		Domestic Bank Borrowing
	Million Tsh (1)	*Percent* (2)	*Million Tsh* (3)	*Percent* (4)	*Million Tsh* (5)[a]
1983	205	2.6	4,398	17.8	3,510
1984	2,278	27.8	1,091	3.7	2,723
1985	2,247	21.5	8,753	29.0	3,399
1986	5,591	44.0	11,382	29.2	3,291
1987	6,241	34.1	16,090	32.0	2,220
1988	7,236	29.5	23,450	35.3	–939

Source: Computed from Bank of Tanzania, *Economic and Operations Report* for the year ended June 30, 1989.

[a] Computed by averaging fiscal year figures.

In Table 13 we exhibit the changes in the domestic lending to marketing of agricultural produce (almost all going to parastatals). It can be clearly seen that between 1982 and 1988, 50 percent of the increase in total commercial lending is accounted for by increases in lending to agricultural marketing parastatals. For 1985–1988, the figure is 49 percent. If we consider the changes in the money supply (M$_2$) from 1985 to 1988 and total commercial bank lending to official entities over the same period, then the latter makes up 80.1 percent of the total change in M$_2$. It therefore appears that indeed the change in domestic money supply is closely associated with bank credit to official, and especially agricultural marketing, parastatals. This obviously makes agricultural marketing reform an item with important macroeconomic consequences.

Table 14 shows the modes of financing of the external deficit during 1983–1988. It is obvious that the accumulation of arrears and debt rescheduling have been the main methods of financing a growing current account deficit since the onset of the ERP. The current account deficit has grown from –5.4 percent of GDP at market prices in 1985, to –12.0 percent in 1988, and capital flows have not ameliorated the situation by much. It must be recalled that own-funded imports are counterbalanced by an equivalent current transfer item on the credit side, so that they do not affect the overall current account balance. The figures show the unsustainability of the external deficit and the reliance on debt rescheduling.

TABLE 13

Tanzania: Contribution of Lending for Agricultural Marketing to Total Domestic Lending Changes (in million Tsh).

	Change in Total Domestic Lending by Commercial Banks from Previous Year (1)	Change in Total Lending to Marketing of Agricultural Produce (2)	Contribution of Agricultural Marketing (2)/(1) x 100
1983	1,064	834	78.4
1984	2,312	1,054	45.6
1985	4,574	2,029	44.4
1986	10,323	–4,639	–44.9
1987	27,220	30,071	110.5
1988	18,386	2,103	11.4
Change 1982–1988	62,815	31,452	50.1
Change 1985–1988	55,779	27,210	48.8

Source: Bank of Tanzania, *Economic and Operation Report* for the year ended June 30, 1989.

TABLE 14

Tanzania: Financing of the Current Account Deficit (in million Tsh, unless noted).

	1983	1984	1985	1986	1987	1988
Current account	-3,394	-5,491	-6,500	-10,633	-28,655	-37,323
Capital account (MLT) net	2,038	-1,133	-323	-688	-450	3,932
Supplier's credit (net)	1,134	1,679	-559	-1,816	321	477
Imprt. sup. and exc. finance	675	751	1,048	2,720	2,744	9,998
Errors and omissions	-664	1,768	-560	-2,154	7,982	-4,217
Overall balance	-211	-2,426	-6,894	-12,571	-18,058	-27,133
As a percent of GDPMP	-4.8	-6.2	-5.4	-6.7	-13.1	-12.0
As a percent of GDPMP	-0.3	-2.7	-5.7	-7.9	-8.2	-8.7
Financing						
IMF (net)	-333	-421	-248	429	2,506	-5,563
Reserve decrease (-increase)	-168	47	175	-816	-643	4,448
Arrears (+ increase)	713	2,800	6,967	-27,635	-64	15,379
Debt rescheduling	0	0	0	37,479	12,081	12,870
Others	-1	0	0	3,114	4,178	-1

Source: Bank of Tanzania, *Economic and Operations Report* for the year ended June 30, 1989.

THE HIDDEN ECONOMY IN TANZANIA

One of the major problems facing the analyst of the Tanzanian economy is the fact that the numbers that presumably describe the evolution of aggregate variables suffer from inaccuracies due to incomplete coverage, as well as inaccurate estimates of the activities covered. This is particularly so in agriculture, mining, manufacturing, construction, and trade.

In Tanzania, because of the post-1967 emphasis on development through public ownership and control of the major enterprises producing and distributing goods and services and the subsequent nationalizations, a large segment of the formerly active private sector either stopped producing or went underground, in the sense that it kept producing but with higher costs due to the cost of evading the various government controls. Given the official policy, however, these activities were not officially recognized, and hence no effort was made to estimate them. The resulting "hidden" or "second" or "parallel" or "underground" economy in Tanzania (the terms will be used interchangeably below) is thought to have gradually grown as public controls became more binding and especially as shortages of various goods became widespread with the post-1979 foreign exchange crisis. A question of major macroeconomic relevance is whether the hidden economy has followed the fluctuations of the officially observed economy, and if not, whether it has tended to compensate for accentuate the observed secular decline in economic activity.

In the past decade, there has been an active literature concerned with estimates of the underground economy in developed countries (see Tanzi [1982] for an early survey and Bhattacharyya [1990] for a recent analysis). This is usually defined as that economy which is not measured by official GDP statistics. It covers legal but unreported or unmeasured activities, such as those of many small-scale enterprises, usually known as the "informal sector," as well as illegal activities, such as production and smuggling of official export crops, illegal mining, hunting, and so forth. In Tanzania, given the legal monopoly over marketing and distribution of agricultural crops and the legal monopoly of parastatal production of many consumer and intermediate items, parallel markets quickly arose. The problem has been analyzed extensively by Maliyamkono and Bagachwa (1990), who attempted several techniques in an effort to measure the size and evolution of the second economy. There are four major methods used for estimating the second economy: those based on differences between survey-based incomes and expenditures; those based on labor participation; those based on monetary estimates; and those based on analyzing tax returns (see Frey and Pommerehne 1982). Maliyamkono and Bagachwa (MB) used the first two in their analysis of Tanzania. In this report we shall review their results and present some new estimates.

In their first approach, MB used one of the simplest available methods, based on the assumption that the currency-to-demand-deposit ratio stays unchanged over time (Guttman 1977). On the basis of that assumption and using 1977 as a base year (a year in which the second economy was assumed to be negligible), they found that as a share of official GDP the second economy grew from 9.8 percent in 1978 to between 22 and 29 percent in the period 1980–1986 and reached 31.4 percent in 1986. However, if one uses the same technique and base year to compute the second economy in years before 1977, one finds that between 1970 and 1972 the unofficial economy was between 20 and 30 percent of GDP, while between 1973 and 1979 the second economy was smaller than 10 percent of GDP, which seems unlikely in view of the fact that controls were quite extensive during that period. The problems with this technique, as well as any other that assumes fixed monetary ratios, are well known and are readily acknowledged by MB. A preferable method is one based on the estimation of a demand-for-currency equation (Tanzi 1983; Bhattacharyya 1990). However, MB report that they were unable to estimate such an equation for Tanzania.

MB also reported the results of a household survey in 1986, which measured expenditures and incomes for a sample of urban and rural households. By blowing up their expenditure figures to the national level, they found that officially reported, private final consumption was underestimated in 1986 by about 30 percent. Given that the aggregate marginal propensity to consume is around 0.93 in Tanzania (Lipumba et al. 1988), this implies a 33 percent underestimate of GDP.

One major aspect of the second economy is parallel exports. There is a large, unrecorded set of activities that generate domestic product and income and which result in exports that are not recorded. The large overvaluation of the currency in the 1970s and 1980s, combined with the wide border with countries where Tanzanian goods could be exchanged, made the control of exports almost an impossible task. MB, as well as Bagachwa, Luvanga, and Mjema (1990), report that there are several categories of illegal exports in Tanzania, including agricultural products (maize, wheat, beans, goats, sheep), cattle, traditional export crops (coffee, cardamon, cotton), hides and skins, products of hunting (ivory), mining products (gold, diamonds, other precious stones), tourism (via parallel cashing of foreign exchange), housing services provided to foreigners, and over- and under invoicing of official exports and imports. Goods obtained in exchange include basic consumer goods, which were in short supply in the 1970s and 1980s, luxury consumer goods, and some intermediate goods.

A glimpse of the size of parallel exports can be obtained by examining the figures for "own-funded imports," which started in 1984. Import under this category are funded with the importers' own foreign exchange. It was thought in the early years of the scheme that such imports would exhaust much of the foreign exchange that residents had accumulated through the parallel market. However, own-funded imports not only did not slow down, but in fact increased substantially, after 1986. The conclusion follows that the foreign exchange for these imports must have come from a flow of unrecorded export earnings. Below we utilize this idea and a methodology based on the income approach to balance-of-payment adjustment to estimate the missing GDP that is consistent with the large inflow of own-funded imports.

The methodology, which we shall term the "missing income" methodology, starts by assuming that second-economy GDP is not supply-constrained as total economy GDP or official GDP would be (Ndulu 1988; Lipumba et al. 1988), but instead adjusts to satisfy demand for it, much as in the Keynesian economic model. There is no government interference in it since by definition it escapes public control. A simple ex-post equation that states the macroeconomic balance between unofficial GDP (denoted by Y_u) and the expenditure on it is the following:

$$Y_u = C_u + E_u - M_u \tag{3.1}$$

where C_u is unofficial, unrecorded consumption of the product generated by the second economy; E_u is unofficial, unrecorded exports; and M_u is unofficial, unrecorded imports.

We make the traditional assumptions that consumption and imports depend on generated income.

$$C_u = C_u\,(Y_u) \tag{3.2}$$

$$M_u = M_u\,(Y_u)\,. \tag{3.3}$$

Hence (3.1) can be written,

$$Y_u - C_u\,(Y_u) + M_u\,(Y_u) = E_u\,. \tag{3.4}$$

Taking the total differential of (3.4), we obtain:

$$dY_u = \frac{dE_u}{1 - \alpha + \mu} \tag{3.5}$$

where α is the marginal propensity to consume and μ is the marginal propensity to import out of income. If we can estimate values for the parameters α and μ, then by utilizing some estimates for the size of parallel exports we could infer the size of unofficial GDP (Y_u) required to support this level of imports.

To implement our method, we utilize estimates of the income elasticity of aggregate private consumption expenditures and the income elasticities of imports of consumer and intermediate goods arrived at by Lipumba et al. (1988) using data for the officially reported aggregate series from 1968 to 1984. To use these estimates, we must assume that the same parameters are also valid for second-economy transactions, which we do. The reported values in Lipumba et al. (1988) are the following:

$$e_C = 0.296, e_{MC} = 0.571, e_{MI} = 0.739$$

where e_C is the income elasticity of private consumption expenditures, and e_{MC} and e_{MI} are the elasticities with respect to official GDP of imports of consumer and intermediate goods respectively.

The next step is to combine the two import elasticities to form an elasticity of aggregate, second-economy imports. We assume that imports that came through clandestine routes were mainly consumer and intermediate goods. We then utilize the breakdown of no-payment imports for the period July 1984 to December 1985 reported by Ndulu and Hyuha (1986) and estimate that the share of intermediate imports (including spares and building materials) in total imports of intermediate and consumer goods is 0.40, leaving a share of 0.60 for consumer goods. These, along with the above estimates of elasticities, imply an elasticity of parallel imports with respect to parallel income of 0.64.

To transform the estimated elasticities to marginal propensities, we utilize the average propensity to consume and the average propensity to import computed from official data of the period 1976–1983. This period includes both the euphoria of 1976–1978 and the post–1980 crisis years. The resulting estimates are, for the marginal propensity to consume, $\alpha = 0.68$ and for the marginal propensity to import, $\beta = 0.13$, resulting in a value of 0.45 for the denominator of (3.5).

The final step involves estimating parallel exports. For lack of any better numbers, we utilize the figures for the dollar value of own-funded imports from 1985 to 1988 reported by Bagachwa, Luvanga, and Mjema (1990). They also report figures for 1984, but the program operated for only half of that year, and the agents were still learning; hence that year was dropped. The assumption that the size of parallel, unrecorded exports is close to that of own-funded imports can be justified as follows: on the one hand, the figures would overestimate parallel exports because they also include drawdown from accumulated foreign exchange holdings abroad. On the other hand, however, they could very well underestimate the size of parallel exports because despite the indirect "legalization" of parallel exports, there must still be a substantial amount of products that are exported and bartered directly for unrecorded import goods. This must be so particularly for parallel agricultural exports in the border areas. In any case the estimates are only intended to give ballpark indications of magnitudes.

In Table 15 we indicate the results of our calculations, which give a picture of a huge second economy (almost equal in size to the official GDP) when parallel rates are used to translate own foreign exchange to Tsh (row 8). The size of the second economy ranges between 16 and 45 percent of official GDP when official rates are used (row 7). It is obvious that the Tsh equivalent of parallel exports and own-funded imports should be computed using parallel foreign exchange rates. However, remember that the prices used to compute current market value of GDP are still mostly official prices, which for many products do not represent

TABLE 15
Tanzania: Estimates of the Second Economy by the Missing
Income Approach.

	1985	*1986*	*1987*	*1988*
(1) Official GDP at current market prices	120.6	159.6	219.0	311.5
(2) Own-funded imports (million US$)[a]	505.0	476.0	514.0	638.0
(3) Own-funded imports in Tsh at official rates	8.8	15.6	33.0	63.3
(4) Own-funded imports in Tsh at parallel rates	50.9	78.5	92.5	134.0
(5) Implied second-economy GDP from row (3)[b]	19.6	34.7	73.3	140.7
(6) Implied second-economy GDP from row (4)[b]	113.1	174.4	205.6	297.8
(7) row (5) as a share of row (1) (%)	16.3	21.7	33.5	45.2
(8) row (6) as a share of row (1) (%)	93.8	109.3	93.9	95.6
(9) row (6) as a share of adjusted GDP[c]	60.7	67.6	58.9	59.6

Note: Figures are in billion Tsh unless otherwise noted.
[a] *Source:* Bagachwa, Luvanga, and Mjema (1990).
[b] Using equation 3.1 (see text).
[c] See text.

actual market prices. The degree of underestimate of current-market GDP can be inferred by comparing the implied GDP deflator from official statistics and the NCPI. Such a comparison reveals that the NCPI has grown much faster than the GDP deflator, starting around 1980, which is logical given that the crisis started then, and official prices started losing their significance at that time. In fact, the ratio of the NCPI to the implied GDP deflator, which was close to one before 1980, increased to 1.56 by 1984 and has hovered between 1.55 and 1.62 since then.

If we use the ratio of NCPI to the implied GDP deflator to augment the reported current value GDP in Table 15 and also use the Tsh estimates of unofficial exports translated at parallel rates, then we arrive at figures in the last row of the table. They indicate that the second economy, as revealed by unofficial foreign exchange outflows, ranges between 59 and 68 percent of adjusted nominal GDP. This is clearly a very high level and much higher than the estimates reported by MB.

Another estimate of the unobserved economy has been obtained recently by Bagachwa and Naho (1990a) in a paper prepared for this project. They estimated by Ordinary Least Squares (OLS) a demand-for-currency equation as follows:

$$\ln CUR = -9.39 + 2.06 \ln YOFR + 0.941 \ln RPFC - 0.65 \ln NBCB$$
$$\quad\;\; (-23.20)\;\; (3.76) \qquad\quad (3.84) \qquad\qquad (-4.63)$$

$$-\,0.031 \ln INFL + 4.20 \ln (1 + GINT) + 8.161 (1 + ATR)$$
$$\quad (-3.00) \qquad\qquad (4.21) \qquad\qquad\quad (3.59)$$

$$+\,0.11 \ln PEXP \;(3.5.6)$$
$$\quad (1.83) \qquad\qquad\qquad\qquad R^2 = 0.98,\; \text{D.W. } 2.19 \qquad (3.6)$$

where the period of estimation is 1967 to 1988, the figures under the coefficients are t-ratios, and the variables are as follows: *CUR* is real currency holdings outside banks, namely, nominal currency holdings divided by the NCPI; *YOFR* is real nominal income deflated by the GDP deflator; *RPFC* is ratio of private final consumption expenditure to total expenditure on GDP; *NBCB* is index of number of National Bank of Commerce branches; *INFL* is GDP deflator; *GINT* is ratio of parastatal employees over total employees, a measure of government intervention; *ATR* is average tax rate, equal to the ratio of the sum of income and corporate taxes to the sum of compensation of employees and operating surplus, and *PEXP* is ratio of parallel exchange rate to the official one.

The estimated equation appears quite robust, and all the coefficients have the correct signs and are significant. By using the standard technique developed by

Tanzi (1983), they estimate the size of the second economy, first, by estimating through the above regression total currency holdings as predicted by (3.6) with all variables. Then "legal" currency holdings are estimated from (3.6) by omitting the "interference" variables *GINT*, *ATR*, and *PEXP*. The difference gives the amount of currency held for unofficial-economy transactions. By multiplying this by the observed-transactions velocity of money (obtained by dividing official nominal GDP by M_1, which is the sum of currency and demand deposits), they obtain an estimate of the second economy GDP.

Bagachwa and Naho's results are shown in Table 16. Their estimates show a very large size for the second economy, which started from a modest 20–25 percent of nominal GDP in the late 1960s, expanded to around 40–50 percent during the 1970s and early 1980s, and has grown to more than 60 percent of nominal GDP after 1984. Their estimates for this latter period fall between our low and high values indicated in Table 15.

The last two columns in Table 16 show the real value of the second economy, obtained by dividing the estimated second economy GDP by the NCPI, and its share of real GDP. The results indicate that the second economy grew very fast in the early 1970s and that from 1977 to now, it has fluctuated between 35 and 52 percent of real official GDP, with peaks in 1978 and 1985. In absolute real terms, the second economy does not seem to have grown since the onset of reforms in 1986. On a per capita basis, in fact, the absolute size of the second economy has declined, from peaks of 683 Tsh in 1972 and 677 Tsh in 1978 (in 1976 prices), to 598 Tsh in 1985 and 502 Tsh in 1988.

Table 17 presents the results of Table 16 from another viewpoint. What is reported is the total real GDP—that is, the sum of the official real GDP and the second-economy real GDP—the yearly changes in total and official real GDP, and the size of the second economy as a share of the total. It is interesting to note that a very different picture of total GDP is obtained from this table. Years of decline in total real GDP appear to be 1973, 1979, 1982, 1983, and 1986. Growth appears to have been quite strong in 1984, the first year of liberalization, and has continued to be strong since then. The first year of the ERP, 1986, appears to have been marked by a fall in total real GDP, albeit the official figures indicate a rise. Since 1987, however, growth appears to have occurred at rates faster than officially reported.

Of interest also is the last column, which indicates the share of the second economy in the total (official plus unobserved) GDP. It appears that with minor fluctuations, that share has stayed remarkably constant at around 28–32 percent throughout the last two decades. It must, of course, be noted that all these conclusions depend strongly on the method of estimating the second-economy GDP.

TABLE 16

Tanzania: Estimates of Second Economy GDP 1967–1988 (in million Tshs).

					Estimated				
Year	Actual Currency (1)	Legal Currency (2)	Total Currency (3)	Illegal Currency (4)	Income Velocity of Money (5)	Second Economy (6)	Second Economy as Percentage of the Official Nominal GDP (7)	Real Size of Second Economy[a] (base 1976) (8)	Real Second Economy as a Percentage of Real Official GDP (9)
1967	512.0	305.8	516.7	210.8	6.83	1,440.5	21.4	3,996	27.7
1968	528.6	267.6	508.9	241.4	6.93	1,672.4	23.3	4,017	26.5
1969	605.0	269.0	610.9	341.9	5.65	1,932.2	25.9	3,971	25.7
1970	818.4	322.9	799.6	476.7	6.94	3,309.2	40.3	6,633	40.5
1971	986.6	348.9	972.7	623.8	6.23	3,888.6	43.9	7,445	43.7
1972	1,201.1	421.3	1,251.0	831.6	6.49	5,393.5	53.8	9,588	52.7
1973	1,198.6	415.7	1,186.9	771.2	5.77	4,448.7	38.7	7,169	38.2
1974	1,517.3	450.4	1,469.9	1,019.5	5.86	5,977.7	42.7	8,078	42.0
1975	1,755.8	527.1	1,928.1	1,401.0	5.56	7,790.5	45.9	8,320	40.9
1976	2,071.3	548.6	2,096.1	1,547.5	5.68	8,796.6	40.6	8,797	40.6
1977	2,379.7	619.9	2,507.4	1,887.6	5.56	10,492.4	40.8	9,401	43.2
1978	2,915.2	800.2	3,064.9	2,264.7	6.06	13,737.2	48.1	11,546	52.0
1979	4,055.5	871.1	3,828.1	2,951.0	4.46	13,178.9	40.8	9,816	43.0
1980	5,245.4	1,109.2	5,282.8	4,173.6	4.07	16,973.1	45.3	9,705	41.4
1981	6,616.0	1,240.8	6,393.8	5,153.0	4.38	22,566.2	51.4	11,634	49.9
1982	7,988.7	1,408.8	7,135.2	5,726.4	4.47	25,623.1	48.8	9,042	38.6
1983	8,194.2	1,742.7	8,336.0	6,593.3	4.44	29,249.6	46.7	8,124	35.5
1984	10,472.4	2,064.9	10,570.9	8,501.0	6.44	54,798.6	70.1	11,179	47.3
1985	12,719.0	2,755.0	14,210.7	11,455.7	7.06	80,892.7	74.8	12,381	51.0
1986	18,309.7	3,727.2	16,741.0	13,021.8	6.63	86,370.0	61.3	9,983	39.9
1987	24,550.8	5,431.3	22,921.5	17,490.2	6.89	120,490.2	62.4	10,716	41.3
1988	31,786.7	8,211.6	33,951.6	25,740.1	6.48	166,880.1	61.4	11,314	41.8

Source: Bagachwa and Naho (1990a).
[a] Column (6) divided by the NCPI (1977=100).

TABLE 17

Tanzania: Size of Second Economy (in million 1976 Tsh).

	Official Real GDP (1)	Second Economy GDP (2)	Total Real GDP (1)+(2) (3)	Percent Yearly Change of Total GDP (4)	Percent Yearly Change of Official Real GDP (5)	Second Economy GDP as Percentage of Total GDP (6)
1967	14,438	3,996	18,434			21.68
1968	15,186	4,017	19,203	4.17	5.18	20.92
1969	15,465	3,971	19,436	1.21	1.84	20.43
1970	16,362	6,633	22,995	18.31	5.80	28.85
1971	7,046	7,445	24,491	6.51	4.18	30.40
1972	18,192	9,588	27,780	13.43	6.72	34.51
1973	18,748	7,169	25,917	−6.71	3.06	27.66
1974	19,217	8,078	27,295	5.32	2.50	29.60
1975	20,352	8,320	28,672	5.04	5.91	29.02
1976	21,652	8,797	30,449	6.20	6.39	28.89
1977	21,739	9,401	31,140	2.27	0.40	30.19
1978	22,202	11,546	33,748	8.38	2.13	34.21
1979	22,849	9,816	32,665	−3.21	2.91	30.05
1980	23,419	9,705	33,124	1.41	2.49	29.30
1981	23,301	11,634	34,935	5.47	−0.50	33.30
1982	23,439	9,042	32,481	−7.02	0.59	27.84
1983	22,882	8,124	31,006	−4.54	−2.38	26.20
1984	23,656	11,179	34,835	12.35	3.38	32.09
1985	24,278	12,381	36,659	5.24	2.63	33.77
1986	25,008	9,983	34,991	−4.55	3.01	28.53
1987	25,972	10,716	36,688	4.85	3.85	29.21
1988	27,039	11,314	38,353	4.54	4.11	29.50

Source: Computed by authors.

CONCLUSIONS

As must have become clear in the course of this chapter, economic policy during the last decade in Tanzania has been characterized by many controversies. Those ranged from the diagnosis of causes of the crisis to the appropriate policies to follow. From our examination of recent developments, however, it became clear that the Tanzanian government underestimated the magnitude of the crisis, as well as its dependence on external support. It also appears that despite the nominal adoption of a massive adjustment program, actual policy changes have been implemented very slowly, and many distortions still prevail.

Examples are the influence on the money supply of domestic financing of inefficient parastatals, and the still large difference between the parallel and official exchange rates.

Our analysis also raised the issue that official statistics on economic developments do not represent the true underlying trends in the real economy very well. Our estimates of the unobserved or second economy revealed that a very significant part of the economy goes unrecorded. When this part is incorporated in the official figures, it appears that, with the exception of a few crisis years, the economy has fared much better than had been thought. If this conclusion is corroborated by other, especially micro, evidence, it suggests that the crisis in the Tanzanian economy was for the most part a crisis of the formal part and not necessarily the whole economy.

4

PROFILE OF INCOMES AND POVERTY IN TANZANIA

The most recent World Bank *World Development Report* (1990) ranks Tanzania as the fourth-poorest country of the world, with a 1988 per capita income of only US$ 160. Yet in 1980, at the end of a decade of shocks and economic decline, the International Labour Office (ILO 1982) estimated that in the urban areas only about 15 percent of households might be considered as falling below a poverty line. In the rural areas, the estimate was about 25–30 percent, for a countrywide total of about 25 percent. This is not a very high estimate, compared to other developing country poverty levels. In this chapter, we show that poverty is substantially greater than previously estimated. We present a more up-to-date profile of poverty in Tanzania mainland, emphasizing its structural aspects.

Recent household surveys on which to base analysis of patterns of income and consumption are not available in Tanzania. However, there is a very detailed national household survey that was done in 1976/77, the results of which became available only recently. It is very helpful in giving the structure of Tanzanian households. This is especially so because there was another such survey in 1969, with which the 1976/77 survey can be compared. Furthermore, there exist two detailed rural income surveys (Collier et al. 1986; Bevan et al. 1989) done in 1979/80 and 1983, respectively, which can also be used for comparative purposes, despite the fact that they were not representative of the entire country but only certain regions. These four sources provide the bulk of the information for our analysis.

The next section outlines some basic demographic characteristics of the Tanzanian household. In the following section the structure and sources of rural and urban incomes are analyzed. We also analyze income differentiation and we show that income in Tanzania is quite equitably distributed, compared with other countries. In the following section, we discuss the observed pattern of income differentiation. Subsequently we analyze patterns of consumption among different types of households, and we show that most of the food intake of the poor in both rural and urban areas comes out of subsistence production. We compute an absolute poverty line and estimate that a very substantial number of Tanzanian households appear to have expenditures below it. (We also estimate poverty lines for every year until 1989 and show that they amounted to less than even senior civil servant salaries in 1989.) In the final section we summarize our main conclusions.

POPULATION AND SOME HOUSEHOLD CHARACTERISTICS

According to the 1988 population census, the population of mainland Tanzania was 22,533.8 thousand people, and the average household size was 5.3, implying that there were about 4,252 thousand households. The 1978 census revealed a population of 17,036.5 thousand, composed of 3,442 thousand households, with an average of 4.9 members. The 1967 census had revealed a population of 11,958.7 thousand and an average household size of 4.5. While the average intercensal population growth rate between 1978 and 1988 has declined to 2.8 percent from 3.2 percent between 1967 and 1978, the average size of households seems to have increased. It is not clear whether this trend is real or due to a different definition of the household in the different census years.

Most of the Tanzanian population lives in rural areas. Table 18 exhibits the number of households reported as rural and as urban in the 1978 census and in the 1976/77 Household Budget Survey (HBS), by region. The 1988 census preliminary report does not distinguish between rural and urban households. The 1978 census reports 13 percent more households for the mainland, compared with the 1976/77 HBS, the overreporting being similar for the rural and urban categories. The 1978 census, however, reported an average household size of 4.9 for the whole country, while in the HBS it was 5.65. The result is that the HBS implied a total population in 1976/77 of about 17,154 thousand, which is 0.7 percent above the census figure of one year later. While the error in total population does not appear to be very large, it seems that the HBS used a slightly different

TABLE 18

Tanzania: Rural and Urban Households, 1976–1978.

| | Number of Households (in thousands) | | | | | | Average Household Size | | |
| | 1978 Population Census | | | 1976/77 Household Budget Survey | | | Population Census | | Household Budget Survey |
	Rural (1)	Urban (2)	Total (3)	Rural (4)	Urban (5)	Total (6)	1978 (7)	1988 (8)	1976/77 (9)
Tanzania	2,917.91	517.54	3,435.45	2,585.05	453.70	3,038.75	4.90	5.30	5.65
Arusha	157.00	18.72	175.72	117.34	22.46	139.80	5.30	5.40	5.33
Coast	111.45	8.07	119.52	99.45	0.00	99.45	4.30	4.90	5.65
Dar es Salaam	18.39	186.50	204.89	0.00	165.21	165.21	4.10	4.30	5.02
Dodoma	186.43	16.98	203.42	149.10	32.34	181.45	4.70	5.00	5.13
Iringa	184.03	18.25	202.27	157.28	10.88	168.17	4.50	4.80	5.32
Kigoma	105.41	12.23	117.64	95.11	8.05	103.16	5.50	5.80	6.06
Kilimanjaro	152.93	16.59	169.51	148.78	16.96	165.74	5.30	5.40	5.91
Lindi	106.39	11.69	118.07	112.97	6.28	119.24	4.40	4.60	4.90
Mara	106.10	10.73	116.83	109.81	9.74	119.55	6.20	6.70	6.67
Mbeya	196.72	22.09	218.81	176.02	10.81	186.83	5.00	4.90	5.87
Morogoro	173.61	28.52	202.13	151.05	12.93	163.98	4.70	5.30	5.53
Mtwara	156.46	21.82	178.28	166.37	11.22	177.59	4.30	4.40	4.97
Mwanza	206.81	34.15	240.96	209.66	31.54	241.19	6.00	6.40	6.75
Rukwa	86.50	11.36	97.87	64.98	8.92	73.89	5.10	5.30	6.05
Ruvuma	99.68	8.95	108.62	101.85	7.96	109.81	5.20	5.30	4.89
Shinyanga	213.53	12.84	226.37	189.25	14.76	204.00	5.80	6.30	6.57
Singida	119.49	12.88	132.37	95.17	9.93	105.10	4.60	5.30	5.80
Tabora	137.29	24.48	161.76	133.92	15.19	149.11	5.00	5.70	5.52
Tanga	181.90	34.24	216.14	146.21	33.85	180.06	4.70	5.10	5.65
West Lake	217.80	8.46	226.26	160.74	22.66	183.40	4.50	4.90	5.00

Source: Tanzania, *1978 Population Census Preliminary Report*, Tanzania Bureau of Statistics, *Household Budget Survey, 1976/77*.

definition of a household. In 1978, about 87 percent of the population lived in rural areas, compared with 93 percent reported in the 1967 population census. Although recent data have not been analyzed in detail yet, it is thought that the rate of urban growth in the last decade is less than the 9 percent annual rate experienced between 1967 and 1978. About 91 percent of rural households in 1978 lived in registered villages (entities that have legal and corporate status under Tanzanian law), 4.8 percent in unregistered, traditional villages, and only a small proportion outside villages. This is a result of the villagization campaign, as before 1970, most of the rural households lived in unregistered villages or outside villages.

Table 19 shows the frequency distribution of households by size in urban and rural areas circa 1977. It can be seen that, as expected, rural households have, on average, more members (mean size 5.8) than urban households (mean size 5.0). The population census of 1978 showed that about 45 percent of the population is economically active (7,687.4 thousand), of which 88 percent is in agriculture. Clearly, agriculture is the main economic activity for the bulk of Tanzanians.

Table 20 exhibits the educational level of heads of households by sector of activity of head of household. Over half the heads of households (51.6 percent) did not have any education in 1977; 36.9 percent had some primary education; and 9.1 percent had completed primary education. It is clear from the table that almost all of the household heads without school education are in agriculture (94 percent), while the bulk of household heads with post-primary education (86 percent) are engaged in the nonagricultural sectors. Among those with some primary education, agriculture occupies 77 percent. Education, and especially

TABLE 19
Tanzania: Distribution of Rural and Urban Households by Size (percentages).

Household Size	Rural	Urban
1	4.8	12.6
2	9.3	10.9
3–4	25.9	23.9
5–6	25.1	24.7
7–8	17.3	14.8
9–	17.6	13.1
Total number of households (000)	2,585.1	453.7

Source: Household Budget Survey, 1976/1977, Table 4C.

TABLE 20

Tanzania: Household Distribution According to Educational Level and Industry of Head of Household, 1976/77.

Educational Level		Agriculture	Mining and Quarrying	Manufacturing	Public Utilities	Construction	Commerce	Transport and Communication	Finance	Community Services	Total
No school class completed		1,470,900	0	22,790	1,060	6,340	16,060	18,780	270	31,870	1,568,060
	a	57.44	0.00	24.44	9.56	25.02	24.30	37.86	1.73	14.75	51.60
	b	93.80	0.00	1.45	0.07	0.40	1.02	1.20	0.02	2.03	100.00
One to six school classes completed		955,610	570	36,290	4,960	14,060	29,740	14,460	4,530	59,580	1,119,780
	a	37.32	48.72	38.93	44.72	55.49	44.99	29.15	28.98	27.58	36.85
	b	85.34	0.05	3.24	0.44	1.26	2.66	1.29	0.40	5.32	100.00
Completed primary education		123,810	600	30,520	4,810	4,100	13,170	9,820	5,850	83,470	276,160
	a	4.84	51.28	32.74	43.37	16.18	19.92	19.80	37.43	38.64	9.09
	b	44.83	0.22	11.05	1.74	1.48	4.77	3.56	2.12	30.23	100.00
One to three years of secondary education		7,470	0	900	120	70	4,000	4,000	2,710	14,310	33,580
	a	0.29	0.00	0.97	1.08	0.28	6.05	8.06	17.34	6.62	1.11
	b	22.25	0.00	2.68	0.36	0.21	11.91	11.91	8.07	42.61	100.00

										Total
Completed form IV, V, or VI aggregate											
	(count)	1,880	0	2,070	140	770	2,660	2,540	1,640	17,065	28,765
	a	0.07	0.00	2.22	1.26	3.04	4.02	5.12	10.49	7.90	0.95
	b	6.53	0.00	7.19	0.49	2.68	9.25	8.83	5.70	59.30	100.00
Vocational course after primary school or form IV, VI aggregate											
	(count)	920	0	660	0	0	470	0	630	9,720	12,400
	a	0.04	0.00	0.71	0.00	0.00	0.71	0.00	4.03	4.50	0.41
	b	7.43	0.00	5.33	0.00	0.00	3.79	0.00	5.08	78.45	100.00
Total											
	(count)	2,560,590	1,170	93,230	11,090	25,340	66,100	49,600	15,630	216,010	3,038,740
	a	100.00	100.00	100.00	100.00	100.00	100.00	100.00	100.00	100.00	100.00
	b	84.26	0.04	3.07	0.36	0.83	2.18	1.63	0.51	7.11	100.00

Source: Household Budget Survey, 1976/77, Table 27.
Note: Figures in row "a" below numbers correspond to vertical percentages. Figures in row "b" correspond to horizontal percentages.

post-primary education, are thus strongly associated with movement out of agricultural activities. A striking aspect of the table is the small proportion of household heads with post-primary education (only 2.5 percent). These figures describe a poor human capital situation in the late 1970s, despite efforts at universal primary and adult education after the Arusha declaration and the villagization campaign. According to some observers, those policies bore fruit only toward the late seventies. For instance, according to the International Labour Office (ILO 1982), in 1970 general illiteracy was 68 percent, and the primary school enrollment rate was 35 percent. By the late 1970s, illiteracy was down to 10 percent, and primary school enrollment was up to 70 percent (ILO 1982).

STRUCTURE OF INCOME

Tanzanians have diversified patterns of income. Table 21 exhibits the sources of average, per household income in rural and urban Tanzania, including nonmonetary (subsistence) income. About 48 percent of total income in rural areas is nonmonetary income, which is basically consumption of own-produced food. In the urban areas the proportion is much lower at 6.6 percent, as expected. If we count all nonmonetary income as income from agriculture (the actual proportion is 97.5 percent in rural, and 96.7 percent in urban, areas), then own-account agricultural activities (including fishing) accounted for 67.7 percent of average, per-household rural income in 1976/77 and 8.9 percent of average urban household income.

Wages and salaries are the main source of income in urban areas, accounting for 49.9 percent of total income, they account for only 7.7 percent of total, and 16.2 of cash, income in the rural areas. In the rural areas the second major income source is the category of trade, enterprise, and professional activities, accounting for 17 percent of total, and 35.7 percent of cash, income for the average household. Notice that in rural areas, cash income from trade, enterprise, and professions is as important as cash income from crop sales and much more important than cash income from wages. This might be due to the fact that wage labor in Tanzania was illegal for many years and might be underestimated. The same holds for urban areas where 23.9 percent of total income (25.6 percent of cash income) is accounted for by trade, enterprise, or profession. Furthermore, this component of income is one of the most heavily underestimated, especially in urban areas (ILO 1982).

Almost all households in rural areas (86.7 percent) have some cash income from trade, enterprise, or profession, while the same holds for only 59.2 percent of urban households. Also, a fairly large proportion of rural households (36.8 percent) have some income from remittances or gifts.

TABLE 21
Structure of Household Income in Rural and Urban Tanzania, 1976/77.

Source of Cash Income	Average Household Income from Different Sources (in Tsh per household)			Number of Households Making Cash Income from Given Source (in thousands)		
	Rural	Urban	Total	Rural	Urban	Total
Crop husbandry	937 (17.31)	110 (1.20)	814 (13.64)	2061 (79.73)	83 (18.32)	2,144 (70.57)
Animal husbandry	113 (2.09)	26 (0.28)	100 (1.68)	1453 (56.21)	59 (13.02)	1,512 (49.77)
Fishing	39 (0.72)	73 (0.80)	44 (0.74)	99 (3.83)	15 (3.31)	114 (3.75)
Wages and salaries	418 (7.72)	4,557 (49.91)	1,036 (17.36)	756 (29.25)	307 (67.77)	1,063 (34.99)
Trade, own enterprise, or profession	921 (17.01)	2,186 (23.94)	1,110 (18.60)	2,242 (86.73)	268 (59.16)	2,510 (82.62)
Registered cooperatives	148 (2.73)	174 (1.91)	152 (2.55)	584 (22.59)	29 (6.40)	613 (20.18)
Rents, sublets	5 (0.09)	162 (1.77)	29 (0.49)	34 (1.32)	53 (11.70)	87 (2.86)
Interests and dividends	11 (0.20)	63 (0.69)	18 (0.30)	79 (3.06)	18 (3.97)	97 (3.19)
Remittances and gifts	94 (1.74)	234 (2.56)	115 (1.93)	940 (36.36)	141 (31.13)	1,081 (35.58)
Sale of assets	33 (0.61)	90 (0.99)	41 (0.69)	218 (8.43)	37 (8.17)	255 (8.39)

(Table continues on the following page.)

TABLE 21
(continued)

Source of Cash Income	Average Household Income from Different Sources (in Tsh per household)			Number of Households Making Cash Income from Given Source (in thousands)		
	Rural	Urban	Total	Rural	Urban	Total
Lottery, scholarships	1 (0.02)	7 (0.08)	2 (0.03)	32 (1.24)	6 (1.32)	38 (1.25)
Pensions, insurance, provident fund	5 (0.09)	67 (0.73)	14 (0.23)	23 (0.89)	8 (1.77)	31 (1.02)
Loans from family or friends	31 (0.57)	175 (1.92)	53 (0.89)	493 (19.07)	89 (19.65)	583 (19.19)
Loans and overdrafts from banks	20 (0.37)	106 (1.16)	33 (0.55)	55 (2.13)	22 (4.86)	77 (2.53)
Cashing of bank savings, securities, etc.	60 (1.11)	497 (5.44)	126 (2.11)	288 (11.14)	55 (12.14)	343 (11.29)
Total stated	2,836 (52.38)	8,527 (93.39)	3,686 (61.75)			
Nonmonetary income	2,578 (47.62)	604 (6.61)	2,283 (38.25)			
Total income	5,414 (100.00)	9,131 (100.00)	5,969 (100.00)			
Number of households ('000)	2,585.1	453.7	3,038.8	2,585 (100.00)	453 (100.00)	3,038 (100.00)

Source: Computed from Household Budget Survey, 1976/77, Tables 13 and 4A.
Note: Numbers in parentheses below figures in the first three columns denote vertical percentages.

The average reported cash income seems to be much higher for urban households, compared with rural ones, by a ratio of 3 to 1. This, however, is counterbalanced by a more than 4-to-1 advantage in the rural areas as far as nonmonetary income is concerned. When added, the average, total per-household income in the urban areas appears to be almost 70 percent higher than average, per-household rural income. Whether this translates to a corresponding real income differential, of course, depends on quantities and prices of similar types of consumed goods.

The figures in Table 21 hide the fact that within rural and urban areas, there are both farm and nonfarm households with quite different patterns of income. Table 22 exhibits the structure of cash income for these different types of households and compares it with the corresponding structure from the 1969 HBS.

It can be noticed from the table that in the rural areas, sources of income of both farm and nonfarm households shifted between 1969 and 1976/77 toward trade, enterprise, and profession, as well as "other" sources (which includes all the other categories exhibited in Table 21). In the urban areas, the pattern is quite different. First, notice the sharp increase in the number of so-called "farm" households living in urban areas between 1969 and 1976/77. These are households whose heads are employed by agriculture-related enterprises but who are not necessarily farmers. For these, cash income shifted toward crop husbandry and "other," and away from trade or enterprise. For nonfarm urban households, the only noticeable shift is away from wages and trade and toward other sources of income.

The change most noticeable in Table 22, however, is in the total value of cash incomes. In the rural areas, between 1969 and 1976/77, the average cash income per household almost tripled for both farm and nonfarm households. In the urban areas, it appears to have declined in nominal terms for farm households, while it increased by less than 50 percent for nonfarm households. Given that the increase in the national consumer price index during the period was 121.7 percent (obtained by averaging the last two quarters of 1976 and the first two quarters of 1977 [Tanzania Bureau of Statistics, *Economic Survey* 1982]), and that the definitions of a household implied a larger average household size in 1976/77, the data indicate a substantial drop in real per capita incomes in the urban areas, as shown in Table 23. If the degree of underestimation of incomes is the same in both the 1969 and 1976/77 surveys, the data imply a small increase in rural, real per capita incomes and an enormous decline of 68 percent in urban, per capita real incomes. This was also the conclusion reached by the ILO mission in 1982 (ILO 1982).

The structure of rural income, as reported by two other detailed income surveys, done in 1979/80 and 1982/83, is shown in Table 24. In the 1979/80

TABLE 22

Tanzania: Structure of Average Cash Income per Household, Rural and Urban Farm and Nonfarm Households, 1969 and 1976/77 (percentages).

	1969			*1976/77*		
	Farm	*Nonfarm*	*Total*	*Farm*	*Nonfarm*	*Total*
Sources of rural cash household income						
Crop husbandry	36.90	11.94	31.36	38.94	13.04	33.04
Animal husbandry	16.10	2.63	12.53	4.68	1.65	3.98
Wages and salaries	10.58	56.74	22.61	5.68	45.48	14.74
Trade, enterprise, profession	26.91	21.36	24.95	34.67	25.14	32.48
Other	9.87	7.34	9.06	16.03	14.69	15.76
Total	100.00	100.00	100.00	100.00	100.00	100.00
Average cash income per household (Tsh)	851	1,826	982	2,501	5,207	2,836
Number of households ('000)	2,282.7	354.3	2,637	2,264.7	320.4	2,585.1
Sources of urban cash household income						
Crop husbandry	1.89	0.56	0.76	8.44	0.30	1.29
Animal husbandry	1.13	0.37	0.40	2.88	0.58	0.86
Wages and salaries	19.71	63.04	60.39	22.34	57.76	53.44
Trade, enterprise, profession	57.18	28.66	29.22	40.01	23.63	25.64
Other	20.08	7.38	9.23	26.32	17.73	18.78
Total	100.00	100.00	100.00	100.00	100.00	100.00
Average cash income per household (Tsh)	3,800	6,299	6,036	3,434	10,742	8,527
Number of households ('000)	16	136	152	137.5	316.2	453.7

Source: Computed from Household Budget Surveys, 1969 and 1976/77.

survey, the shares of subsistence as well as those of wages and own-business, summarized under own business, appear to be lower than in the 1976/77 HBS, while the livestock share appears to be much higher. In the 1982/83 survey, crop income (including subsistence) appears to be lower, while own-business income is higher than in 1976/77 and 1979/80. The share of livestock income is also quite high. Although the two surveys sighted above are not representative—the 1979/80 survey covering eight regions and the 1982/83 survey covering only four—the very large difference in livestock income share merits some discussion.

TABLE 23
Tanzania: Nominal and Real Per Capita Cash Incomes in 1969 and 1976/77
(Tsh/capita).

	1969		1976/77	
	Rural	*Urban*	*Rural*	*Urban*
Nominal per capita cash income (Tsh)	213	2,414	489.0	1,705.0
Real per capita cash income (1969 base)	213	2,414	221.0	769.0
National CPI	100	100	221.7	221.7

Source: Computed from Household Budget Surveys, 1969 and 1976/77.

TABLE 24
Tanzania: Composition of Rural Household Income, 1980 and 1983
(percentages).

	1979/80	*1982/83*
Net income from crop sales	14.1	48.5[b]
Subsistence crop production	41.4	c
Net livestock income	21.0	13.9
Own-business	19.5[a]	26.3
Wages		6.4
Remittances	4.0	4.8
Per capita annual income (Tsh)	734.3	1,549.0
Mean household size	5.3	d
Per household annual income (Tsh)	3,892.0	d

Sources: For 1979/80, Collier et al. (1986), pp. 65–66; for 1982/83, Bevan et al. (1989), p. 54.
[a] In Collier et al., only total nonfarm earnings are reported.
[b] In Bevan et al. (1990), the crop income is reported as originating from food crops (41.5 percent) and cash crops (7 percent).
[c] In Bevan et al. (1990), 72 percent of all farm income (62 percent of crop income and more than 100 percent of livestock income) is derived from subsistence. This implies that 45 percent of total income is derived from subsistence.
[d] Not indicated in the relevant source.

In both surveys, particularly the 1979/80 survey (p. 64), the problematic nature of livestock income is readily acknowledged. The reason is that although livestock yields normal outputs (such as milk, meat, offals, etc.) that can be valued in a standard way, it is, on the other hand, one of the main assets of rural households. The latter implies that sales of livestock should better be thought of in a separate income category, that of sales of assets, in which sales of any other asset would also be recorded. Similarly, purchases of livestock should be recorded separately and made part of investment expenditures. In the same fashion, stock valuation adjustments, such as livestock births and deaths, should be included as a separate component of income for which there should be a corresponding, equal investment outlay. The separate recording of livestock sales and purchases as asset changes should be done because conceptually the net of these is equivalent to net dissaving in livestock assets, and hence it is not a proper part of current or permanent income.

The 1979/80 survey includes livestock sales as part of current income, does not include livestock valuation, and is not clear as to whether it nets out livestock purchases. If only sales of livestock are included, this would tend to overestimate total income, as well as income from livestock, and indeed this seems to be the case in the results.

The 1982/83 survey (p. 305) correctly included as part of livestock income own-consumption of produce from livestock (such as milk). Net cash sales of stock (sales minus purchases) are also included, but they are again netted out in the stock valuation definition. Hence it appears that livestock income includes, apart from consumption or sales of products, net stock valuations—that is, births plus net gifts (received minus given), minus deaths, thefts, own-consumption (of stock), and stock given to labor. It is not clear why all stock valuations are included as part of current income. While some parts of stock valuation, such as net births or gifts of livestock received, are certainly part of current income, own-consumption of stock or gifts of stock given out are part of household expenditure, not income. Hence counting all stock valuations as part of income will probably bias the "normal" income considerably. For instance, in a bad year a liquidation of livestock herds would count as negative income, and in fact this is what seems to account for the large negative livestock income of the poorer rural households in Bevan et al. (1990). The proper way would have been to record all such asset transactions separately as saving or dissaving and to include as part of current income only those asset changes that result from net births, net transfers of stock, and stock given out as wages.

In fact, this is what appears to have been done in the 1976/77 HBS, as sources of income from asset transactions, including livestock sales, are recorded separately, and correspondingly investments, including purchases of livestock, are recorded separately as part of the total distribution of proceeds from all sources. As can be seen from Table 21, however, in the 1976/77 survey, proceeds from sales of assets are reported to be very low. It is not clear from the survey's methodological explanation exactly how the various income components were measured, and hence it is not clear what exactly is included under livestock income and sales of assets. The conclusion is that some doubt must be cast on the rural livestock income figures, especially those from the 1979/80 and 1982/83 surveys, particularly when one attempts to compare the composition of rural household incomes over time. It appears, nevertheless, that rural crop income, including subsistence consumption, declined as a share of total income from 1976/77 to 1982/83, while the share of income from trade and entrepreneurship seems to have increased.

Table 25 exhibits the different sources of cash income for households with heads employed in the private, cooperative, or public sector. The greatest number of Tanzanian households in 1976/77 had heads who were privately employed, mainly in agriculture. Only 11.4 percent were employed by cooperatives, parastatals, or in other public-sector jobs. The bulk of the cash income of those households came from wages and salaries, and their total cash income was on average more than twice that of households operating in the private sector. Given, however, that most private households are rural, farming households and that subsistence income accounts for about half of their total income (cf. Table 21), the difference in total average income between households whose heads are in the private sector and those in the public sector does not appear to be very large.

The education of the head of household appears to make a significant difference in average household cash income in both rural and urban areas, as well as in the individual sectors, as shown in Table 26. Among rural households, those whose head had completed primary school had cash incomes about twice as high as those with no school education. For those with secondary or vocational post-primary education, the ratio is close to four to one. Those with high-level secondary education (completed form VI) had the highest overall cash incomes, but their numbers were rather small, and they were all concentrated in public service. That education is positively associated with cash incomes was also found by Collier et al. (1986). Table 26 also exhibits the average household cash income by economic sector and industry of the head of household. Households with heads in commerce and finance seem to be the wealthiest overall. There were 66,110 households whose head was in commerce in 1976/77, only 2.2 percent of the total number; only 15,600 households had heads engaged in finance. The bulk of household heads (84.3 percent) were engaged in agriculture.

Table 27 exhibits the annual average cash incomes of Tanzanian households by sector and economic activity of head of household. It is interesting to note that households whose head is engaged in agriculture do not exhibit much cash income differentiation irrespective of whether the head is employed privately or by the public sector in all its various forms. When subsistence income is considered, average income in agricultural households does not seem to be very different irrespective of whether the household head is engaged privately or in an agricultural cooperative, agricultural parastatal, or agricultural public service.

TABLE 25

Tanzania: Annual Cash Income in Private Households by Source of Income and Sector of Head of Household, 1976/77 (Tsh per household).

Source of Cash Icnome	Private	Registered Cooperative	Parastatal	Public Service	Other	Total Stated	Sector not Stated
Crop husbandry	908 (29.94)	693 (9.61)	139 (1.48)	415 (5.42)	43 (0.63)	822 (22.07)	501 (22.71)
Animal husbandry	114 (3.76)	8 (0.11)	7 (0.07)	31 (0.41)	15 (0.22)	101 (2.71)	42 (1.90)
Fishing	51 (1.68)	57 (0.79)	3 (0.03)	6 (0.08)	0 (0.00)	45 (1.21)	7 (0.32)
Wages and salaries	237 (7.81)	4,397 (60.96)	7,417 (79.13)	5,896 (77.06)	5,206 (76.42)	1,052 (28.25)	380 (17.23)
Trade, own enterprise, or profession	1,190 (39.24)	1,340 (18.58)	702 (7.49)	404 (5.28)	839 (12.32)	1,116 (29.97)	881 (39.94)
Registered cooperative	165 (5.44)	121 (1.68)	55 (0.59)	112 (1.46)	27 (0.40)	153 (4.11)	92 (4.17)
Rents, sublets	24 (0.79)	80 (1.11)	68 (0.73)	20 (0.26)	78 (1.15)	28 (0.75)	49 (2.22)
Interests and dividends	20 (0.66)	12 (0.17)	12 (0.13)	6 (0.08)	14 (0.21)	19 (0.51)	8 (0.36)
Remittances and gifts	105 (3.46)	124 (1.72)	161 (1.72)	186 (2.43)	213 (3.13)	114 (3.06)	121 (5.49)
Sale of assets	40 (1.32)	69 (0.96)	81 (0.86)	44 (0.58)	9 (0.13)	42 (1.13)	29 (1.31)

Lottery, scholarships	1 (0.05)	2 (0.05)	23 (0.34)	6 (0.08)	4 (0.04)	0 (0.00)	1 (0.03)
Pensions, insurance, provident fund	13 (0.59)	14 (0.38)	0 (0.00)	22 (0.29)	81 (0.86)	34 (0.47)	10 (0.33)
Loans from family or friends	33 (1.50)	53 (1.42)	150 (2.20)	159 (2.08)	166 (1.77)	147 (2.04)	37 (1.22)
Loans and overdrafts from banks, etc.	16 (0.73)	34 (0.91)	30 (0.44)	55 (0.72)	105 (1.12)	53 (0.73)	28 (0.92)
Cashing of bank savings, securities, etc.	33 (1.50)	128 (3.44)	163 (2.39)	289 (3.78)	372 (3.97)	78 (1.08)	104 (3.43)
Total stated	2,206 (100.00)	3,724 (100.00)	6,812 (100.00)	7,651 (100.00)	9,373 (100.00)	7,213 (100.00)	3,033 (100.00)
Number of households ('000)	76	2,963	68	164	144	287	2,559

Source: Household Budget Survey, 1976/77, Table 23.
Note: Number in parenthesis indicates percentage.

TABLE 26

Tanzania: Annual Cash Income by Educational Level of Head of Household, 1976/77 (Tsh per household).

Educational Level	Rural	Urban	Agriculture	Mining and Quarrying	Manufacturing	Public Utilities	Construction	Commerce	Transport and Communication	Finance	Community Services	Total
No school class completed	2,330	5,494	2,337	0	6,871	7,092	5,806	9,561	7,196	4,622	7,286	2,654
One to six school classes completed	3,030	8,035	2,829	5,156	8,131	9,574	4,714	12,119	8,099	7,793	7,198	3,623
Completed primary education	4,777	9,154	3,584	5,145	7,690	8,334	8,212	13,697	8,721	6,854	8,225	6,330
One to three years of secondary education	10,493	14,106	3,313	0	19,977	9,647	17,033	38,406	8,186	13,184	10,825	12,574
Completed form IV	11,189	24,051	12,066	0	19,891	13,985	8,817	88,776	13,020	17,702	13,739	21,014
Completed form V	0	0	0	0	0	0	0	0	0	0	0	0
Completed form VI	17,101	35,165	0	0	33,812	0	0	63,112	0	20,599	24,337	28,140
Vocational course after primary school	10,443	9,786	2,636	0	12,804	0	0	0	0	0	11,659	10,403
Vocational course after form IV	10,961	22,919	0	0	34,871	0	0	56,665	0	17,889	13,717	18,485
Vocational course after form VI	0	29,267	0	0	0	0	0	27,218	0	45,649	25,565	29,267
Total	2,870	8,544	2,591	5,150	8,220	8,857	5,714	16,617	8,139	10,380	8,735	3,686

Source: Household Budget Survey, 1976/77, Tables 27 and 33.

TABLE 27

Tanzania: Annual Cash Income in Private Households by Economic Activity and Sector of Head of Household, 1976/77 (Tsh per household).

Industry of Head of Household	Private	Registered Cooperative	Parastatal	Public Service	Other	Total Stated	Sector not Stated
Agriculture	2,580	5,176	4,847	5,203	4,315	2,603	2,206
	80.969	0.069	0.239	0.303	0.196	81.776	2.486
Mining and quarrying	6,182	0	6,527	4,205	3,949	5,150	0
	0.003	0.000	0.014	0.012	0.009	0.039	0.000
Manufacturing	8,646	8,956	8,512	7,749	7,028	8,220	0
	0.667	0.227	1.214	0.469	0.491	3.068	0.000
Public utilities	25,298	6,913	9,888	5,971	8,791	8,857	0
	0.026	0.013	0.094	0.173	0.059	0.365	0.000
Construction	3,104	3,941	9,640	5,901	8,013	5,714	0
	0.212	0.066	0.090	0.357	0.108	0.834	0.000
Commerce	18,164	8,001	7,477	2,591	8,502	16,617	0
	1.844	0.121	0.085	0.003	0.122	2.175	0.000
Transport and communication	16,128	3,914	9,093	7,279	6,688	8,139	0
	0.113	0.070	0.525	0.397	0.528	1.632	0.000
Finance	18,465	7,840	10,005	10,363	8,987	10,308	0
	0.037	0.105	0.242	0.101	0.023	0.508	0.000
Community services	9,906	7,339	10,375	8,083	6,771	8,735	0
	0.330	0.275	2.242	3.575	0.685	7.108	0.000
Total	3,033	7,213	9,373	7,651	6,812	3,724	2,206
	84.202	0.945	4.745	5.390	2.222	97.504	2.486
Number of households ('000)						3,038.880	
						100.000	

Source: Household Budget Survey, 1976/77, Table 25.

This also seems to hold for those households whose heads are engaged in mining, manufacturing, and community services. However, for the households whose head is engaged in public utilities, commerce, transport, and finance, the private sector seems to offer much better average incomes than the public sector. For construction, the reverse seems to be the case. For those households whose head is engaged in construction via parastatals, average annual cash income is more than three times that of households whose head is engaged in private construction activities.

DISTRIBUTION OF INCOME

The 1976/77 Household Budget Survey compiled information about both cash and noncash incomes. Earlier attempts to look at income distribution, such as that of the ILO (1982), were hampered by the availability of cash income statistics only at the time.

Table 28 exhibits household income statistics for Tanzania mainland for 1976/77. It is interesting to note that most income differentiation is due to the cash component. The ratio of average per capita nonmonetary income between the highest income group and the lowest is 5.5, while the same ratio for per capita cash income is 43.9, and for total income is 20.6. It clearly appears that despite government efforts during the 1970s, there was substantial income differentiation and inequality in Tanzania in 1976/1977. Nonmonetary income was much more equitably distributed than cash income. That is to be expected, as almost all nonmonetary income consists of subsistence food production, which depends largely on labor. Nevertheless, it is interesting to note that higher-income households have higher per capita cash incomes as well as nonmonetary incomes. This could be due to a product composition effect—namely, that higher-income households also produce higher value foods (e.g., livestock products).

In 1976/77, average total income per household in Tanzania stood at 5,969 Tsh, of which 2,283 Tsh or 38.2 percent, was nonmonetary income. The figures show the importance of subsistence agriculture in the economy. It is to be noted that for the lowest three income groups, which account for 34 percent of the population, average per capita subsistence income was equal to, or greater than, per capita cash income. Only in the highest three household income groups, which account for only 16 percent of the population, was the share of subsistence in total per capita income less than 30 percent. Given that traditionally, household budget surveys underestimate incomes, particularly those of high-income groups, this figure also most likely is an underestimate. At the very bottom of the distribution, 8 percent of households, or 5 percent of the people, enjoyed 2 percent of total income. Forty-one percent of households, or 33 percent of people,

TABLE 28

Tanzania: Distribution of Income in Tanzania Mainland, 1976/77 (Tsh).

	Income Group									
	0–999	1,000–1,900	2,000–3,900	4,000–5,999	6,000–7,999	8,000–9,999	10,000–24,999	25,000–39,999	40,000 and Over	Total
No. of households ('000)	14.91	234.18	985.41	864.33	399.68	191.37	313.12	22.44	13.32	3,038.75
No. of household members ('000)	28.97	809.02	4,779.01	4,876.47	2,623.20	1,320.45	2,426.11	184.06	106.68	17,153.97
Average household size	1.94	3.45	4.85	5.64	6.56	6.90	7.75	8.20	8.01	5.65
Average total income per household (Tsh)	769.00	1,611.00	3,061.00	4,911.00	6,874.00	8,850.00	14,295.00	31,395.00	65,183.00	5,969.00
Cash income per household (Tsh)	301.00	697.00	1,542.00	2,753.00	3,984.00	6,049.00	10,002.00	23,446.00	54,525.00	3,686.00
Nonmonetary income per household (Tsh)	468.00	913.00	1,519.00	2,159.00	2,890.00	2,801.00	4,292.00	7,949.00	10,658.00	2,283.00
Per capita total income (Tsh)	395.83	466.33	631.16	870.45	1,047.34	1,282.59	1,844.94	3,828.00	8,138.94	1,057.38
Per capita cash income (Tsh)	154.94	201.76	317.95	487.95	607.01	876.65	1,290.88	2,858.78	6,808.15	652.96
Per capita nonmonetary income	240.90	264.28	313.21	382.67	440.33	405.94	553.93	969.22	1,330.79	404.42
Percentage of households	0.49	7.71	32.43	28.44	13.15	6.30	10.30	0.74	0.44	100.00
Percentage of people	0.17	4.72	27.86	28.43	15.29	7.70	14.14	1.07	0.62	100.00
Percentage of income	0.06	2.08	16.63	23.40	15.15	9.34	24.67	3.88	4.79	100.00
Cumulative % of households	0.49	8.20	40.63	69.07	82.22	88.52	98.82	99.56	100.00	100.00
Cumulative % of people	0.17	4.89	32.74	61.17	76.46	84.16	98.31	99.38	100.00	100.00
Cumulative % of income	0.06	2.14	18.77	42.17	57.32	66.65	91.33	95.21	100.00	100.00
										0.36[a]
										0.26[a]

Source: Computed from Household Budget Survey, 1976/77, Table 43.

[a] Denote Gini coefficients.

at the low end enjoyed 19 percent of total income. At the very high end of the distribution, 1 percent of households comprising 2 percent of the people, enjoyed 5 percent of total income, which is probably an underestimate. Eleven percent of households, comprising 16 percent of the people, had 33 percent of total income at the top. These figures imply a rather equitable distribution of income compared with other countries. In fact, the Gini coefficient, computed on the basis of cumulative incomes attributed to households in Table 28, is 0.363; the Gini coefficient computed on the basis of incomes accruing to people is only 0.264.

It must be realized at this point that the income statistics exhibited in Table 28 aggregate rural and urban households. We could not obtain detailed, similar statistics by rural and urban classifications. It might be argued that the cost of living is higher in the cities; incomes ought to be higher there, and hence the picture exhibited in Table 28 is distorted. On the other hand, however, while the cost of food is higher in the cities, the cost of nonfood items is higher in the rural areas. Since food is a very large component of expenditures in Tanzania, the relative cost of living is probably higher in the cities, on balance. However, the distortion would tend to overestimate inequalities. Hence the low Gini coefficient found could be considered an overestimate of the true one.

Earlier income distribution studies (e.g., those reviewed in ILO 1982) used data on cash incomes only and utilized numbers of households, not people. For instance, the Gini coefficient that was computed by the ILO mission (based on preliminary results on cash income of rural households from the 1976/77 HBS) was 0.49 (ILO 1982). That compares with 0.364 computed here, utilizing full income figures and aggregating over all households. As will be seen below, however, total incomes (cash and subsistence) are much more equitably distributed.

Table 29 exhibits regional income distribution statistics computed from data similar to those of Table 28. With the exception of Kigoma and Mara, all regions exhibit Gini coefficients similar, to or smaller than, the one for the whole of Tanzania. Kigoma exhibits a high Gini coefficient, due to inequalities in reported nonmonetary income, which might imply something suspect about the data. In per capita income terms, Dar es Salaam, Kigoma, Kilimanjaro, Mara, Morogoro, Rukwa, Tabora, and West Lake exhibit per capita incomes above the average for Tanzania as a whole.

Table 30 exhibits the distribution of per capita incomes in Tanzania mainland in 1976/77. Because of household composition effects, this distribution is not expected to be the same as that derived from analyzing household incomes. For instance, Table 28 indicates that in all of Tanzania only 28,970 people, or only 0.2 percent of the population, lived in households whose total annual income was

TABLE 29

Tanzania: Regional Income Distribution Statistics, 1976/77 (Tsh).

	Number of Households	Cash Income Per Household	Nonmonetary Income Per Household	Total Income Per household	Total Income Per Capita	Gini Coefficient Based on Household Income	Gini Coefficient Based on Personal Income
Arusha	139.8	2,881	2,228	5,109	958	0.274	0.224
Coast	99.4	2,481	1,342	3,824	676	0.243	0.122
Dar es Salaam	165.2	10,988	319	11,306	2,251	0.297	0.228
Dodoma	181.4	1,829	2,196	4,025	784	0.373	0.241
Iringa	168.2	1,961	2,326	4,287	806	0.275	0.093
Kigoma	103.2	2,814	7,317	10,131	1,672	0.504	0.553
Kilimanjaro	165.7	5,492	2,665	8,157	1,381	0.231	0.095
Lindi	119.2	1,960	1,837	3,797	775	0.247	0.146
Mara	119.6	5,843	1,784	7,627	1,144	0.438	0.518
Mbeya	186.8	2,874	2,192	5,066	863	0.253	0.165
Morogoro	164.0	4,607	1,938	6,545	1,183	0.289	0.194
Mtwara	177.6	2,143	2,037	4,180	841	0.278	0.208
Mwanza	243.2	3,205	1,869	5,074	758	0.299	0.202
Rukwa	73.9	3,634	5,226	8,860	1,463	0.322	0.175
Ruvuma	109.8	2,599	2,477	5,076	1,039	0.305	0.227
Shinyanga	204.0	2,706	2,237	4,943	753	0.335	0.218
Singida	105.1	1,881	2,657	4,538	782	0.348	0.251
Tabora	149.1	4,319	2,816	7,135	1,294	0.360	0.235
Tanga	180.1	3,638	1,599	5,237	927	0.271	0.128
West Lake	183.4	4,834	2,058	6,892	1,377	0.332	0.193
Tanzania	3,038.8	3,686	2,283	5,969	1,057	0.363	0.264

Source: Computed from Household Budget Survey, 1976/77.

TABLE 30

Tanzania: Distribution of Per Capita Income, 1976/77.

| | Per Capita Income Group | | | | | | | | | |
	0–50	51–100	101–200	201–300	301–400	401–500	501–1,000	1,001–2,000	2,000– and Above	Total
Number of households ('000)	0.703	0.122	15.670	61.537	174.635	238.040	1,167.615	921.046	459.306	3,038.674
Number of people ('000)	2.814	1.461	164.265	556.318	1,404.981	1,768.159	7,325.905	4,497.686	1,431.981	17,153.570
Average household size	4.003	11.975	10.483	9.040	8.045	7.428	6.274	4.883	3.118	5.645
Percentage of households	0.023	0.004	0.516	2.025	5.747	7.834	38.425	30.311	15.115	100.000
Percentage of people	0.016	0.009	0.958	3.243	8.191	10.308	42.708	26.220	8.348	100.000
Cumulative percentage of households	0.023	0.027	0.543	2.568	8.315	16.149	54.574	84.885	100.000	
Cumulative percentage of people	0.016	0.025	0.983	4.226	12.416	22.724	65.432	91.652	100.000	0.140[a]
Income per capita	25.000	75.000	150.000	250.000	350.000	450.000	750.000	1,500.000	3,106.000	
Percentage of income	0.000	0.001	0.136	0.767	2.711	4.386	30.290	37.193	24.520	100.000
Cumulative percentage of income	0.000	0.001	0.137	0.904	3.614	8.001	38.291	75.484	100.000	

Source: Computed from Household Budget Survey, 1976/77, Table 43.

[a] Denotes Gini coefficients.

less than 1,000 Tsh. The per capita income of this household group is 396 Tsh. In Table 30, however, we observe that in 1976/77 there were 2.1 million Tanzanians, or 12.4 percent, living in households whose per capita income was less than 400 Tsh. This implies that within each household income class, there are many households whose per capita income is much below the mean per capita income for the household class as a whole. The 1976/77 HBS tables we obtained did not specify the mean per capita income of households in each per capita income class. To compute the Gini coefficient of the personal income distribution in Table 30, we assumed that the mean in each per capita income group is the unweighted average of the bounding per capita incomes. For the top income group, the mean was estimated so that the total income computed is equal to that reported. The Gini coefficient thus computed is 0.14, which is quite small by international standards. Despite the possible underestimation of inequality inherent in household budget surveys, per capita income in Tanzania around 1976/77 appears to have been quite evenly distributed.

Up to now, we have considered only income. We were not able to break down the distribution of income by rural or urban location. We have, however, obtained data on distribution of household cash expenditures by rural and urban divisions. Admittedly, it would have been better to have households classified by their per capita expenditures, rather than per-household expenditures, but those data were not available. The subsequent analysis is therefore carried out on the basis of groups classified according to per-household expenditures.

Table 31 presents a breakdown of rural and urban households into cash expenditure categories. The first thing to notice is that rural households with low cash expenditures (less than 4,000 Tsh) have, on average, higher total per capita consumption than urban households of similar average cash expenditures. This, of course, is due to the much higher amount of subsistence consumption in the lower-income rural households. By contrast, urban households with high monetary expenditures have much higher total consumption expenditures than rural households with similar expenditures. This last result must be qualified, however, because rural households in the categories with cash expenditures above 40,000 Tsh are reported to have average monetary consumption smaller than the lower bounds of their respective ranges. It is not clear why this is the case. Another observation from the table is that although in the rural areas the nonmonetary income per household is fairly uniform across expenditure classes, it tends to decline for higher-expenditure households in urban areas.

Inequality seems to be much higher in urban areas than in rural ones. Thus the ratio of mean per capita total incomes between the highest and lowest cash expenditure groups in the rural areas is 4.6, while in the urban areas it is 20.3. Slightly over 70 percent of urban households had total incomes below the mean

TABLE 31

Tanzania: Distribution of Rural and Urban Households According to Cash Expenditures (Tsh).

					Expenditure Categories					
	0–999	1,000– 1,999	2,000– 3,999	4,000– 5,999	6,000– 7,999	8,000– 9,999	10,000– 24,999	25,000– 39,999	40,000– and Over	Total
Rural households										
Number of households ('000)	415	723	887	307	112	54	80	6	2	2,585
Percentage of households	16	28	34	12	4	2	3	0	0	100
Number of household members per household	4	5	6	6	7	8	8	10	12	6
Cash income per household	607	1,446	2,578	4,344	6,217	8,122	13,131	28,868	33,576	2,836
Nonmonetary income per household	2,406	2,898	2,430	2,232	2,780	2,862	2,983	3,202	4,502	2,578
Total income per household	3,013	4,344	5,008	6,576	8,997	10,983	16,115	32,060	38,078	5,414
Per capita total income	701	804	835	1,061	1,285	1,308	1,918	3,375	3,200	933
Monetary consumption expenditures per household	616	1,388	2,615	4,367	6,084	7,932	10,692	14,048	14,032	2,704
Subsistence consumption per household	2,340	2,855	2,378	2,178	2,698	2,799	2,903	3,104	4,392	2,523
Total consumption expenditure per household[a]	3,001	4,260	5,009	6,566	8,825	10,738	13,607	17,175	18,424	5,249
Per capita total consumption	698	789	835	1,059	1,261	1,278	1,620	1,808	1,548	905

Urban households

Number of households ('000)	25	37	86	89	60	54	85	10	9	454
Percentage of households	6	8	19	20	13	12	19	2	2	100
Number of household members per household	4	5	5	4	5	6	6	6	7	5
Cash income per household	636	1,384	2,989	4,973	7,241	9,228	15,033	29,211	69,171	8,527
Nonmonetary income per household	1,346	1,392	953	475	375	276	246	197	603	604
Total income per household	1,983	2,776	3,942	5,448	7,615	9,504	15,279	29,408	69,774	9,131
Per capita total income	472	603	857	1,238	1,523	1,697	2,681	4,668	9,558	1,826
Monetary consumption expenditures per household	608	1,432	2,934	4,835	6,845	8,788	14,506	29,807	48,231	7,904
Subsistence consumption per household	1,297	1,347	898	438	324	221	170	131	433	548
Total consumption expenditure per household[a]	1,932	2,800	3,843	5,280	7,183	9,016	14,695	29,950	48,668	8,465
Per capita total consumption	460	609	835	1,200	1,437	1,610	2,578	4,754	6,667	1,693

Source: Computed from Household Budget Survey, 1976/77, Tables 2 and 3.
[a] Includes some other minor items.

urban household income of 9,131 Tsh, while over 85 percent of rural households had total income below the rural mean of 5,414 Tsh. Note, however, that average household size in rural areas is a much stronger positive function of average household income than in urban areas. This implies that the share of people living in households with cash expenditures below the mean is about the same in rural and urban areas.

The Gini coefficient computed from Table 31 on the basis of households and cumulative total household incomes (both monetary and subsistence) is 0.208 in rural areas and 0.418 in urban areas. The Gini coefficient computed on the basis of income accruing to people (that is, after taking into account household size) is only 0.129 in rural areas and 0.382 in urban areas. While these statistics certainly underestimate inequality, because households are not ranked according to total expenditure or income but only according to cash expenditure, they indicate that inequality is much greater in urban than in rural areas and that, absolutely speaking, inequality in rural areas appears to have been low in 1976/77 by international standards.

The presence of subsistence income moderates inequality significantly. For instance, had we computed the Gini coefficient in rural areas on the basis of cash incomes only, a procedure that was tried by the ILO mission (ILO 1982), we would find a figure of 0.413—twice as high as the Gini computed on the basis of total incomes.

Table 32 exhibits the sources of cash income in various cash expenditure categories. Given that for most expenditure and income groups (especially in the lower range) cash expenditure is quite close to cash income (see Table 31), it is quite clear that households with low cash expenditure (and income) derive the bulk of their income from nonmonetary sources, chiefly subsistence agriculture. This was already apparent from Table 28, where for the three lowest income groups, more than half of total income came from subsistence agricultural production. What is of interest in Table 32, however, is that for all expenditure groups, cash income from agriculture (including animal husbandry and fishing) is never more than 45 percent of total cash income. For the lowest three cash expenditure classes, it is 34 percent, 43 percent, and 40 percent, respectively; for the highest two, it is only around 2 percent. Clearly, then, the poor derive a proportionately higher share of cash, as well as total, income from agriculture. However, all income groups have a well diversified pattern of cash earnings. It is interesting to note in this context that the largest nonagricultural component of cash income in low-income households is from trade, enterprise, or profession. Wage and salary income seems to be insignificant at lower incomes and is important only for the higher-expenditure households.

TABLE 32

Tanzania: Sources of Cash Income of Households According to Cash Expenditure Categories, 1976/77 (Tsh/household).

Source of Cash Income	Cash Expenditure Group										
	0–999	1,000– 1,999	2,000– 3,999	4,000– 5,999	6,000– 7,999	8,000– 9,999	10,000– 24,999	25,000– 39,999	40,000– and Over	Total
Crop husbandry	179	562	928	1,039	1,355	1,328	1,630	285	510	814
	(6.06)	(13.16)	(18.88)	(16.43)	(15.91)	(12.97)	(10.39)	(0.94)	(0.80)	(13.64)
Animal husbandry	26	49	126	144	225	109	99	39	747	100
	(0.88)	(1.15)	(2.56)	(2.28)	(2.64)	(1.06)	(0.63)	(0.13)	(1.17)	(1.68)
Fishing	4	13	40	78	92	185	80	196	0	44
	(0.14)	(0.30)	(0.81)	(1.23)	(1.08)	(1.81)	(0.51)	(0.65)	(0.00)	(0.74)
Wages and salaries	41	95	343	1,512	2,293	3,985	6,476	10,182	6,785	1,036
	(1.39)	(2.23)	(6.98)	(23.91)	(26.92)	(38.92)	(41.29)	(33.54)	(10.64)	(17.36)
Trade, own-enterprise, or profession	256	551	853	1,152	1,618	2,057	3,269	13,750	27,992	1,110
	(8.66)	(12.91)	(17.36)	(18.22)	(19.00)	(20.09)	(20.84)	(45.30)	(43.92)	(18.60)
Registered cooperatives	12	46	99	204	268	196	651	249	6,176	152
	(0.41)	(1.08)	(2.01)	(3.23)	(3.15)	(1.91)	(4.15)	(0.82)	(9.69)	(2.55)
Rents, sublets	1	4	12	23	71	62	78	390	2,253	29
	(0.03)	(0.09)	(0.24)	(0.36)	(0.83)	(0.61)	(0.50)	(1.28)	(3.53)	(0.49)
Interests and dividends	0	3	9	15	54	47	101	209	420	18
	(0.00)	(0.07)	(0.18)	(0.24)	(0.63)	(0.46)	(0.64)	(0.69)	(0.66)	(0.30)
Remittances and gifts	53	62	102	143	219	226	344	215	94	115
	(1.79)	(1.45)	(2.08)	(2.26)	(2.57)	(2.21)	(2.19)	(0.71)	(0.15)	(1.93)
Sale of assets	13	10	29	28	99	79	204	80	1,139	41
	(0.44)	(0.23)	(0.59)	(0.44)	(1.16)	(0.77)	(1.30)	(0.26)	(1.79)	(0.69)

(Table continues on the following page.)

TABLE 32
(continued)

Source of Cash Income		Cash Expenditure Group								
	0–999	1,000–1,999	2,000–3,999	4,000–5,999	6,000–7,999	8,000–9,999	10,000–24,999	25,000–39,999	40,000– and Over	Total
Lottery, scholarships	1 (0.03)	1 (0.02)	2 (0.04)	5 (0.08)	3 (0.04)	4 (0.04)	11 (0.07)	0 (0.00)	0 (0.00)	2 (0.03)
Pensions, insurance, provident fund	0 (0.00)	0 (0.00)	5 (0.10)	16 (0.25)	12 (0.14)	0 (0.00)	119 (0.76)	616 (2.03)	0 (0.00)	14 (0.23)
Loans from family or friends	10 (0.34)	17 (0.40)	29 (0.59)	69 (1.09)	102 (1.20)	179 (1.75)	183 (1.17)	143 (0.47)	1,761 (2.76)	53 (0.89)
Loans and overdrafts from banks	3 (0.10)	3 (0.07)	7 (0.14)	9 (0.14)	8 (0.09)	38 (0.37)	294 (1.87)	1,157 (3.81)	1,325 (2.08)	33 (0.55)
Cashing of bank savings, securities, etc.	11 (0.37)	27 (0.63)	32 (0.65)	50 (0.79)	153 (1.80)	183 (1.79)	570 (3.63)	1,579 (5.20)	13,207 (20.72)	126 (2.11)
Total stated	609 (20.61)	1,443 (33.80)	2,615 (53.22)	4,485 (70.92)	6,573 (77.18)	8,678 (84.75)	14,109 (89.95)	29,088 (95.82)	62,408 (97.91)	3,686 (61.75)
Nonmonetary income	2,346 (79.39)	2,826 (66.20)	2,299 (46.78)	1,839 (29.08)	1,944 (22.82)	1,562 (15.25)	1,576 (10.05)	1,268 (4.18)	1,332 (2.09)	2,283 (38.25)
Total income	2,955 (100.00)	4,269 (100.00)	4,914 (100.00)	6,324 (100.00)	8,517 (100.00)	10,240 (100.00)	15,685 (100.00)	30,356 (100.00)	63,740 (100.00)	5,969 (100.00)
Number of households ('000)	440.3	759	972.9	395.7	171.8	107.7	164.4	16.1	10.7	3,038.8

Source: Computed from Household Budget Survey, 1976/77, Table 21.

The figures elaborated above are corroborated by the results of the rural household survey reported by Collier et al. (1986). In that analysis, poorer rural households were found to rely for about three-quarters of their total income (cash and subsistence) on crop income, of which 95 percent was subsistence consumption. Nonfarm income was found to be more important as a source of cash income than crop and livestock product sales for both poor and rich rural households. The same result was found in a later survey (Bevan et al. 1990) conducted in 1983. For the poorer households, nonfarm income from own-business and wages appeared to be greater than income from cash crop sales. However, the proportion of total income derived from cash crop sales was found to be greater among low-income groups than among higher-income ones.

INCOME DIFFERENTIATION

The structure of income analyzed in the previous sections exhibited moderate inequality in rural areas but substantial inequality in urban ones. What are the underlying components of this differentiation? An answer cannot be given with the average figures so far presented, although education and wage employment appear to be significantly related to income differences.

A thorough analysis of patterns of rural differentiation was made by Collier et al. (1986). In that study, it was shown that most of the income differences between rural poor and nonpoor could be traced to differences in ownership of assets. However, size of landholding did not appear to be highly associated with income differences. This can be expected in a land-abundant economy, such as that of Tanzania. Ownership of livestock appeared to be a far greater factor, followed by education. It is not clear, however, whether ownership of livestock is the cause or the result of income differentiation. Since livestock is one of the main forms of investment, it seems quite reasonable that richer households should have more assets, namely livestock, as a result of savings or investment decisions. Access to wage employment was seen in that study as a major explanatory factor of nonfarm income in rural areas. Unit returns for sales of different farm products did not appear to be very different between poor and nonpoor; thus prices are not significantly different between poor and nonpoor. The poor were far more likely to engage in their own business than the nonpoor, but the returns from such activities were much lower for the poor than for the nonpoor. It was thus concluded that the poor were somehow forced into a range of marginal, nonfarm activities.

That the size of landholding was not strongly associated with total per capita income among rural households was also shown in the study of Bevan et al. (1990). The per capita total income (cash and subsistence) from food and cash crops in households operating very small landholding was never less than half the per capita income of households operating landholding 10 or more times larger. Per capita income deriving from nonfarm sources, however, including own-business and wages, was much larger in households operating smaller landholding.

CONSUMPTION PATTERNS

The consumption patterns in Tanzania, as revealed by the 1976/77 Household Budget Survey, exhibit several interesting features. Table 33 exhibits expenditure shares on 10 broad classes of expenditure, by expenditure category in rural areas. Table 34 exhibits the same information for urban areas. The shares are exhibited for both monetary and subsistence consumption and for combined expenditures.

Among both rural and urban households, food expenditures dominate, comprising 75 percent of total spending in rural areas and 66 percent in urban areas, on average. The high food expenditure of the richest rural class must be an aberration, since per capita total, and especially monetary, expenditures in that class appear much lower than those of the next two wealthy classes; that could easily bias the estimation of the shares. While food constitutes about 97 percent of subsistence expenditures, for most expenditure classes, whether rural or urban, it constitutes a much lower share of monetary expenditures—50 percent in rural areas and 63 percent in urban areas, on average. In rural areas, the share of monetary expenditures on food does not vary much by expenditure class; it varies considerably in urban areas, from 65 percent in the lowest cash expenditure class, to 42 percent in the highest.

Among other expenditure categories, the second-most-important expenditure share, in both rural and urban areas and for all expenditure classes except the very highest, is clothing and footwear, accounting for an average of 30 percent of total cash expenditures in rural areas and 13 percent in urban areas. Other important items of monetary consumption expenditures among the expenditure classes are fuel, light and water, furniture, and utensils. Rents are important in urban areas only for high-expenditure households, while household operations also become important for high-expenditure classes.

Another interesting feature of the tables is revealed by the figures for per capita consumption and for total expenditure in the various classes, which appear in the bottom of the tables. The consumption expenditures category refers to expenses in all 10 consumption categories listed in the tables. Total expenditure includes spending for education, other investments, and savings in various forms. The figures reported for total expenditures in Table 31 correspond (apart form

TABLE 33

Tanzania: Expenditure Shares on Various Consumption Categories by Different Income Groups, Rural (percentages).

					Income Group				40,000– and Over	Total
Expenditure	0–999	1,000– 1,999	2,000– 3,999	4,000– 5,999	6,000– 7,999	8,000– 9,999	10,000– 24,999	25,000– 39,999		
Monetary										
Food	48.82	47.84	51.53	53.67	49.70	53.12	43.35	47.74	63.94	50.32
Drinks and tobacco	4.72	3.77	3.01	2.95	2.97	3.95	2.84	1.93	1.52	3.20
Rents	0.08	0.08	0.16	0.20	0.54	1.06	0.71	4.66	0.00	0.35
Fuel, light, and water	4.89	4.17	3.63	3.04	3.39	2.24	2.53	6.52	10.91	3.48
Clothing and footwear	28.66	31.22	28.55	28.38	30.93	24.77	35.24	22.08	10.60	29.51
Furniture and utensils	5.53	5.67	4.76	5.06	5.18	5.67	5.03	3.41	1.98	5.09
Household operations	4.15	3.05	2.29	1.74	1.40	1.36	1.87	2.10	2.03	2.19
Personal care and health	2.05	2.39	2.35	1.80	2.14	1.93	2.10	4.94	4.30	2.20
Recreation and entertainment	0.08	0.26	0.90	0.79	1.06	1.62	0.98	1.06	0.91	0.82
Transportation	1.01	1.55	2.82	2.37	2.68	4.27	5.35	5.55	3.81	2.84
Total	100.00	100.00	100.00	100.00	100.00	100.00	100.00	100.00	100.00	100.00
Subsistence										
Food	97.13	97.25	97.14	96.85	97.77	96.58	96.48	86.03	90.50	97.10
Other	2.87	2.75	2.86	3.15	2.23	3.42	3.52	13.97	9.50	2.90
Total	100.00	100.00	100.00	100.00	100.00	100.00	100.00	100.00	100.00	100.00
Monetary and subsistence										
Food	87.52	82.08	74.69	69.49	66.48	65.79	57.61	55.97	73.74	74.69
Drinks and tobacco	1.02	1.54	1.77	2.12	1.97	2.83	2.20	1.60	1.62	1.78
Rents	0.02	0.02	0.08	0.13	0.35	0.75	0.52	3.66	0.00	0.17

(Table continues on the following page.)

TABLE 33
(continued)

Expenditure	Income Group								40,000– and Over	Total
	0–999	1,000– 1,999	2,000– 3,999	4,000– 5,999	6,000– 7,999	8,000– 9,999	10,000– 24,999	25,000– 39,999		
Fuel, light, and water	3.12	2.79	2.91	2.76	2.91	2.42	2.53	5.59	7.44	2.86
Clothing and footwear	5.70	9.59	14.06	17.98	20.13	17.55	25.79	18.28	7.77	14.14
Furniture and utensils	1.10	1.74	2.35	3.21	3.37	4.02	3.68	2.99	1.48	2.44
Household operations	0.83	0.94	1.13	1.11	0.91	0.97	1.38	2.28	1.62	1.05
Personal care and health	0.43	0.74	1.17	1.16	1.42	1.38	1.56	4.38	3.14	1.07
Recreation and entertainment	0.02	0.08	0.45	0.50	0.69	1.15	0.71	0.83	0.58	0.39
Transportation	0.25	0.48	1.41	1.55	1.75	3.13	4.02	4.42	2.62	1.39
Total	100.00	100.00	100.00	100.00	100.00	100.00	100.00	100.00	100.00	100.00
Per capita consumption expenditure (Tsh)	679.5	762.9	780.5	958.4	1102.6	1,141.3	1,287.2	1,505.2	999.5	834.8
Monetary	135.2	234.3	384.3	607.2	717.6	808.6	941.8	1,181.7	630.7	399.8
Subsistence	544.3	528.6	396.2	351.2	385.0	332.7	345.4	323.5	368.8	435.0
Per capita total expenditure (Tsh)	687.5	785.8	832.2	1,055.7	1,254.5	1,277.5	1,618.5	1,805.4	1,548.1	901.2

Source: Computed from Household Budget Survey, 1976/77.

TABLE 34

Tanzania: Expenditure Shares on Various Consumption Categories by Different Income Groups, Urban (percentages).

	Income Group									
Expenditure	0–999	1,000–1,999	2,000–3,999	4,000–5,999	6,000–7,999	8,000–9,999	10,000–24,999	25,000–39,999	40,000–and Over	Total
Monetary										
Food	64.58	70.37	67.74	63.37	68.92	70.08	63.75	51.29	42.34	63.14
Drinks and tobacco	2.81	2.76	2.14	1.99	1.40	1.74	2.93	4.32	3.02	2.46
Rents	0.26	0.42	1.66	4.53	3.33	3.05	4.64	7.16	11.21	4.56
Fuel, light, and water	6.61	4.58	5.14	6.15	6.08	7.14	6.35	6.17	8.19	6.40
Clothing and footwear	17.42	15.68	16.20	14.82	12.42	11.19	12.85	12.45	9.26	12.90
Furniture and utensils	4.02	1.69	2.49	3.69	2.63	1.79	2.00	2.78	0.71	2.29
Household operations	2.55	2.33	1.61	1.58	1.37	1.33	2.19	6.41	8.04	2.60
Personal care and health	0.88	1.09	1.31	1.44	1.30	1.15	1.30	2.70	1.48	1.40
Recreation and entertainment	0.06	0.05	0.58	1.22	0.55	0.41	0.58	1.40	1.93	0.79
Transportation	0.81	1.04	1.12	1.20	2.00	2.11	3.42	5.33	13.83	3.46
Total	100.00	100.00	100.00	100.00	100.00	100.00	100.00	100.00	100.00	100.00
Subsistence										
Food	97.60	96.89	96.48	96.14	97.31	97.23	93.91	94.93	96.00	96.59
Other	2.40	3.11	3.52	3.86	2.69	2.77	6.09	5.07	4.00	3.41
Total	100.00	100.00	100.00	100.00	100.00	100.00	100.00	100.00	100.00	100.00
Monetary and subsistence										
Food	84.65	83.61	74.89	66.43	70.44	70.91	64.25	51.61	43.25	66.00
Drinks and tobacco	1.10	1.40	1.62	1.82	1.33	1.69	2.91	4.30	2.99	2.27
Rents	0.10	0.21	1.25	4.11	3.15	2.96	4.56	7.10	11.02	4.17

(Table continues on the following page.)

TABLE 34
(continued)

| | Income Group | | | | | | | | 40,000– | |
Expenditure	0–999	1,000– 1,999	2,000– 3,999	4,000– 5,999	6,000– 7,999	8,000– 9,999	10,000– 24,999	25,000– 39,999	and Over	Total
Fuel, light, and water	4.01	3.75	4.71	5.88	5.89	7.01	6.29	6.14	8.07	6.11
Clothing and footwear	6.85	7.85	12.17	13.44	11.75	10.85	12.64	12.36	9.10	11.80
Furniture and utensils	1.57	0.85	1.87	3.34	2.49	1.74	1.97	2.76	0.70	2.09
Household operations	1.01	1.16	1.21	1.44	1.30	1.29	2.16	6.36	7.91	2.38
Personal care and health	0.36	0.58	0.99	1.32	1.23	1.11	1.29	2.69	1.47	1.29
Recreation and entertainment	0.02	0.03	0.44	1.11	0.52	0.40	0.57	1.39	1.89	0.73
Transportation	0.32	0.55	0.85	1.11	1.89	2.05	3.36	5.29	13.60	3.17
Total	100.00	100.00	100.00	100.00	100.00	100.00	100.00	100.00	100.00	100.00
Per capita consumption expenditure (Tsh)	508.2	586.6	784.3	1,062.8	1,207.9	1,291.6	1,821.0	2,784.9	3,518.4	1,283.2
Monetary	199.3	293.8	589.0	963.3	1,143.1	1,252.1	1,791.2	2,764.0	3,459.0	1,173.6
Subsistence	308.9	292.8	195.3	99.5	64.8	39.5	29.8	20.9	59.4	109.6
Per capita total expenditure (Tsh)	453.8	604.1	833.2	1,198.4	1,433.8	1,608.9	2,574.7	4,752.4	6,666.8	1,690.3

Source: Computed from Household Budget Survey, 1976/77.

minor rounding) to the bottom lines of Tables 33 and 34. It is quite revealing, but also expected, that households in the lower expenditure categories reported consumption expenditures quite close to total expenditures; in other words, very little saving. In fact, for the lowest urban class dissaving is reported, on average. In contrast, households in the top three or four expenditure classes report substantial excess of expenditure over consumption, hence substantial savings. Nevertheless, almost all classes report some savings, albeit in most cases they are small.

A final feature of the tables is the breakdown of per capita consumption between monetary and subsistence. Among rural households, per capita subsistence consumption is highest among low-cash-expenditure groups, and declines for higher-expenditure groups, as expected. For the lowest two cash expenditure groups, subsistence consumption constitutes 80 percent and 70 percent, respectively, of total consumption. However, even for the highest expenditure groups, subsistence still constitutes a substantial share of total consumption (more than 20 percent). This is quite different than in urban areas. For the lowest-expenditure households there, subsistence constitutes 61 percent of total consumption expenditures, but for the four highest expenditure groups it is less than 3 percent. Clearly, then, a substantial portion of the total consumption of the poorest households in Tanzania is shielded from price fluctuations.

Given that food constitutes an overwhelming share of consumption in Tanzania, the next item of discussion concerns the composition of food consumption. Table 35 exhibits the consumption of 12 categories of foods in kilograms per capita per year, by cash expenditures class in the rural areas. Table 36 exhibits the same data for the urban areas. Cereal and starchy root consumption per capita (the two major staple classes) seem to be quite even in the rural areas, irrespective of expenditure class. The composition of cereal and starch consumption changes, however, with rice becoming more important and sorghum flour less important as expenditures rise. Among starches, cassava and sweet potatoes become less important, while cooking bananas rise in importance as expenditure rises. All other food items exhibit a positive expenditure elasticity, as expected, since they are largely nonstaple. In the urban areas, a rather similar pattern emerges.

Tables 37 and 38 exhibit the total daily per capita calorie intakes of various kinds of food by monetary expenditure category in rural and urban areas, respectively. These are computed by multiplying the respective quantities consumed by appropriate calorie content coefficients and converting them to daily equivalents. The first major observation is that daily per capita calorie intake in the rural areas is quite evenly and narrowly distributed among expenditure classes around the mean of 2,153 kilocalories per capita per day. In fact, it appears that wealthier rural households consume fewer calories per capita than

TABLE 35

Tanzania: Annual Consumption in Private Households, 1976/77, by Food Items by Household Expenditure Group, Rural (quantities in kilogram/capita/year).

	Expenditure Class (Tsh)								40,000– and Over	Total
	0–999	1,000– 1,999	2,000– 3,999	4,000– 5,999	6,000– 7,999	8,000– 9,999	10,000– 24,999	25,000– 39,999		
Cereals	134.9	144.6	125.2	142.3	137.7	146.3	105.4	91.8	133.1	133.1
Maize, grain	10.7	14.3	17.0	20.2	30.3	42.7	15.8	3.3	10.4	17.1
Maize, flour	77.2	93.0	68.3	74.7	72.6	64.0	54.0	56.5	69.1	75.5
Sorghum, flour	25.3	10.9	9.2	12.9	4.1	2.0	2.0	0.1	2.3	11.2
Cereal products	0.0	0.2	0.5	0.8	1.1	1.8	1.4	1.4	0.6	0.5
Starchy roots and starches	90.9	93.1	104.2	76.0	106.7	102.1	120.6	104.9	47.0	96.2
Cassava	32.1	23.3	19.7	10.8	11.9	15.2	13.5	11.2	4.4	19.8
Sweet potatoes	14.0	17.8	22.0	15.5	13.1	12.0	21.5	30.0	5.1	18.3
Cooking bananas	7.2	20.0	30.3	31.8	47.4	62.3	69.0	60.2	4.0	28.4
Sugar and sweets	1.4	2.6	4.2	6.6	6.6	7.9	11.2	14.9	7.9	4.3
Pulses, dry	43.5	40.0	20.7	22.1	22.9	15.2	19.4	15.7	35.5	28.3
Nuts	3.3	2.2	2.7	2.6	2.3	3.2	3.7	3.4	0.9	2.6
Vegetables	11.4	14.1	12.5	13.4	11.7	11.3	11.0	22.1	8.2	12.8
Fruits	4.0	5.6	6.8	8.2	9.0	11.9	9.9	9.6	8.5	6.7
Meat, meat products, poultry	4.0	5.7	9.3	13.5	13.0	14.0	16.3	16.2	16.2	9.0
Fish and shellfish	1.6	2.2	2.8	3.4	2.7	2.7	2.6	3.3	2.3	2.6
Milk and dairy products	8.1	4.8	6.5	3.9	11.3	12.0	9.6	21.9	0.6	6.6
Oils and fats	0.2	0.6	0.3	0.6	0.9	1.5	1.3	2.9	1.2	0.5

Source: Computed from Household Budget Survey, 1976/77.

TABLE 36

Tanzania: Annual Consumption in Private Households, 1976/77, by Food Items by Household Expenditure Group, Urban (quantities in kilogram/capita/year).

	Expenditure Class (Tsh)									
	0–999	1,000– 1,999	2,000– 3,999	4,000– 5,999	6,000– 7,999	8,000– 9,999	10,000– 24,999	25,000– 39,999	40,000– and Over	Total
Cereals	115.0	110.9	94.8	88.2	91.8	97.0	106.1	97.6	99.2	98.4
Rice, husked	6.4	10.2	12.4	21.1	27.8	33.0	40.4	45.1	41.4	26.0
Maize, grain	5.2	10.0	18.5	15.2	7.4	8.6	6.5	8.7	2.9	10.6
Maize, flour	43.1	44.6	48.3	48.2	52.0	52.1	54.7	34.0	30.0	49.2
Sorghum, flour	46.7	27.6	10.4	0.7	0.6	0.4	0.4	0.2	0.0	6.4
Cereal products	1.7	1.7	4.1	9.3	32.2	16.3	21.1	26.0	16.3	14.6
Starchy roots and starches	35.2	59.1	67.8	37.5	31.0	31.4	38.6	31.0	52.3	43.2
Cassava	13.8	34.6	21.1	9.8	6.6	6.3	11.8	4.1	3.3	13.0
Sweet potatoes	15.2	12.8	12.6	6.1	6.8	6.8	8.4	3.8	5.3	8.8
Cooking bananas	0.5	0.9	13.5	13.4	9.4	9.6	11.1	13.8	24.1	10.6
Sugar and sweets	3.6	4.6	7.0	11.4	13.6	15.7	19.8	20.5	24.1	13.0
Pulses, dry	9.5	9.8	12.2	13.0	15.0	13.6	16.7	14.6	19.9	13.8
Nuts	5.2	5.2	6.5	11.6	18.4	21.3	25.1	18.3	4.2	15.0
Vegetables	7.4	9.6	14.8	14.8	17.2	18.0	24.4	31.1	24.9	17.6
Fruits	3.1	3.7	5.0	6.4	9.6	12.3	16.1	26.0	22.9	10.2
Meat, meat products, poultry	6.7	7.0	10.7	13.4	14.6	16.1	20.4	27.1	22.7	14.8
Fish and shellfish	1.2	2.2	3.3	5.2	4.4	3.8	4.7	3.3	1.8	4.0
Milk and dairy products	3.3	5.4	3.9	1.8	1.2	0.7	1.6	3.2	6.4	2.4
Oils and fats	0.0	0.0	0.4	0.9	1.0	1.3	2.5	5.4	7.5	1.4

Source: Computed from Household Budget Survey, 1976/77.

TABLE 37

Tanzania: Daily Per Capita Calorie Intake of Rural Households, 1976/77, by Household Cash Expenditure Class.

	Cash Expenditure Class (Tsh)									
	0–999	1,000–1,999	2,000–3,999	4,000–5,999	6,000–7,999	8,000–9,999	10,000–24,999	25,000–39,999	40,000 and Over	Total
	Kilocalories/capital/day									
Cereals	1,333.69	1,434.23	1,237.91	1,400.56	1,359.48	1,441.03	1,037.04	915.65	1,305.74	1,316.24
Cereal products	0.00	1.98	5.34	8.62	12.21	19.08	15.26	14.62	6.29	5.53
Starchy roots and starches	334.08	338.76	375.56	263.50	377.92	365.30	426.94	362.36	175.40	345.27
Sugar and sweets	15.29	28.41	45.66	72.47	72.02	86.11	122.64	163.81	86.57	47.24
Pulses, dry	405.10	372.60	192.51	205.83	212.92	141.94	180.76	146.10	330.33	263.39
Nuts	49.32	34.40	36.30	32.61	28.88	38.68	47.46	53.53	13.81	35.71
Vegetables	14.05	17.35	15.41	16.50	14.44	13.94	13.50	27.25	10.15	15.73
Fruits	4.87	6.85	8.42	10.14	11.10	14.68	12.18	11.81	10.46	8.29
Meat, meat products, poultry	28.16	40.89	66.48	96.51	92.60	100.07	116.18	115.47	115.53	63.86
Fish and shellfish	14.27	19.48	24.84	29.70	23.80	24.01	22.96	28.61	19.89	22.67
Milk and dairy products	20.07	11.87	16.03	9.54	27.83	29.65	23.78	53.99	1.45	16.15
Oils and fats	5.73	13.70	8.22	15.91	21.14	38.16	32.29	72.67	29.01	12.75
Total	2,224.64	2,320.52	2,032.70	2,161.89	2,254.33	2,312.64	2,050.98	1,965.87	2,104.63	2,152.84

Percent of Total

Cereals	59.95	61.81	60.90	64.78	60.31	62.31	50.56	46.58	62.04	61.14
Cereal products	0.00	0.09	0.26	0.40	0.54	0.83	0.74	0.74	0.30	0.26
Starchy roots and starches	15.02	14.60	18.48	12.19	16.76	15.80	20.82	18.43	8.30	16.00
Sugar and sweets	0.69	1.22	2.25	3.35	3.19	3.72	5.98	8.33	4.11	2.19
Pulses, dry	18.21	16.06	9.47	9.52	9.44	6.14	8.81	7.43	15.70	12.23
Nuts	2.22	1.48	1.79	1.51	1.28	1.67	2.31	2.72	0.66	1.66
Vegetables	0.63	0.75	0.76	0.76	0.64	0.60	0.66	1.39	0.48	0.73
Fruits	0.22	0.30	0.41	0.47	0.49	0.63	0.59	0.60	0.50	0.39
Meat, meat products, poultry	1.27	1.76	3.27	4.46	4.11	4.33	5.66	5.87	5.49	2.97
Fish and shellfish	0.64	0.84	1.22	1.37	1.06	1.04	1.12	1.46	0.95	1.05
Milk and dairy products	0.90	0.51	0.79	0.44	1.23	1.28	1.16	2.75	0.07	0.75
Oils and fats	0.26	0.59	0.40	0.74	0.94	1.65	1.57	3.70	1.38	0.59
Total	100.00	100.00	100.00	100.00	100.00	100.00	100.00	100.00	100.00	100.00

Source: Computed from Household Budget Survey, 1976/77.

TABLE 38

Tanzania: Daily Per Capita Calorie Intake of Urban Households, 1976/77, by Household Cash Expenditure Class.

	Cash Expenditure Class (Tsh)									
	0–999	1,000–1,999	2,000–3,999	4,000–5,999	6,000–7,999	8,000–9,999	10,000–24,999	25,000–39,999	40,000 and Over	Total
	Kilocalories/capital/day									
Cereals	1,131.40	1,092.21	933.77	875.82	912.25	967.34	1,061.97	972.43	985.83	977.16
Cereal products	17.81	18.58	44.13	99.56	344.05	173.63	224.95	278.15	174.18	156.00
Starchy roots and starches	129.92	229.39	251.34	134.57	109.53	108.95	134.90	99.00	163.50	154.92
Sugar and sweets	39.14	50.03	76.24	124.53	149.04	172.21	217.26	224.40	264.21	142.47
Pulses, dry	88.71	91.13	113.40	120.67	139.73	126.42	155.25	136.03	185.03	128.55
Nuts	59.69	58.01	73.08	126.21	199.73	234.49	270.80	203.35	50.37	161.26
Vegetables	9.10	11.79	18.23	18.21	21.21	22.24	30.06	38.36	30.74	21.70
Fruits	3.82	4.56	6.16	7.85	11.84	15.19	19.90	32.09	28.20	12.58
Meat, meat products, poultry	47.49	49.55	75.88	95.52	104.00	114.48	144.97	193.35	161.98	105.42
Fish and shellfish	10.44	19.06	28.59	45.83	38.58	32.88	41.53	29.22	15.61	35.07
Milk and dairy products	8.22	13.40	9.65	4.48	2.96	1.76	3.89	7.83	15.88	5.92
Oils and fats	0.00	0.00	10.72	22.42	24.66	30.82	60.56	133.07	185.78	34.52
Total	1,545.73	1,637.71	1,641.19	1,675.68	2,057.56	2,000.41	2,366.03	2,347.28	2,261.31	1,935.55

Percent of Total

Cereals	73.20	66.69	56.90	52.27	44.34	48.36	44.88	41.43	43.60	50.48
Cereal products	1.15	1.13	2.69	5.94	16.72	8.68	9.51	11.85	7.70	8.06
Starchy roots and starches	8.41	14.01	15.31	8.03	5.32	5.45	5.70	4.22	7.23	8.00
Sugar and sweets	2.53	3.05	4.65	7.43	7.24	8.61	9.18	9.56	11.68	7.36
Pulses, dry	5.74	5.56	6.91	7.20	6.79	6.32	6.56	5.80	8.18	6.64
Nuts	3.86	3.54	4.45	7.53	9.71	11.72	11.45	8.66	2.23	8.33
Vegetables	0.59	0.72	1.11	1.09	1.03	1.11	1.27	1.63	1.36	1.12
Fruits	0.25	0.28	0.38	0.47	0.58	0.76	0.84	1.37	1.25	0.65
Meat, meat products, poultry	3.07	3.03	4.62	5.70	5.05	5.72	6.13	8.24	7.16	5.45
Fish and shellfish	0.68	1.16	1.74	2.73	1.87	1.64	1.76	1.25	0.69	1.81
Milk and dairy products	0.53	0.82	0.59	0.27	0.14	0.09	0.16	0.33	0.70	0.31
Oils and fats	0.00	0.00	0.65	1.34	1.20	1.54	2.56	5.67	8.22	1.78
Total	100.00	100.00	100.00	100.00	100.00	100.00	100.00	100.00	100.00	100.00

Source: Computed from Household Budget Survey, 1976/77.

poorer ones. This could be due to household composition effects, as rural households with larger families tend to have higher overall consumption, without necessarily implying a higher per capita consumption. Nevertheless, it appears that the rural poor do not consume fewer calories than the rural rich. This is not so in urban areas, where the average daily per capita calorie intake of the poor is much lower than that of the urban, high-expenditure categories. The mean daily per capita calorie intake in urban areas is estimated at 1,936 kilocalories, which is 10 percent lower than the average figure for the rural areas.

Cereals (and products) constitute a rather uniform 61 percent of total daily calorie intake in the rural areas across expenditure classes, while in the urban areas, albeit on average cereals and products constitute 59 percent of daily calorie intake, this varies considerably, from a high of 74 percent for the poorest households to a low of 51 percent for the richest. Starches and pulses are the second major source of calorie intake in rural areas, with the other categories contributing only minor shares. In urban areas, however, sugar, nuts, and meat also contribute a substantial share of daily calorie intake that rises significantly with household expenditure.

A most interesting revelation from the 1976/77 HBS concerns the shares of the various foods consumed that are from subsistence production or purchased. We used information on monetary and subsistence consumption (which is valued at average prices for similar products) from the HBS (Tables 3C and 3D), to disaggregate each category of food expenditure into a portion purchased for cash and a portion obtained from own-production by expenditure class.

Tables 39 and 40 exhibit the shares of total consumption and of various food groups consumed in rural and urban areas, respectively, that are obtained for cash. In the rural areas, for the lowest expenditure classes, only 21 percent of their total consumption is obtained through monetary purchases, and only 12 percent of food and drink consumption. However, there is a sharp differentiation in the shares purchased among various food categories. For the same, lowest rural expenditure class, only 6 percent of cereals consumption, 3 percent of pulses, 5 percent of vegetables, 1 percent of starch, and 5 percent of dairy consumption are purchased; the rest is obtained from own-production. By contrast, 97 percent of cereal products, 94 percent of sugar, 65 percent of meat, 92 percent of fish, and 82 percent of oils and fats are purchased. For higher-expenditure rural households, the shares of staples purchased is considerably higher—37–43 percent for cereals, 14–80 percent for starches, 24–53 percent for pulses, 48–79 percent for vegetables, and 43–95 percent for milk. For nonstaples, the shares purchased are as high or higher than those of the lower-expenditure classes. Surprisingly, the same pattern emerges among urban households, with poorer ones purchasing only a

TABLE 39

Tanzania: Fractional Shares of Household Total and Food Consumption Purchased for Money by Household Expenditure Class, Rural, 1976/77.

	Cash Expenditure Class									
	0–999	1,000– 1,999	2,000– 3,999	4,000– 5,999	6,000– 7,999	8,000– 9,999	10,000– 24,999	25,000– 39,999	40,000– and Over	Total
Total consumption	0.21	0.33	0.52	0.67	0.69	0.74	0.79	0.82	0.76	0.52
Food and drink consumption	0.12	0.19	0.35	0.50	0.50	0.59	0.56	0.67	0.55	0.33
Cereals	0.06	0.09	0.21	0.29	0.32	0.43	0.39	0.37	0.38	0.19
Cereal products	0.97	0.78	0.98	0.99	0.98	1.00	0.97	0.74	1.00	0.96
Starchy roots and starches	0.01	0.03	0.10	0.18	0.22	0.16	0.14	0.80	0.23	0.09
Sugar and sweets	0.94	0.96	0.98	1.00	0.99	0.96	0.99	0.89	0.94	0.98
Pulses, dry	0.03	0.06	0.18	0.28	0.30	0.46	0.32	0.53	0.24	0.14
Nuts	0.09	0.27	0.39	0.58	0.62	0.61	0.75	0.78	0.42	0.38
Vegetables	0.05	0.10	0.20	0.38	0.41	0.54	0.48	0.79	0.76	0.20
Fruits	0.28	0.30	0.37	0.57	0.53	0.57	0.67	0.89	0.56	0.43
Meat, meat products, poultry	0.65	0.71	0.74	0.89	0.93	0.96	0.91	0.90	0.86	0.81
Fish and shellfish	0.92	0.88	0.90	0.93	0.97	0.94	0.97	0.99	0.94	0.91
Milk and dairy products	0.05	0.15	0.27	0.56	0.33	0.62	0.43	0.73	0.95	0.32
Oils and fats	0.82	0.89	0.91	0.96	0.96	1.00	0.93	0.58	0.88	0.93

Source: Computed from Household Budget Survey, 1976/77, Tables 3C and 3D.

TABLE 40

Tanzania: Fractional Shares of Household Total and Food Consumption Purchased for Money by Household Expenditure Class, Urban, 1976/77.

	Cash Expenditure Class									
	0–999	1,000–1,999	2,000–3,999	4,000–5,999	6,000–7,999	8,000–9,999	10,000–24,999	25,000–39,999	40,000 and Over	Total
Total consumption	0.32	0.52	0.77	0.92	0.95	0.98	0.99	1.00	0.99	0.94
Food and drink consumption	0.31	0.43	0.68	0.87	0.93	0.96	0.98	0.99	0.96	0.88
Cereals	0.16	0.28	0.54	0.71	0.86	0.92	0.95	0.97	0.90	0.76
Cereal products	1.00	0.95	0.97	1.00	0.99	1.00	1.00	1.00	0.99	0.99
Starchy roots and starches	0.05	0.14	0.35	0.68	0.79	0.83	0.94	0.96	0.88	0.64
Sugar and sweets	0.98	0.99	1.00	1.00	1.00	1.00	1.00	1.00	1.00	1.00
Pulses, dry	0.26	0.39	0.55	0.85	0.86	0.96	0.97	0.97	0.93	0.83
Nuts	0.56	0.72	0.88	0.97	0.98	0.99	1.00	1.00	1.00	0.97
Vegetables	0.16	0.26	0.57	0.83	0.93	0.96	0.97	0.99	0.98	0.85
Fruits	0.40	0.48	0.77	0.88	0.92	0.91	0.95	0.92	0.87	0.90
Meat, meat products, poultry	0.48	0.78	0.94	0.99	0.97	0.99	0.99	1.00	0.98	0.97
Fish and shellfish	0.88	0.67	0.90	0.98	0.96	0.98	0.98	1.00	1.00	0.95
Milk and dairy products	0.28	0.06	0.51	0.99	0.98	0.99	1.00	1.00	1.00	0.94
Oils and fats	0.99	0.99	1.00	1.00	1.00	1.00	1.00	1.00	1.00	1.00

Source: Computed from Household Budget Survey, 1976/77, Tables 3C and 3D.

very small share of their basic foods, although they purchase 31 percent of their total food and drink consumption.

Tables 41 and 42 present an even more vivid demonstration of the importance of subsistence consumption of foods for poor household in both rural and urban areas. The tables exhibit the daily calories per capita that are obtained from cash purchases or subsistence production. In Table 39, it was seen that the poorest rural households obtained only 12 percent of their total food consumption through cash purchases. From Table 41, it appears that the corresponding share of total calories consumed is only 6.9 percent. In other words, for the poorest rural groups, only a minuscule portion of their total daily calorie intake is obtained for cash. Surprisingly, the same appears to be the case with poor urban groups. For the two poorest urban classes, over 70 percent of their daily calorie intake is from subsistence production. Whether this comes from own-production or food remittances from rural relatives is not specified. It seems doubtful, however, that poor urban households could rely for as much as 80 percent of their calorie consumption on remittances.

The share of calories obtained for cash in rural areas can be seen from Table 41 to be almost always lower than the share of total food and drink obtained with cash, as reported in Table 39. The same seems to hold for the urban areas, when one compares Table 42 with Table 40. There is significant differentiation, however, between rural and urban areas in the proportion of calories obtained from the market. For any given household cash expenditure category, the share of calories obtained for cash is always substantially higher in the urban areas. On average, rural households obtain only 20.9 percent of their calories from the market, while for the average urban household, the share is 80.8 percent.

POVERTY LINE AND EXTENT OF POVERTY

Given the exposition of income and expenditure distribution statistics and the analysis of consumption patterns of the previous sections, this section attempts to estimate a poverty line circa 1976/77 and to estimate the incidence of poverty in rural and urban mainland Tanzania. Although the year 1976/77 is quite far removed from current conditions, it is the only year for which a detailed national household budget survey is available. An analysis of poverty in that year will reveal structural patterns that can be used to update the poverty line in later years, given information on prices.

An early analysis of poverty in Tanzania was done by the ILO mission (ILO 1982), which calculated a poverty line by costing three different subsistence diets for 1980 and supplementing these with some nonsurvey information about nonfood costs. It was thus calculated that the basic needs income (BNI) circa 1980

TABLE 41

Tanzania: Daily Per Capita Calorie Intake of Various Foods in Rural Households from Subsistence and Purchases, 1976/77, by Expenditure Class (kilocalories/capita/year).

	Cash Expenditure Class (Tsh)									
	0–999	1,000–1,999	2,000–3,999	4,000–5,999	6,000–7,999	8,000–9,999	10,000–24,999	25,000–39,999	40,000–and Over	Total
Monetary										
Cereals	76.08	109.40	231.91	342.64	396.74	548.31	328.32	291.71	386.47	218.94
Cereal products	0.00	1.55	5.23	8.52	11.97	19.07	14.79	10.84	6.29	5.31
Starchy roots and starches	5.25	10.24	36.52	47.89	82.70	65.83	55.11	285.19	21.89	31.60
Sugar and sweets	14.36	27.16	44.86	72.40	71.54	82.84	121.64	146.32	81.31	46.27
Pulses, dry	12.44	21.33	34.94	57.17	63.79	64.59	57.52	77.81	78.53	36.96
Nuts	5.86	11.37	17.38	20.77	19.91	26.15	34.71	43.50	3.51	15.84
Vegetables	0.68	1.72	3.14	6.26	5.90	7.54	6.45	21.51	7.71	3.08
Fruits	1.35	2.09	3.09	5.75	5.89	8.34	8.11	10.55	5.86	3.54
Meat, meat products, poultry	18.22	29.18	49.33	85.80	86.33	96.43	105.50	103.98	99.20	51.42
Fish and shellfish	13.12	17.14	22.31	27.72	23.11	22.55	22.22	28.38	18.67	20.68
Milk and dairy products	1.09	1.83	4.32	5.39	9.12	18.25	10.25	39.54	1.38	5.18
Oils and fats	4.73	12.13	7.51	15.29	20.24	38.07	29.87	41.98	25.42	11.82
Total	153.17	245.13	460.54	695.59	797.24	997.96	794.48	1,101.29	736.25	450.64
Share of total calorie intake (%)	6.90	10.60	22.70	32.20	35.40	43.20	38.70	56.00	35.00	20.90

Subsistence

Cereals	1,257.62	1,324.83	1,006.00	1,057.92	962.74	892.72	708.72	623.94	919.27	1,097.30
Cereal products	0.00	0.43	0.11	0.10	0.24	0.01	0.48	3.78	0.00	0.22
Starchy roots and starches	328.83	328.52	339.04	215.61	295.22	299.47	371.84	77.17	153.51	313.67
Sugar and sweets	0.94	1.26	0.80	0.07	0.47	3.27	1.00	17.49	5.26	0.97
Pulses, dry	392.66	351.28	157.57	148.67	149.12	77.35	123.24	68.29	251.80	226.43
Nuts	43.45	23.02	18.92	11.84	8.98	12.53	12.74	10.03	10.30	19.87
Vegetables	13.37	15.63	12.27	10.24	8.54	6.40	7.06	5.74	2.45	12.64
Fruits	3.53	4.76	5.34	4.40	5.20	6.34	4.07	1.26	4.61	4.75
Meat, meat products, poultry	9.94	11.71	17.15	10.70	6.27	3.64	10.68	11.49	16.33	12.44
Fish and shellfish	1.15	2.34	2.53	1.97	0.68	1.46	0.74	0.23	1.22	1.99
Milk and dairy products	18.98	10.04	11.71	4.15	18.71	11.40	13.53	14.45	0.07	10.98
Oils and fats	1.00	1.57	0.71	0.62	0.89	0.09	2.42	30.70	3.58	0.93
Total	2,071.46	2,075.39	1,572.16	1,466.30	1,457.09	1,314.68	1,256.51	864.58	1,368.38	1,702.20
Share of total calorie intake (%)	93.10	89.40	77.30	67.80	64.60	56.80	61.30	44.00	65.00	79.10

Source: Computed by authors.

TABLE 42

Tanzania: Daily Per Capita Calorie Intake of Various Foods in Urban Households from Subsistence and Purchases, 1976/77, by Expenditure Class (kilocalories/capita/day).

	Cash Expenditure Class (Tsh)									
	0–999	1,000–1,999	2,000–3,999	4,000–5,999	6,000–7,999	8,000–9,999	10,000–24,999	25,000–39,999	40,000–and Over	Total
Monetary										
Cereals	148.07	277.43	454.70	610.73	767.10	880.85	1,000.66	938.85	778.25	705.05
Cereal products	17.76	17.60	42.87	99.37	340.89	173.09	224.76	278.02	171.79	155.11
Starchy roots and starches	5.09	29.27	81.26	86.60	82.84	90.29	123.88	94.23	135.20	91.16
Sugar and sweets	38.21	49.72	76.23	124.50	148.37	172.21	216.88	224.36	263.77	142.21
Pulses, dry	22.99	35.88	61.94	102.76	120.33	121.19	150.05	132.14	172.26	106.33
Nuts	44.40	49.36	67.77	124.65	198.57	232.56	270.12	203.31	50.25	158.57
Vegetables	1.50	3.05	10.32	15.08	19.69	21.24	29.31	37.84	30.13	18.41
Fruits	1.53	2.18	4.73	6.90	10.92	13.79	18.96	29.37	24.66	11.31
Meat, meat products, poultry	22.86	38.61	71.55	94.18	100.96	113.65	144.03	192.69	158.73	102.34
Fish and shellfish	9.20	12.74	25.68	44.86	37.16	32.24	40.64	29.22	15.61	33.31
Milk and dairy products	2.32	0.75	4.90	4.42	2.90	1.75	3.89	7.83	15.88	5.57
Oils and fats	0.00	0.00	10.70	22.40	24.60	30.80	60.30	133.00	185.58	34.44
Total	313.93	516.60	912.65	1,336.46	1,854.33	1,883.67	2,283.50	2,300.86	2,002.11	1,563.80
Share of total calorie intake (%)	20.30	31.50	55.60	79.80	89.70	94.20	96.50	98.00	88.50	80.80

Subsistence										
Cereals	983.33	814.78	479.07	265.09	145.16	86.49	61.31	33.58	207.58	272.11
Cereal products	0.05	0.99	1.26	0.19	3.17	0.54	0.18	0.13	2.39	0.89
Starchy roots and starches	124.83	200.12	170.08	47.96	26.68	18.66	11.02	4.77	28.30	63.76
Sugar and sweets	0.93	0.31	0.01	0.03	0.67	0.00	0.37	0.03	0.44	0.25
Pulses, dry	65.72	55.24	51.47	17.91	19.39	5.23	5.20	3.89	12.77	22.22
Nuts	15.29	8.65	5.31	1.56	1.16	1.93	0.68	0.04	0.11	2.69
Vegetables	7.60	8.74	7.90	3.13	1.52	0.99	0.75	0.52	0.61	3.29
Fruits	2.29	2.37	1.44	0.95	0.92	1.40	0.94	2.73	3.54	1.27
Meat, meat products, poultry	24.62	10.94	4.33	1.34	3.04	0.83	0.94	0.65	3.25	3.08
Fish and shellfish	1.23	6.32	2.90	0.97	1.42	0.64	0.88	0.00	0.00	1.76
Milk and dairy products	5.90	12.65	4.74	0.06	0.06	0.01	0.00	0.00	0.00	0.35
Oils and fats	0.00	0.00	0.03	0.02	0.06	0.02	0.26	0.07	0.20	0.08
Total	1,231.80	1,121.11	728.54	339.22	203.23	116.74	82.53	46.42	259.20	371.75
Share of total calorie intake (%)	79.70	68.50	44.40	20.20	10.30	5.80	3.50	2.00	11.50	19.20

Source: Computed by authors.

was 600 Tsh per month for a family of five, or 1,440 Tsh per capita per annum. On the basis of that figure and aggregate income statistics, it was estimated that about 15 percent of urban households and 25–30 percent of rural households fell below BNI around 1980, a rather mild degree of poverty. It will be seen below, however, that these figures were most likely large underestimates of the degree of poverty.

Two methodologies are followed here. The first one will consider calorie intake and relate it to food expenditure and total expenditures. The second will consider the relation of food expenditures to total income or total consumption expenditures. The relation of calorie intake to total food expenditures (both monetary and subsistence) was proposed and used by Greer and Thorbecke (1986) to derive a food poverty line using cross-section, household-level data. In the case at hand, we did not have information at the level of households, but only by cash expenditure classes of households, as already exhibited in the previous sections. We therefore used the interval means from the aggregated data for the analysis.

The first step in the analysis involves relating per capita total calorie intake to per capita total expenditure and per capita total food expenditure. The following relationships were estimated.

$$TCALPC = \alpha + \beta \ln PCFE \qquad (4.1)$$

$$TCALPC = \alpha + \beta \ln PCTE \qquad (4.2)$$

where *TCALPC* is total calories consumed per capita; *PCFE* is total (monetary and subsistence) per capita food consumption expenditures; and *PCTE* is per capita total consumption expenditures (monetary and subsistence) excluding savings.

The data used have been exhibited in the previous two sections. The OLS estimates of the above equations are exhibited in Table 43. It can be seen that there does not appear to be any significant relation between per capita calorie intake and food expenditures or total per capita expenditures in rural areas, but that a significant and positive relation appears to exist for urban households. Several other functional forms were estimated, but the results were quite similar. The elasticity of per capita calorie intake with respect to food expenditures in the urban areas, from the estimated equations, is 0.34, while the elasticity of calorie intake with respect to total expenditures is 0.17. By solving equations (4.1) and (4.2) for per capita food, or total, expenditure consistent with a given per capita calorie level, we can obtain an estimate of a possible food, or total, poverty line, that is, a level of per capita expenditure consistent with a given per capita calorie intake. The results of these calculations for the urban areas are exhibited in Table 44 for five different levels of per capita calorie intake.

Based on FAO/WHO energy recommendations and the age and sex composition of the Tanzanian population, it has been estimated that the average daily per

TABLE 43

Tanzania: Econometric Estimates of Calorie Expenditure Cross–Section Relations, 1976/77.

Dependent Variable	Constant	ln PCFE	ln PCTE	$\bar{R}^{2b}$	N.O.[c]
		Independent Variables			
Rural					
TCALPC	3886.8	−263.4		−0.064	9
	(1.623)[a]	(−0.722)			
TCALPC	3423.7		−179.6	0.124	9
	(3.950)		(−1.461)		
Urban					
TCALPC	−2523.0	663.6		0.883	9
	(−4.410)	(7.833)			
TCALPC	−486.3		331.6	0.787	
	(−1.098)		(5.533)		

Source: Computed by authors.
[a] Figures in parenthesis denote t–statistics.
[b] Adjusted R-squared.
[c] Number of observations.

TABLE 44

Tanzania: Per Capita Food and Total Expenditures in Urban Areas Consistent with a Given Per Capita Calorie Intake in 1976/77.

	Per Capita Calorie Intake (kilocalories/capita/day)				
	1,800	*1,900*	*2,000*	*2,100*	*2,200*
(1) Per capita food expenditure (Tsh/annum)	675	785	912	1,061	1,233
(2) Per capita total expenditure (Tsh/annum)	987	1,335	1,804	2,439	3,298
Ratio (1)/(2)	0.68	0.59	0.51	0.44	0.37

Source: Computed by authors.

capita calorie requirement circa 1980 was 2,229 kilocalories (Tanzania 1987b, Agriculture and Livestock). On the basis of the data in Tables 37 and 38, it appears that almost every rural household, irrespective of expenditure class, achieves or comes close to this level, while only the three highest household expenditure classes in urban areas achieve the standard. It might well be that calorie requirements in rural areas are, on average, higher than in urban areas. But even if we arbitrarily adopt an urban minimum calorie standard of 2,000 kilocalories, it is only about 48 percent of urban households (cf. Tables 38 and 31), those with cash household expenditures above 6,000 Tsh, that achieve it. These are the households that exhibit average per capita daily calorie intake above 2,000 kilocalories in Table 38.

Notice, however, that the second line in Table 44 indicates that daily per capita calorie consumption of 2,000 kilocalories is consistent with an annual per capita expenditure level of 1,804 Tsh. From Table 31, it appears that this average per capita expenditure level is achieved in the urban areas only by households with total cash expenditures of 8,000 Tsh and above, or only about 35 percent of urban households. Based on these considerations one must conclude that in 1976/77 about 50–60 percent of urban households could be classified as poor. This figure is substantially higher than what was estimated by ILO for 1980, but given that 1976/77 was a much better year in Tanzania than 1980, the ILO underestimate is bound to be even greater.

To check the consistency of the above estimates and to obtain a poverty estimate for rural areas also, we use the second methodology, which relates per capita food expenditures to per capita total expenditures and total income, as reported for the respective intervals in the 1976/77 HBS. For this purpose we estimated by OLS the following two sets of equations:

$$ln\ PCFE = \alpha + \beta ln\ PCTE \tag{4.3}$$

$$ln\ PCFE = \alpha + \beta ln\ PCTY \tag{4.4}$$

where *PCFE* and *PCTE* are as defined earlier, and *PCTY* is per capita total income (including savings). Table 45 exhibits the estimates of parameters α and β.

The results indicate significant and positive relations between per capita food expenditures and total expenditures, as well as total income, in both rural and urban areas, with the best fits between per capita food expenditures and per capita total consumption expenditures. The good fit in the rural areas, when contrasted with the poor, earlier fit between per capita calorie intake and food expenditures, indicates that as total per capita expenditures increase in rural areas, the composition of food intake changes in favor of higher-quality foods, even though the

TABLE 45

Tanzania: Econometric Estimates of Relations Between Total and Food
Expenditures.

Dependent Variable	Independent Variables				
	Constant	ln PCTE	ln PCTY	$\bar{R}^{2b}$	N.O.^{c}
Rural					
ln PCTE	4.094	0.350		0.875	9
	(12.502)^a	(7.534)			
ln PCTE	5.205		0.188	0.688	9
	(16.520)		(4.316)		
Urban					
ln PCTE	2.929	0.519		0.974	9
	(13.221)	(17.300)			
ln PCTE	3.216		0.475	0.944	9
	(10.574)		(11.668)		

Source: Computed by authors.
^{a} Figures in parenthesis denote t–statistics.
^{b} Adjusted R-squared.
^{c} Number of observations.

total calorie intake stays roughly constant. This is noticeable in Table 35, where
it can be seen that as household cash expenditures increase in rural areas, more
sugar, fruits, and meats are consumed. Within the starchy root component, it can
be seen that as expenditures rise, a substitution away from cassava and into sweet
potatoes takes place, while within cereals, rice consumption rises at the expense
of maize.

The elasticity of per capita food expenditures with respect to total per capita
consumption expenditures is 0.35 in rural and 0.52 in urban areas, whereas the
income elasticities of food expenditures are lower, at 0.19 in rural and 0.48 in the
urban areas. These figures are consistent with growing savings as income rises.

The estimated equations can be used to derive a level of poverty by using the
ratio of food expenditure to total expenditure or total income as the variable
determining poverty. Notice in Table 44 that, using the calorie method, the ratio
of food expenditure to total expenditure for a household with mean per capita
daily calorie intake of 2,000 kilocalories, in urban areas, is 0.51. Table 34,
however, indicates that it is only the two highest cash expenditure classes in
urban areas that achieve a ratio as low or lower, while all the others have a much
higher ratio. Among rural households, no class achieves a ratio as low as this, as
can be seen from Table 33.

We can use different values of this ratio to derive from the estimated equations
corresponding poverty lines in rural and urban areas. Notice that equation (4.3)
can be written as follows:

$$PCTE = \exp\left(\frac{1}{\beta - 1}(ln\,\rho - \alpha)\right) \tag{4.5}$$

where

$$\rho = \frac{PCFE}{PCTE} \tag{4.6}$$

and exp (·) denotes the exponential function. Using alternative values of ρ, we can estimate the corresponding values for per capita total expenditures. Table 46 exhibits the results of such calculations.

The results are interesting in many ways. First, notice that the estimated poverty lines are not very different between rural and urban households. This is probably so because such a large share of consumption at low levels of income in both rural and urban areas is out of subsistence production. In fact, for the three highest ratios of food to total expenditures, the rural poverty line is above the urban poverty line.

As shown in Table 44, in urban areas, a per capita daily calorie intake of 2,000 kilocalories implied a ratio of food to total expenditure of 0.51 and a per capita poverty level of 1,804 Tsh. In fact equation (4.5) implies a poverty level for $\rho = 0.51$ of 1,789 Tsh, which is quite close to what was estimated with the first method. This implies that the two methods give compatible results, and the definition of a poverty level depends on what one assumes about either minimum daily per capita calorie intake or the ratio of food expenditures to total expenditures. We shall use the latter method, as it indicates poverty levels for both rural and urban households.

Since it appears that the estimated poverty lines are quite similar in rural and urban areas, we can use Table 30, showing the distribution of per capita incomes in Tanzania. Although the information set out in Table 30 aggregates rural and urban households, it is the only table we have obtained that specifically considers

TABLE 46

Tanzania: Poverty Levels Estimated According to the Ratio of Food to Total Expenditure (Tsh/capita/annum).

	Ratio of Food to Total Per Capita Expenditure						
	0.50	*0.55*	*0.60*	*0.65*	*0.70*	*0.75*	*0.80*
Total expenditure							
Rural households	1,579	1,364	1,193	1,055	941	846	766
Urban households	1,864	1,529	1,276	1,080	926	802	702

Source: Computed by authors.

per capita, and not per household, incomes or expenditures. We use simple linear interpolation to estimate the proportion of households or people in poverty when the poverty line falls at a given income interval. Notice that Table 30 describes the distribution of per capita incomes and not expenditures. We could have used the second set of regressions, exhibited in Table 45, to relate the ratio of food expenditures to total income via a procedure similar to what is indicated in (4.5). However, we believe that the expenditure data are less biased, especially at the high levels and hence the resulting regressions are more reliable. Second, as was exhibited in Table 31, with the exception of very high levels of income and expenditure, household total expenditures are quite close to household incomes. Hence the bias arising from our procedure is small and, if anything, it underestimates the degree of poverty.

Table 47 exhibits the estimates of the percentage of households and people in Tanzania mainland circa 1976/77 that were living in poverty. We have used a weighted average poverty level from Table 46. The weights are the proportions of population living in rural and urban areas, which, using figures from the earlier section ("Population and Some Household Characteristics") are 0.87 and 0.13, respectively.

The results indicate very high levels of poverty even for extreme assumptions. For instance, even if we assume a definition of poverty according to which the ratio of food to total expenditures is 0.8, an admittedly extreme situation, 36 percent of households or 55 percent of people would have been classified as poor in 1976/77. Although in rural areas this would not imply severe calorie undernutrition, it would mean very severe undernutrition in urban areas.

The ILO mission, in its estimates of the BNI, used a ratio of food to total expenditure of 0.66. As shown in Table 47, it appears that for this ratio, 56.3

TABLE 47

Tanzania: Percentage of People and Households in Poverty in 1976/77 Using Poverty Lines According to the Ratio of Food to Total Expenditure.

	Ratio of Food to Total Expenditure						
	0.50	*0.55*	*0.60*	*0.65*	*0.70*	*0.75*	*0.80*
National poverty line (Tsh/capita/year)	1,616	1,385	1,204	1,058	939	840	758
Percentage of households below poverty line	73.2	66.2	60.8	56.3	49.9	42.3	36.0
Percentage of people below poverty line	81.6	75.5	70.8	67.0	60.2	51.8	44.8

Source: Computed by authors.

percent of households and 67 percent of people in Tanzania would be classified as poor. These poverty levels are clearly much higher than what was estimated by the ILO mission, which did not have the results of the full 1976/77 HBS and used aggregate data. Taking our estimated national per capita total expenditure of 1,058 Tsh, which corresponds to a food-to-total-expenditure ratio of 0.65 (similar to the ILO assumption), and using the National Consumer Price Index (NCPI) averaged over 1980/81, we obtain that the corresponding per capita poverty line in 1980 (the year of the ILO estimate) is about 1,871 Tsh, or 30 percent higher, than the 1,440 Tsh that the ILO had estimated. If their estimate is deflated to 1976/77, it yields a per capita poverty line of 814 Tsh, which, according to Table 47, would imply that about 40 percent of households and 49 percent of people were living in poverty. Clearly then, poverty is substantial in Tanzania and can be grossly underestimated using aggregate national income data.

To obtain an idea of what constituted poverty in 1989, we have used the component price series of the NCPI, which gives an index for each of the 10 categories of consumer goods indicated in Tables 33 and 34, and the group-specific weights indicated in those tables for the five lowest cash expenditure classes. The average per capita total annual expenditure in any of these classes in 1976/77, rural or urban, does not exceed 1,208 Tsh, which implies (based on the figures in Table 47) that we are examining the consumption patterns of the five poorest classes of rural and urban households. Using this methodology, we computed the corresponding per capita total annual expenditure in 1989 that would be equivalent in purchasing power to the average per capita annual expenditure in each of the five lowest 1976/77 classes. The results are indicated in Table 48. Assuming that the highest interval exhibited in Table 48 illustrates the poverty threshold, and using an average household size of 5.3 (from the 1988 census), it follows that a household would be classified as poor in 1989 if it had monthly total (monetary and subsistence) income of less than 8,258 Tsh in the rural areas and less than 8,885 Tsh in the urban areas. For reference, in 1987/88, 89 percent of all civil servants had monthly salaries of 3,610 Tsh (Level MS 3) or less, and the highest grade civil servants (MS 17–19) made, on average, only 7,980 Tsh. It is quite clear that a 1989 household headed by a civil servant needed other sources of income it were not to be poor.

CONCLUSIONS

The upshot of the analysis in this chapter is, first, that poverty in 1976/77, a relatively good year from a macroeconomic and agricultural production stand-point, was extensive, and much more so than has been previously estimated. It

TABLE 48

Tanzania: Poverty Lines in 1989, Household Cash Expenditure Category in 1976/77 (Tsh/capita/annum).

	0–999	1,000–1,999	2,000–3,999	4,000–5,999	6,000–7,999
Average per capita total expenditure, 1976/77					
Rural	680	763	781	958	1,103
Urban	508	587	784	1,063	1,208
Average per capita total expenditure, 1989					
Rural	11,720	13,130	13,352	16,359	18,698
Urban	8,756	10,056	13,267	17,587	20,118

Source: Computed by authors.

appears that in that year poverty was quite widespread, and hence that income distribution was quite even. A major factor in this evenness was the prevalence of subsistence consumption in the rural areas but also among the urban poor.

It also appeared from our analysis that inequality was greater in the urban areas than in the rural ones. Given that a large share of the incomes of urban middle- and upper-class, and rural nonfarm, households comes from wages and salaries, much of that from the formal sector, it seems that changes in the wider public sector performance can have a significant impact on these households, as will be demonstrated later.

5

PERFORMANCE OF AGRICULTURE

In order to evaluate the performance of the Tanzanian economy before and after adjustment, a correct assessment of agricultural growth is crucial given the large share of agriculture in GDP. Ever since the mid-1970s, Tanzania's agricultural sector has—according to official estimates—grown at rates above those of the nonagricultural sector and has increased its share in the GDP at the expense of the nonagricultural sectors (see Tables 2 and 9). Such a pattern runs counter to what is usually considered a "normal" pattern of economic growth. This atypical growth of the agricultural sector is attributed to increases in the production of food crops, since stagnation has characterized the performance of export crops.

In this chapter we start with a brief overview of the changes in the institutional setting of agriculture over the last three decades. We then present an analysis of the trends in food and export crop production and show that the claim of consistent expansion in food crop production is not consistent with other types of information. We also show that agrarian structure and technology seem to have stayed remarkably constant during the period of institutional upheaval and crisis. Finally, although we will argue that agricultural producers were clearly affected negatively by the stagnation and deterioration of Tanzania's economy before adjustment, some of the main potential benefits of structural adjustment were not effectively transmitted to the majority of agricultural producers.

THE INSTITUTIONAL SETTING

Tanzania's agricultural sector performed remarkably well in the 1950s and the early 1960s. However, the advent of a state-controlled economy after the Arusha declaration in 1967 created an environment that was generally repressive for agriculture. The socialist policies adopted turned against private production and marketing of export crops and substituted for them state farms and monopsonistic marketing boards. The inefficient operation of the various agricultural parastatals virtually decimated Tanzania's export crop sector. Given that agricultural exports accounted for approximately 80 percent of total exports, the collapse of the export crop sector can be seen as a major endogenous cause of the macroeconomic crisis of the early 1980s.

Tanzania's peasant farm sector (as opposed to estate plantation and other large-scale operations) provides around 85 percent or more of the following major export crops: coffee, cotton, cashews, tobacco, and pyrethrum. Additionally, peasant farms are responsible for approximately 25 percent of tea production, 50 percent of the officially marketed rice production, and virtually all of the legally marketed maize production. During the 1950s and 1960s, this peasant sector expanded its share in agricultural exports considerably and dominated the country's export performance (World Bank 1983). However, the existence of a considerable number of plantations and large-scale farm enterprises gives Tanzania a diverse mix of agricultural producers. This typical mix of peasant and estate farming was basically already in place by the end of German colonial rule.

At independence, the marketing structure was characterized by a combination of private traders and a strongly emerging cooperative structure, much as had been the case earlier in the century. After independence, the "improvement approach," as defined in the First Five-Year Plan of the newly independent state, strongly emphasized the cooperative movement, probably partially because it was seen as an appropriate countervailing power against "non-African" elements, namely, Tanzanians of Indian and Arab origin. Partly as a result of high prices during the drought of the 1960/61 season, the government decreed in 1962 the Agricultural Products Control and Marketing Act, which defined what became known as the *three-tier single-channel marketing system*. At the apex level, crop-specific *marketing boards* were established, which were responsible for the final sale of agricultural produce. The marketing boards bought from *regional cooperative unions*, who in turn were supplied by *primary cooperatives* or directly by private producers. Crops falling under this regime had their prices set by the government and were called "scheduled" crops. They included maize, paddy, wheat, oilseeds, cashew nuts, and cotton. All but cotton were marketed by the National Agricultural Products Board (NAPB). Final marketing of all other crops (i.e., cotton, tobacco, coffee, pyrethrum, sisal, and tea) took place through crop-specific marketing boards, which derived producer prices from actual export sales.

Under the three-tier single-channel marketing system, there existed significant geographical price differences due to variable marketing costs. Pricing was only fixed with respect to the price that the marketing boards paid to the regional cooperative unions for the final delivery of produce (the "into-store" price of the marketing board). Unions and co-ops deducted their (officially approved) marketing costs (e.g., transportation) and farmers received the residual.

The vigor with which the government promoted the cooperative form of organization resulted, as earlier in the century, in a cooperative structure which became increasingly government dominated. Especially with respect to the domestic marketing of food crops, cooperative marketing had no comparative marketing advantages, and as a result the structure had to be virtually imposed from above. Additionally, when registration standards for cooperatives relaxed, the quality, performance of the cooperative organizations plummeted, and there were increased fraud and nonrepayment of credit.

By 1973, the three-tier single-channel marketing system consisted of about 2,300 primary co-ops (which usually combined several villages and marketed several crops), 20 regional cooperative unions, and agricultural marketing boards for coffee, oilseeds, cashew nuts, cotton, pyrethrum, sisal, sugar, tea, tobacco, and cereals. In 1973, the government replaced the marketing boards with parastatal crop authorities, possibly in an attempt to reduce cooperative control over marketing. The NAPB was also abolished in 1973, and the National Milling Corporation (NMC), which until that time had been only involved in milling, took over the NAPB marketing functions.

Whereas the unions had specialized geographically by region, the crop authorities were specialized by crop, nationwide. In the 1974/75 crop season, the "into-store price," which had resulted in differential pricing at the regional level, was replaced by a "producer price," which became fixed for the whole nation (a "pan-territorial price"). Additionally, the list of scheduled crops was extended to include sorghum, bulrush millet, finger millet, and cassava—the so-called "drought crops." Various pulses were added to the list later in the 1970s. The pan-territorial pricing policy, which affected producers as well as consumers, was in effect from 1974 to 1981 for all scheduled crops with the exception of coffee and sisal.

The Village Development Act was passed in 1975, after "Operation Sogeza" (planned villagization), and the village became a legal person able to enter into contracts with other legal entities.

All marketing functions of the cooperative system were transferred to crop authorities, which received considerable funding from western donors. At the same time, most private retail shops in rural areas were closed under "Operation Maduka," and Regional Trading Corporations become responsible for the retail distribution of food and consumer goods. Due to the general inefficiency of the new system, consumer goods rationing soon followed. Many observers point to the induced disincentives for production of such rationing (see, for example, Bevan el al.1989). This combination of restrictions with respect to the marketing of agricultural produce and supply of consumer goods must have amplified the attractiveness of parallel markets in general and illegal export/import in particular.

By 1983, the parallel, open markets had become so active that the government, in a last-ditch effort to reassert its control over the economy, declared a "War on Economic Saboteurs," that is, private traders. The effects of increased controls and roadblocks temporarily reduced the quantities traded on the open market and caused open market prices to increase.

In 1984, a first set of liberalization measures took effect. For instance, the amount of food grains allowed to be privately traded was raised to 500 kilograms, and the roadblocks were removed. Although the reinstated cooperatives formally held a marketing monopoly, the government implicitly allowed traders to deal with villagers.

In 1985, the government relaxed its control over international trade by implementing the own-funded import scheme. As a result, private imports of trucks jumped by 300 percent in 1986. Open markets for maize grew sharply, as transportation problems decreased when fuel and spare parts became more readily available. According to estimates for Tandale market in Dar es Salaam, open-market sales doubled to over 50 percent of total quantity traded from 1984 to 1987 (Gordon 1989).

After several increases, all remaining quantity restrictions on interregional private grain trade were lifted when the permit system was abolished in March 1987. However, the official marketing channels were still under obligation to purchase all quantities offered for sale. Moreover, in the more remote main maize-producing regions, the official producer prices were above the open-market producer price, as a result of the increases in quantity available in the open market and favorable weather conditions over the 1985–1987 period. During the 1984–1987 period, NMC stocks of maize reached record levels (up to about 200,000 tons) with average increases in official purchases of 40 percent per year. NMC's domestic maize sales were depressed, because the official consumer price was higher than the open-market consumer price. In an effort to decrease its accumulated stocks, the NMC opened over 100 retail shops in December 1988, selling at below-open-market prices.

In June 1988, the NMC officially lost its monopoly of the grain trade. Officially, private traders were still not allowed to buy directly from primary cooperatives. However, the private sector did not seem very interested in purchasing from the unions, given the price situation in the open markets. Thus, the unions continued to rely on the NMC to sell their produce. Both the unions and the NMC realized considerable losses on their marketing transactions in the 1988/89 and 1989/90 seasons. Moreover, in December 1988, the government was forced to assume responsibility for the substantial overdrafts of the NMC.

In September 1989, the government freed maize marketing at the primary cooperative level: private traders were allowed to buy directly from primary co-ops. By 1990, considerable food grain stocks (approximately 250,000 tons) were stranded, predominantly in the regions of Arusha, Rukwa, and Shinyanga. NMC operations virtually came to a halt in 1990 after the government prohibited it from undertaking unprofitable operations. The financial losses of the NMC's and other parastatals had risen to such levels that they were posing a threat to the Tanzanian banking system.

OFFICIAL SOURCES OF AGRICULTURAL DATA

An assessment of agricultural performance in Tanzania can be based on three sources of information. First, several Tanzanian government agencies regularly publish regionally and nationally aggregated agricultural data. Second, one can use a number of studies that contain agricultural production estimates obtained through nationally representative surveys. Third, one can obtain corroborating evidence from a number of indirect sources; for example, agricultural price information, international trade statistics, health statistics, and the like. In this chapter, we will explore a number of these sources and ascertain whether it is possible to arrive at a consistent picture of the performance of agriculture over the last 25 years.

Various official agricultural output series exist, produced by a number of government agencies. Sometimes the differences between these series are minimal; sometimes the discrepancies are quite substantial. One of the problems for users of such statistics is that it is not easy to discern from the publications exactly how the different output series were generated. The publications are often rather cursory on methodological information. Only through direct interviews with the relevant officers in the government can one ascertain how certain series are estimated.

At present, the situation does not seem to have improved. The Bureau of Statistics produces its own agricultural statistics on food crops, derived from a nationally representative sample survey undertaken by the bureau in 1986/87. However, for the computation of the national accounts, the bureau does not use its own information, but uses instead production estimates from the Early Warning and Crop Monitoring Bureau (EWCMB) of the Ministry of Agriculture. The EWCMB estimates food production on the basis of a yield estimate obtained from a physiological crop model that uses rainfall data and certain agronomic parameters. The yield estimate is combined with area estimates from the agricultural extension agents to obtain total production. The main pitfall of the model is that it is not regularly calibrated to objective production estimates in the field. Nonetheless, the EWCMB estimates are widely accepted as the best estimates available and are therefore used to construct the national accounts. The Marketing Development Bureau of the Ministry of Agriculture also accepts and reports the EWCMB estimates.

All the different agencies, including the EWCMB, rely on the estimates from the Village Extension Officers and the District and Regional Agriculture and Livestock Development Officers (RALDOs). These agents do not employ objectifiable methods of area, yield, and production measurement. Given the nature of some of the major farming systems in Tanzania (viz., the savannah and semiarid systems), it is likely that the agents have a reasonable grasp of year-to-year qualitative changes in overall production levels for a given village ("higher", "lower," "about the same") but a less-reliable estimate of quantitative changes in area and yields per hectare. Additionally, the various agencies employ different methods to compile or "correct" the RALDO estimates.

A second source of error might be that the initial evaluation of the extension officer is usually presented to the village authorities before it is officially reported. Village authorities may have an interest in influencing the estimates upward, since the party awards prizes for record agricultural production. Similarly, the government has issued a number of decrees that might have influenced the reliability of the area and production estimates, particularly during the Ujamaa period. Thus, the Rural Lands (Planning Utilization) Act of 1973 established certain rules and bylaws stating minimum and compulsory areas for certain crops. At times, stringent fines or imprisonment have been imposed on defaulters (Mtetewaunga 1986). The compulsory minimum acreage may have produced a phantom growth of those crops in an understandable effort to appease the authorities. The growth in per capita food crop production recorded during the height of Ujamaa policies, (1973–1976), may be partially the result of such politicized production estimates.

A FIRST ASSESSMENT BASED ON OFFICIAL STATISTICS

Using the official agricultural statistics as a reference, the following broad picture of agricultural performance over the last 25 years emerges. Per capita production of food and export crops is graphed in Figure 4 for the period 1966–1989 using Divisia (value share weighted) indices. The overall conclusion, based on the official series, is that a dramatic decline in the per capita marketing of the major export crops was compensated by an equally dramatic rise in per capita food crop production.

FIGURE 4

Per Capita Production of Food Crops and Purchases of Export Crops.

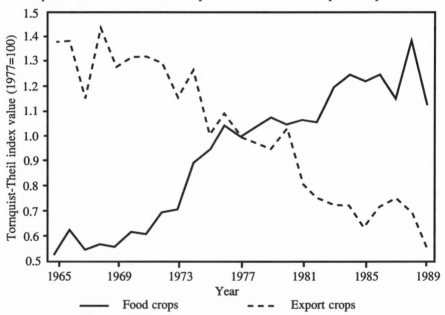

Source: Authors' calculations.

Notes: The Tornquist-Theil index is a discrete approximation of the Divisia index. The index was chained and based to 1977. The index is used in this and all following figures. Divergence with the corresponding Laspeyres index were found to be negligible in all cases. Food crops composing the index: maize, paddy, wheat, sorghum, millet, cassava, and beans. Export crops: coffee, cotton, cashew, pyrethrum, tea, tobacco, and cocoa. Sisal was excluded. Sisal production has decreased dramatically over the period. For export crops, official purchases are recorded as production.

The decline in officially marketed export crop production in Tanzania has been well-documented, and a broad consensus exists on the basic facts. However, the data refer to official purchases only; no direct estimates for actual production or area figures exist. Consequently, there is no direct or indirect information on the size of unofficial markets for export crops over time. Thus we have no data about the extent to which parallel exports have been able to compensate for the decline in the official export crop marketings.

Per capita export crop purchases showed a gradual, and at times steep, decline between 1966 and 1975—the period of nationalization of private estates. The period 1976–1980 saw relatively high world market prices for export crops and was characterized by stabilization of per capita export crop marketings. A steep decline from 1980 to 1984 was followed by a temporary recovery from 1985 to 1987, after which the decline seemed simply to continue on its earlier path. In spite of certain temporary ups and downs, then, over the entire 1965–1989 period, per capita export crop production was more than halved.

Turning to per capita food crop production, we can distinguish the following subperiods. Food production kept up with relatively high population growth from 1966 until 1971, a period during which the government outlined its basic development strategy, highlighted by the Arusha declaration of 1967. Rapid growth in food production is also reported in the official series between 1972 and 1976, when many of the socialist policies were actually, and at times forcefully, implemented (e.g., monopsonistic cooperative marketing, villagization, relocation of urban unemployed to rural areas, compulsory minimum acreage, pan-territorial pricing). The drought of 1973/74 also fell in this period but seems to have had little effect on official production figures.

The period between 1977 and 1983 is characterized by stagnation in per capita food production. These are the years of "boom and bust," the coffee boom and the events that led to the economic crisis of the early 1980s: the abolition of the cooperatives, the war with Idi Amin, the second oil crisis, and the general failure of state socialism to generate economic growth.

The unsustainability of the official marketing system was accentuated during the 1981/82 and 1982/83 droughts. When the government in effect liberalized private grain marketing in 1984, a dramatic surge in production was recorded for 1983/84. After 1984, however, a decline in per capita food production seems to have set in, although 1988/89 was recorded by the EWCMB as an extraordinarily good year.

Summarizing, over the entire 1966–1989 period, we observe that the official statistics report a doubling of national per capita food crop production, primarily caused by a rapid increase in the mid-1970s.

AN ALTERNATIVE SCENARIO

Some observers broadly agree with the trends implied by the official data. They contend that food production in Tanzania has consistently outpaced population growth since the 1950s and has in fact accelerated since the mid-1970s (Odegaard 1985, Lundahl and Ndulu 1987). In the context of a food-versus-cash-crop argument, they posit that a major increase in food production has occurred, mainly caused by government price policies that favored the food crops, which resulted in a shift of resources away from export crops to food crops.

Other observers have entirely dismissed the assertion of positive growth in per capita food production and posit a negative trend. Thus, Collier, Radwan, and Wangwe (1986) make the argument that food production per capita must have declined over the 1967–1978 period, partly because of the limited potential for substitution of labor out of export crops.

Could we formulate an alternative scenario with respect to agricultural growth in Tanzania? In particular, it seems that acknowledging the existence of positive incentives for an increase in food production need not preclude questioning the magnitude of the increase. For instance, rapid per capita growth was recorded during the 1971–1976 period, concurrent with a major drought, villagization, and the abolition of the cooperative structure. It is the 1971–1976 period, in particular, that accounts for a significant portion of the total increase in per capita food production from 1966 to 1989, during which time the index shows a doubling of aggregate per capita food production. Note, moreover, that this acceleration in food crop production in the 1970s is supposed to have come on top of an already impressive growth rate during the 1960s, when Tanzania had the highest rate of increase of domestic food production of the entire African continent (see also Lofchie 1988).

In contrast to the thesis of rapid per capita growth of food crop production, and to that of declining per capita food production, one could entertain a third hypothesis. For the period up to the mid-1980s, one could posit a scenario of stagnation and modest increases in per capita food production based on two related arguments: first, the profitability of off-farm, income-generating activities declined, increasing the relative profitability of farm activities and inducing an increase in the availability of farm labor. Additionally, the relative profitability of export crop production declined, causing a shift of resources from export to food crops. So far, the thesis is a basic cash-versus-food-crop argument.

However, second, farmers did not continuously expand per capita food crop production significantly above subsistence levels due to the increasing uncertainty of the economic environment in the period 1971 to 1984. That period saw decreasing availability of incentive goods, an inability of the official marketing system to assure producers a consistently profitable market, and often-high risks associated with using the parallel markets. In other words, the increase of the relative profitability of food crop production did not result in a continued expansion of food crop production over and above subsistence levels.

A small but significant increase in food crop production above former subsistence levels may, nevertheless, have occurred if farmers perceived the overall riskiness of the market environment to have increased. To hedge against such risks, they may have increased food production with the objective of increasing on-farm food stocks. Moreover, the intermittent availability and increasing price of incentive goods may have induced farmers to hold more liquid assets, including food stocks.

Producers' reactions to market failures may have included a continuous increase in on-farm food stocks. In the absence of large increases in real incomes, such increased storage constitutes the only hypothesis that simultaneously allows for a modest increase in per capita food production and a protracted increase in the real price of food on the open markets.

We will further investigate these hypotheses below, confronting them with data from various sources.

PRICES

In discussions of Tanzanian agriculture, one often encounters debates about the importance of "non-price" factors, such as the weather, the effects of villagization, labor shortages, lack of processing capacity, transportation problems, and scarcity of consumer, or incentive, goods. Care should be taken, however, to define exactly what is meant by "price." For instance, transportation bottlenecks affect the transformation of market or consumer prices into producer, or farm gate, prices. In a situation where transportation is very poor or lacking, it may be tempting to say that non-price factors are important, using the term to draw attention to the large margin between official market prices and farm gate, producer prices. Yet the fact that the manipulation of official prices may not substantially affect the actual profitability of rural farming is hardly proof of the importance of non-price factors.

Evidence for low estimates of elasticities of supply in sub-Saharan Africa is usually derived from simulation models, which assume direct resource trade-offs between food and cash crop production and/or rigidities in produce and factor markets. Thus, for Tanzania, Renkow, Leonard, and Franklin (1983) simulate a household model and come up with own-price marketed food supply elasticities well below 1 (from .11 to .74). The empirical validity of the trade-off assumption is highly dependent, however, on the particular crops under consideration.

In Tanzania, the empirical definition of price is of even greater than usual importance, given the particular marketing environment, which includes substantial parallel markets. In this respect, references to "supply elasticities" should often be interpreted as meaning the elasticity of quantities marketed through parastatals, with respect to officially announced producer prices. The empirical econometric evidence for Tanzania on the magnitude of this type of elasticity of supply runs contrary to the estimations derived from the simulation exercises undertaken by Renkow, Leonard, and Franklin (1983). In general, econometrically estimated supply elasticities are positive and quite high. Ndulu (1980) estimates short-run supply functions for the main maize surplus regions which vary from 3.2 to 7.2. Gerrard and Roe (1983) give 2.29 for the own-price elasticities of maize and rice production. Lundahl and Ndulu (1987) give price elasticities of officially marketed quantities of maize and paddy of 1.67 and 3.1, respectively. However, all of the above empirical evidence is based on the officially recorded data. The apparently substantial responsiveness of Tanzanian food crop marketing to official price may thus exaggerate the responsiveness of total production. Inclusion of open market information in the regression model is likely to reduce the estimates. For instance, using the relative price of maize on the open market with respect to the official price of annual export crops, Odegaard (1985) comes to a considerably lower price elasticity of officially marketed supply of 1.04.

Estimates of price elasticities for export crops should be more reliable than those for food crops, given the lesser significance of parallel markets and more reliable recording of marketed quantities. Gwyer (1971) and Malima (1971) arrive at positive elasticities for sisal and cotton (e.g., 2.5 for cotton). Moreover the period-by-period consistency between the price and quantity indices of export crops, as depicted in Figure 5, seems to make it inappropriate to downplay the impact of the producer price factor on the decline of the export crop sector. From Figure 5 it is apparent that decline and stagnation have characterized the trend in real producer prices of export crops for the entire period, with the exception of a temporary boom in 1975/1976. A modest and fragile increase was recorded from 1984 to 1987. The modesty of this upward trend is associated with the low transmission of real export crop price increases to the producer level. To see this, notice that during 1984 to 1987 producer prices of both Arabica and Robusta coffee should have risen considerably, due to a combination of favorable world market prices and the effects of devaluation. However, as can be gleaned from Table 49, these gains were not passed on to producers. In the 1986/87 and 1987/88 marketing

FIGURE 5

Export Crops, Price, and Quantity Index, 1965–1989.

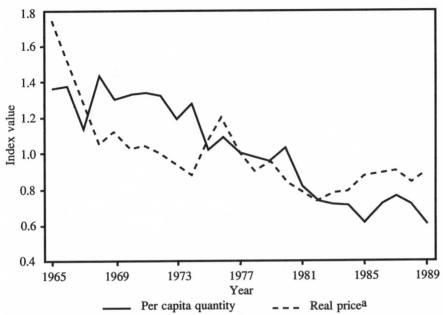

― Per capita quantity　― ― ― Real price[a]

[a] Nominal price index deflated by the NCPI.
Source: Authors' calculations.

seasons, the share of world prices received by producers declined substantially compared with the five previous seasons. A similar process occurred for the other major export crops. The benefits of structural adjustment policies have mainly been gobbled up by the parastatal sector.

Not surprisingly, then, per capita export crop production continued its decline, interrupted only temporarily by a positive supply response in the early stages of the adjustment period. The early, but temporary, supply response seems to confirm the arguments of Collier and Gunning (1989) that during the initial years of recovery, increased availability of consumer goods provided the economic incentives that explain the positive supply reaction. In the long run, however, real prices need to improve in order to sustain the supply reaction.

Figure 6 exhibits the aggregate real price of food crops in the parallel and official markets from 1967 to 1989. The deflator used is the nonfood component of the National Consumer Price Index (NCPI). When food imports increased in the mid-1970s, the government actively used price incentives to stimulate the production of food crops. Starting in the 1974/75 crop season, a pan-territorial

TABLE 49

Tanzania: Price Analysis, Arabica and Robusta Coffee.

	1981/82	1982/83	1983/84	1984/85	1985/86	1986/87	1987/88
				Arabica			
Average export price (official exchange rates)	20.97	26.06	39.16	55.61	72.36	150.00	171.99
Parchment equivalent price (80%)	16.78	20.85	31.33	44.49	57.89	120.00	137.59
Producer price (advance + interim + final, clean) (Tsh/kg)	17.38	18.96	28.59	37.10	57.25	75.94	82.50
Producer price/export price (percent)	83	73	73	67	79	51	48
				Robusta			
Average export price (official exchange rates)	16.38	22.22	40.38	46.67	52.78	126.90	131.04
Parchment equivalent price (50%)	8.19	11.11	20.19	23.33	26.39	63.45	65.52
Producer price (advance + interim + final, clean) (Tsh/Kg)	11.14	21.10	32.70	30.14	36.60	65.00	75.40
Producer price/export price (percent)	68	95	81	65	69	51	58

Source: United Republic of Tanzania, Marketing Development Bureau, *Annual Review of Coffee (Kahawa) 1988*, Tables 13 and 15.
Notes: All prices are in TSh/kilogram unless otherwise indicated.

FIGURE 6

Food Prices, 1969–1989, Official and Parallel Real Prices.

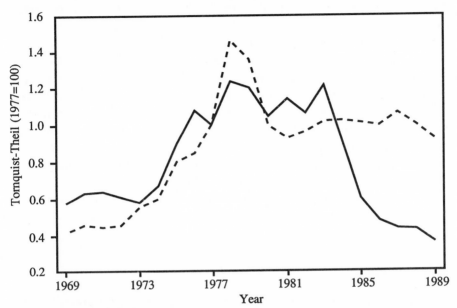

Source: Authors' calculations.

Note: Nominal prices deflated by the nonfood component of the NCPI. Official price index is composed of maize, paddy, wheat, sorghum, millet, cassava, and beans. Parallel price index is composed of maize, paddy, and beans only.

price system came into effect, and compulsory minimum acreage were declared. From 1979/80 to 1983/84, however, official prices fell, in real terms, and the "dual signal" policy system of official prices and compulsory acreage sent out conflicting signals to producers (Lundahl and Ndulu 1987; Bank of Tanzania 1984).

If we compare the real price level in the parallel market at the end of the 1960s with that of the early 1980s, we find a considerable appreciation. Parallel market prices rose steeply in the mid-1970s in response to the inefficiencies of the official marketing system and remained at approximately the same high levels until the government relaxed enforcement of the official marketing channels in 1984.

The observed price trends of food and export crops seem only partially compatible with a cash-versus-food-crop argument. On the one hand, the relative price of food on the parallel market with respect to the official price of export crops (not shown) rose considerably during the period 1973/74–1975/76 and between 1981/82 and 1984/85, and export crop production fell steeply during those periods. This part of the food-versus-export-crop thesis seems uncontested. However, any thesis that posits a complementary, rapid increase of per capita food production in the 1970s needs to address the consistent, simultaneous increase of the real price of food on the open markets. The prolonged increase in real food prices contradicts high official food production growth rates: food production per capita cannot have increased dramatically, because that would have been reflected in a general decline in real food prices on the parallel market, at unchanged or declining per capita income levels. Only a significant, and highly unlikely, per capita real income growth could be compatible with a higher per capita food output with real food price increases on the parallel market, where most of the surplus is marketed.

The impact of food market liberalization on food prices after 1984 supports our reasoning. At that time the increased supply immediately caused real food prices to fall.

SURVEY DATA

Comparisons between the Household Budget Surveys in 1969 and 1976/77 imply an annual growth of per capita consumption of the main food crops (excluding bananas) of 3.5 percent in the rural areas, and 3.1 percent in the urban areas. Given that population growth averaged 3.3 percent, this implies that production of these crops must have grown by well over 6 percent per year over the period 1969 to 1976/77. This is a respectable growth rate. According to the index based on the series of the Ministry of Agriculture and Livestock Development, however, per capita food production was supposed to have increased even more over this period, by over 11 percent per year.

We have compared the most commonly cited official series—namely, the ones originating from the Early Warning and Crop Monitoring Bureau (EWCMB) of the Ministry of Agriculture and Livestock Development—with the results of the recently published Agricultural Sample Survey 1986/87 (AGSASU) (Tanzania Bureau of Statistics 1989). The AGSASU methodology used a nationally representative sample and employed objective area and yield measurement methods. Note, however, that the AGSASU estimates include neither production on large-scale farms nor production by "urban farmers," that is, persons cultivating plots in peri-urban and rural areas, but not resident in those areas.

If we compare the official EWCMB estimates for some selected crops with the results of the AGSASU study, we see that for 1986/87 the official series reported a national production of 2,359,000 metric tons of maize, whereas AGSASU reports

2,017,000 metric tons. The estimates seem reasonably close. However, looking at the estimates for paddy, we see that the Ministry of Agriculture arrives at an estimate of 644,000 tons, and AGSASU reports only 445,000 tons—a difference of 30 percent. Wheat was not included in AGSASU. For the nontraded food crops, the trend of cassava production is the most remarkable: the official figure is 1,875,000 metric tons, but AGSASU reports only 305,000 metric tons. Beans production is officially estimated to be 347,000 tons; AGSASU reports 282,000 tons. Millet and sorghum together account for 570,000 tons according to the official series, but AGSASU estimates their production to be closer to 431,000 tons. Across the board, then, the series reported by EWCMB are significantly above the numbers reported by AGSASU.

Another way to compare the estimates is to convert the various crop quantities into calories by using standard calorie contents and assuming certain fixed conversion rates, such as that for the conversion of maize grain to maize flour. The results of such an exercise are depicted in Figure 7. It should be noted that the figures do not include a number of crops important in the calorie budget, such as sweet potatoes, cooking bananas, nuts, vegetables, fruit, meat, fish, dairy products, oils and fats, and a number of minor cereals and pulses. The graph is solely meant as a crude check on consistency, not as an indication of total calorie production in the country.

In Figure 7, total calories available from gross production are plotted over the 1966–1989 period and this trend is compared with three independent observations: the two consumption estimates from the Household Budget Surveys (HBS) in 1969 and 1976/77, and the production estimate from the Agricultural Sample Survey conducted in 1986/87. The comparisons suggest that whereas in 1969, official production statistics seemed to imply per capita calorie intakes similar to the 1969 HBS, in later years official production statistics seem to consistently and substantially overestimate the availability of staple food crops. The three independent observations, taken from HBS and AGSASU respectively, seem to indicate that food production per capita increased significantly between 1969 and 1976. Between 1976 and 1986, however, it showed a gradual decline, or stayed approximately constant if one assumes that production by urban residents (around 14 percent of the national population) would add 15 percent to the AGSASU figure.

IMPORTS

Another check on consistency is provided by data on cereal imports over the period under consideration. The agroclimatic conditions of Tanzania should normally not warrant any structural food aid. Emergency food aid should only

FIGURE 7

Caloric Comparison between Official Series and Survey Estimates, Major
Cereals, Cassava, and Beans.

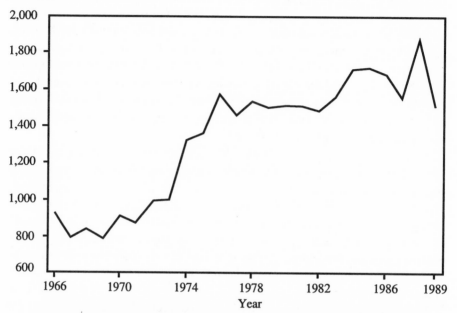

Sources: Marketing Development Bureau and other Ministry of Agriculture and Livestock
Development publications; Household Budget Surveys: International Labour Office, 1982;
Bureau of Statistics: Agricultural Sample Survey, 1986/87.
Notes: HBS = Household Budget Survey; and AGSASU = Agricultural Sample Survey. Crops
and calorie contents used: maize 3,630; paddy, 3,540; wheat, 3,440; sorghum, 3,350; millet,
3,360; cassava, 1,530; beans, 1,040.

be required in exceptionally bad years. Nonetheless, considerable amounts of
food grains have been imported during a number of years, over and above what
would be expected in light of the official production data. Figure 8 shows two
periods of considerable grain imports, namely, 1974 and 1980–1986. Note that
Tanzania imported 291,000 tons of maize in 1974/75. This is nearly 40 percent
of total production the previous season, or 20 percent of that of the 1974/75
season. Odegaard (1985, 151) attributes the increase in imports wholly to a shift
in food marketing from official market channels to the parallel food markets
coupled with a decline in wheat production in the large-scale farming sector. In
other words, the increase in imports in the mid-1970s, according to one ob-
server, was mainly caused by a failure of the official marketing system to supply
Tanzania's urban consumers with food.

FIGURE 8

Net Cereal Imports, 1966–1990.

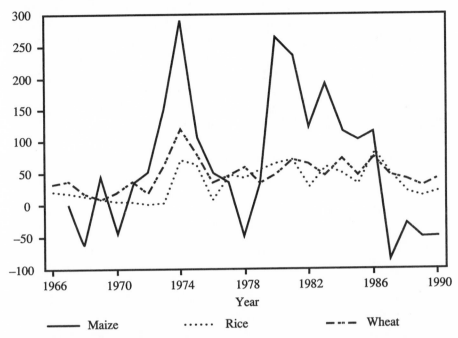

Source: Internal files, Economic Research Service, United States Department of Agriculture.

The next, more prolonged period of food imports took place in the period 1980/81 until 1986/87. During this period, maize imports averaged around 165,000 metric tons per year, which is about 8–9 percent of average annual production over the same years. Note that around 16 percent of the total population lived in urban areas during the period, and Dar es Salaam itself constituted around 5–6 percent of the total population. If one assumes that food imports were mainly destined for urban maize consumption, one is left with an unexplainable growth in national production—and hence nonurban consumption—since total maize production, according to official estimates, rose from 1,839,000 tons in 1980 to 2,359,000 tons in 1986, a total of 28.3 percent, or 10.3 percent more than population growth.

PARALLEL EXPORTS

Some of the major maize-producing areas are on Tanzania's borders. During the period of consumer goods shortages (mid-1970s until mid-1980s), considerable quantities of maize are likely to have been traded for incentive goods with Kenya, Zambia, Zaire, Malawi, and Rwanda (Lofchie 1988; 1989). The Marketing Development Bureau (MDB) of the Ministry of Agriculture undertook a study of the parallel markets for food grains in 1983 and identified northern Zambia and southern Kenya as the main target areas of parallel grain exports. Imports were consumer goods, such as soap, batteries, and cloth. The MDB estimated that 40,000 to 100,000 metric tons of maize, rice, and beans might have ended up in parallel export markets (Tanzania 1983). Given that the official production estimate for these three crops combined was around 2,300,000 metric tons in 1982/83, the MDB estimate implies that only 1.75 to 4.38 percent of total production was exported illegally.

Thus although there is evidence that parallel exports of food crops to neighboring countries were significant, they cannot by themselves explain the dramatic rise in officially recorded food production, given the high transaction costs associated with illegal, parallel export markets.

For some export crops, substantial parallel markets did exist, however. Coffee is Tanzania's most important export crop: during the 1980s, the value of coffee exports constituted between 25 and 50 percent of the value of all exports. Moreover, an estimated 1.78 million people depend on coffee for their livelihood (Agland Investment Services 1989). Although producers have reportedly doubled Tanzania's coffee area in the last 15 years, to around 234,000 hectares (Kristjanson et al. 1990), recorded yields have declined dramatically. While reduced yields may be partly the result of a failure of farmers to regenerate their coffee farms, it is likely that some of the yield reduction is in fact imaginary and reflects an increase of parallel exports, particularly of Arabica coffee from Arusha and Kilimanjaro to Kenya.

Supporting this hypothesis is the fact that the quality of Tanzanian coffee has fallen rapidly. In 1968/69, 87 percent of the mild Arabica production was of medium quality or higher. In 1986/87, the share was only 50 percent. Moreover, high-quality coffee (class 1–5) has dropped from 16 percent to 1.62 percent of the total (Agland Investment Services 1989, 30). Part of the fall in quality is attributed to the lack of a premium for quality in the official marketing system. Part, however, may also be attributable to an increase in parallel exports to the Kenyan, and to a much lesser extent, Ugandan and South African, markets (the latter would be reached via Zambia).

There is substantial anecdotal evidence of a lively coffee smuggling trade from Kilimanjaro and Arusha regions to Kenya. Interviews with coffee traders in Moshi revealed that coffee smuggling was virtually nonexistent in 1975 and 1976 but picked up afterward, due to rapidly increasing prices in Kenya. Such price differences did not remain great, but the shortage of consumer goods in

Tanzania in the late 1970s and early 1980s provided powerful incentives for parallel barter exports. In 1983 and 1984, parallel exports dropped, due to the official crackdown on parallel trade and the re-registration of the original cooperative unions. After 1985, however, parallel exports again steadily increased.

These anecdotes seem entirely consistent with the price trends depicted in Figure 9, which show that price incentives did indeed rise steeply from 1975 until 1977. During the years of the crisis, price incentives were less, but it seems logical to assume that the general consumer goods shortage in Tanzania compensated for this converging trend. The fact that after devaluation of the Tanzanian shilling relative producer prices in Tanzania worsened is also brought out by Figure 9.

FIGURE 9

Real Coffee Prices, 1970–1988 (NCPI); Parallel Market and Official Producer Price.

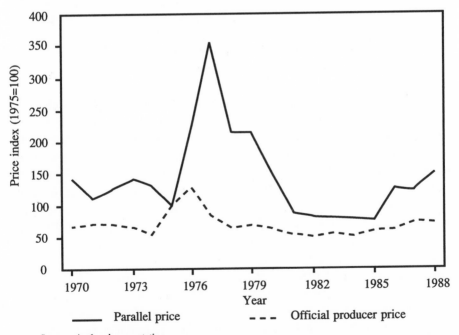

Source: Authors' computation.

Note: Parallel prices were computed by changing Kenyan producer prices to Tanzanian currency at parallel rates. Both official and parallel nominal prices were deflated by the NCPI.

Whereas such parallel markets are quite substantial for some high-value export crops, they tend to have a highly regional character. Producers in regions with access to parallel export markets, such as Arusha and Kilimanjaro, certainly took advantage of them to compensate for the crisis of the official economy in Tanzania. Thus compensating effects from parallel export incomes have had a considerable regional bias. This points again to the overriding importance of a realistic assessment of the performance of the food crop sector for the economic analysis of agricultural producer welfare in Tanzania.

MALNUTRITION

A recent World Bank/FAO mission reported a puzzling "calorie overhang" in Tanzania. Relying on official production estimates and increasing the FAO/WHO-recommended food requirement from 600 grams to 700 grams per person per day "in order to allow for post-harvest losses," the mission concluded that in 1988/89, national food production was above food requirements by about 39 percent. Energy requirements were exceeded by about 22 percent, even using the latest 1985 FAO/WHO/UNU recommendation of 2,780 kilocalories per person per day (an increase of 21 percent over the old level of 2,300 kilocalories). In other words, energy requirements were exceeded by 22 percent (reported surplus), plus 17 percent (postharvest losses), plus 21 percent (increase in the FAO/WHO/UNU recommendation)—a grand total of 60 percent above the recommended level of 2,300 kilocalories per person per day (Yambi, Kavishe, and Lorri 1990).

Paradoxically, the same mission also reported that 50 percent of the children below the age of 5 years are underweight. According to the same mission, "the rates of malnutrition in different areas of the country are not correlated with agricultural production," and it is concluded that "adequate aggregate food availability at national level does not translate into household food security for all" (Yambi, Kavishe, and Lorri 1990, 1). Is it possible that another explanation exists for the high prevalence of malnutrition in Tanzania, that is, that aggregate per capita food production is below what is reported? Our analysis in chapter 4 (see Tables 37 and 38) suggested that in the good year of 1976/77, daily calorie intakes were, on average, below the 2,300 kilocalorie FAO/WHO/UNU recommendation. It seems difficult to believe that after a decade of almost continuous crisis, calorie intake could have increased as much as the mission suggests. Or is intrahousehold inequality, and in particular the use of grain to make beer consumed by male household heads in Tanzania, so large that it can by itself explain the phenomenon? That is difficult to accept on a national scale.

AGRICULTURAL STRUCTURE AND TECHNOLOGY

In a relatively land-abundant setting, such as can be found in Tanzania, a dramatic increase in per capita food production should normally be associated with an increase in farm area, holding technology constant. To investigate this hypothesis, one can compare changes in farm size and size distribution between 1971/72 and 1986/87, as revealed by the Bureau of Statistics Agricultural Census and the Agricultural Sample Survey (AGSASU) respectively (see Figures 10 and 11).

Between 1971/72 and 1986/87, there appear to be few significant changes with respect to farm size distribution, apart from an increase in the number of farms smaller than 0.50 hectares which seems to have come mainly from the 0.50–2.00 hectares category. Similarly, a look at the changes in area actually cultivated reveals that there has not been a net increase. In fact, except for farms larger than 10 hectares, crop land per holding actually seems to have declined (Figure 12). Overall increases in farm area, or distributional shifts capturing economies of scale seem, therefore, unlikely candidates to explain high agricultural growth rates in Tanzania. What is perhaps most striking is that according to these data, the highly interventionist agricultural policies during the period under consideration seem to have had little actual impact in terms of the size and distribution of farm area per household.

On-farm labor resources have increased somewhat during the period 1971/72–1986/87 (see Figure 13). This would seem to be in line with the slowing of urban population growth from 10.7 percent during the years 1967–1978 to 5.4 percent for 1978–1988. The increase in on-farm labor resources seems to have been absorbed mainly by the farms larger than 2 hectares. Labor resources per hectare have also increased (see Figure 14), but only marginally, and again mostly in the larger size classes.

In order to ascertain whether a shift of land resources from cash to food crops has taken place, one can first examine changes in the area under food crops. The comparison of the two surveys in terms of net cultivated area under food crops is technically difficult, given differences in definitions between the two censuses. However, since the two different estimates that we constructed produced approximately the same overall pattern, we only report the results of one (see Figure 15). If we compare the area recorded for the main season, that is, the *masika* season, in 1986/87 with the 1971/72 data, there is evidence that the area devoted to food crops actually decreased over the period. The decrease becomes less prominent, of course, if for 1986/87 the combined area of *masika* and *vuli* seasons is used, but the decreasing trend still remains. However, given the different ways in which the results were reported in the two surveys, one should

FIGURE 10

Changes in Farm Size Distribution, 1971/72–1986/87.

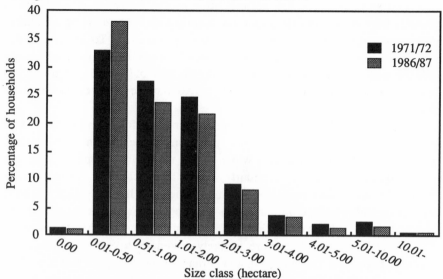

Sources: Computed from data in the Tanzania Bureau of Statistics, Agricultural Census 1971/72 and Agricultural Sample Survey of Tanzania Mainland 1986/87.

FIGURE 11

Changes in Farm Size, 1971/72–1986/87.

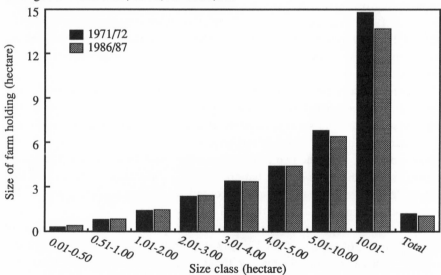

Sources: Computed from data in the Tanzania Bureau of Statistics, Agricultural Census 1971/72 and Agricultural Sample Survey of Tanzania Mainland 1986/87.

FIGURE 12

Crop Land per Holding, 1971/72–1986/87.

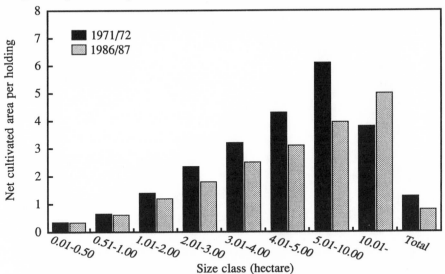

Sources: Computed from data in the Tanzania Bureau of Statistics, Agricultural Census 1971/72 and Agricultural Sample Survey of Tanzania Mainland 1986/87.

FIGURE 13

Changes in On-Farm Labor Availability per Holding, 1971/72–1986/87.

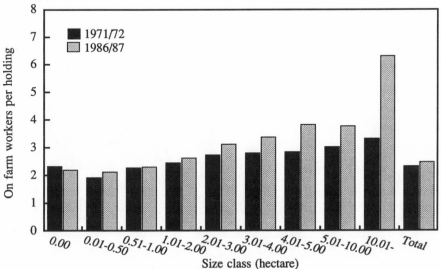

Sources: Computed from data in the Tanzania Bureau of Statistics, Agricultural Census 1971/72 and Agricultural Sample Survey of Tanzania Mainland 1986/87.

FIGURE 14

Changes in On-Farm Labor Availability per Hectare, 1971/72–1986/87.

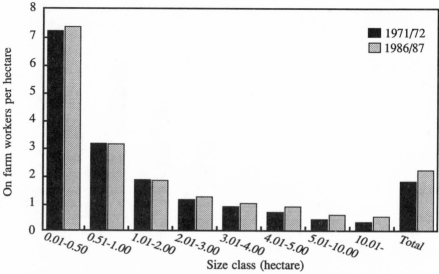

Sources: Computed from data in the Tanzania Bureau of Statistics, Agricultural Census 1971/72 and Agricultural Sample Survey of Tanzania Mainland 1986/87.

FIGURE 15

Changes in Cultivated Area under Food Crops, 1971/72–1986/87.

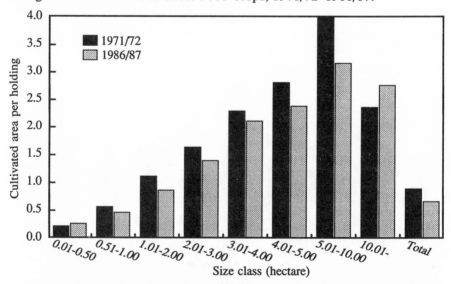

Sources: Computed from data in the Tanzania Bureau of Statistics, Agricultural Census 1971/72 and Agricultural Sample Survey of Tanzania Mainland 1986/87.

not place undue importance on this finding. There is some evidence of a different pattern at the high end of the farm size distribution: large farms above 10 hectares actually seemed to have increased their area under food crops.

Did this increase at the high end of the farm size scale come from a redistribution of resources away from cash crops, as has been implied in the literature on Tanzania? Or, alternatively, did the larger farms have to absorb a higher share of unemployed labor? Unfortunately, AGSASU did not cover cash crops. AGSASU does report on the total area under permanent crops, which might give us a rough indication of area trends of the perennial export crops, such as coffee, cashew nut, tea, and coconut. To obtain a measure of comparability, we have distilled from the 1971/72 census tables the areas under pure stands of permanent crops and the areas of crop mixes that included a permanent crop, and compared them with the 1986/87 figure.

According to the results shown in Figure 16, the average area devoted to permanent crops, either pure or intercropped, has increased from 0.14 hectares to 0.18 hectares per holding, that is, by 28.5 percent from 1971/72 to 1986/87. This increase has taken place predominantly in the larger-farm size classes, those above 5 hectares. It should be noted that farms larger than 10 hectares, again, show a pattern markedly different from the other size classes. The largest farms seem to have significantly increased their total area devoted to permanent crops.

It was hypothesized above that increased levels of economic risk, as perceived by producers, may have induced an increase of on-farm food stocks. Supporting this hypothesis is the observation that the area under cassava, a crop particularly suited for such an on-farm storage strategy, has seen substantial increases across all farm sizes (see Figure 17). However, it could also be argued that the trend observed is indicative of a shift away from the more permanent cropping system that was envisaged by the villagization policies of the 1970s.

Next, we need to consider developments in agricultural technology to gauge the impact of the increase in relative labor availability on the farm. Changes in agricultural technology could potentially account for both the increase in food production reported and for the increased application of labor per hectare of the larger farms. The use of chemical fertilizers may provide an indication of changes in agricultural techniques. Between 1971/72 and 1986/87, the number of households that reported use of chemical fertilizers nearly doubled, although it remains at a low level in absolute terms, growing from 7.3 to 14.0 percent of households.

The use of fertilizer is typically skewed toward the smaller farms, a pattern that has not changed over time. The increase of labor resources on the larger farms, then, was not accompanied by a concurrent increase in the use of fertilizers. This makes an increase of labor productivity on the larger farms somewhat

FIGURE 16
Changes in Pure or Mixtures of Permanent Crops, 1971/72–1986/87.

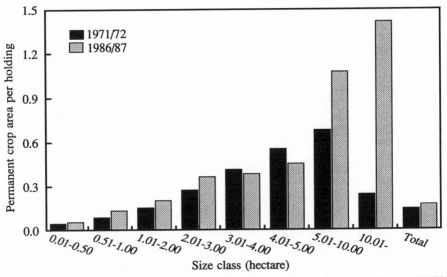

Sources: Computed from data in the Tanzania Bureau of Statistics, Agricultural Census 1971/72 and Agricultural Sample Survey of Tanzania Mainland 1986/87.

FIGURE 17
Changes in Area under Cassava, 1971/72–1986/87.

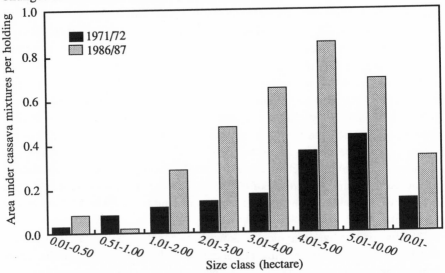

Sources: Computed from data in the Tanzania Bureau of Statistics, Agricultural Census 1971/72 and Agricultural Sample Survey of Tanzania Mainland 1986/87.

implausible. On the other hand, we have no information on the quantities actually applied. The mere reporting of the existence or not of fertilizer use may not be a good indication of its actual impact.

Other changes in agricultural techniques may be associated with an increase of the use of animal traction. The different reporting formats of the two surveys make it difficult to take a direct look at the issue of animal traction, in terms of the actual use of implements, such as ploughs and weeders. Given the fact that animal traction has been a component of many agricultural development programs, the mere presence of a plough on the farm may not say much about its actual use. Moreover, AGSASU reports ploughs, but is not clear whether they are drawn by tractors or animals. It is also not clear whether this refers to ploughs only or also includes weeders. However, both surveys report the incidence of oxen (male castrated animals) on the farm. If we assume that these are employed as draft animals, we can also use the oxen variable as a proxy for the actual use of animal traction.

The figures suggest that in 1986/87, on average, there were actually more households reporting the presence of a plough than reporting the presence of oxen. This confirms our suspicions that a significant number of the implements may not actually be used. In general, the holdings on which animal traction is used seem to have increased from an overall 4–5 percent of holdings in 1971/72 to approximately 8 percent in 1986/87.

The same conclusion can be drawn for the use of tractors in farming. One of the justifications put forward for the villagization program was the potential for mechanization of large, consolidated farms. However, tractor use has actually gone down from 0.29 percent in 1971/72 to 0.11 percent of all peasant holdings in 1986/87.

Summarizing our results, we can say the following. First, there were apparently no significant changes in farm size and its distribution. Second, there are indications that the net cultivated area per holding has actually gone down between 1971/72 and 1986/87. This tendency is also reflected in data on the area under food crops: according to our comparison of the two surveys, it is even possible that there has been a reduction in that area. Only the largest farms may have increased their area in food production. Moreover, if there has been an increase in food production, it seems unlikely that it has come about by a shift of land resources away from permanent crops to temporary crops in terms of area per holding. Third, although some of the relative increases are significant, the absolute levels of the use of fertilizer and mechanized traction cannot lead us to conclude the existence of a structural change in agricultural technology.

CONCLUSION

Since the mid-1970s, official estimates of the performance of Tanzanian agriculture show remarkable growth of the food sector. On a macro-level, this growth is reflected in a pattern of economic development in which agriculture consistently increases its share in GDP. However, we have submitted several reasons why one should doubt the validity of the official production estimates for the food sector. It seems that the period-by-period trends, as they appear in the official series of agricultural production, are reasonably accurate. However, when we look at the net, aggregate effect of the various trends, there seems to be a consistent contradiction between the official estimates, which show a doubling of per capita food crop production over the period 1966 to 1989, and survey estimates, caloric comparisons, price data, malnutrition rates, grain import figures, and information on structure and technology. None of the latter sources seems to support the claimed dramatic increase in food production. Thus, the evidence we have so far used does not corroborate the food-versus-cash-crop thesis that a rapid decline in export crop production was offset by an equally rapid increase in food crop production. Export crop production did decline, but food crop production did not compensate for the decline.

Independent survey estimates, import data, health statistics, estimates of parallel exports, open market price information, and changes in agricultural structure and technology seem to point, at best, to a slight increase in per capita food production. However, the modest increases may not have compensated for the general increase in risk levels, as perceived by the farmers. Such an increase in the overall level of risk perceived by producers could have been caused by a general failure of official marketing channels for both production and consumption goods, coupled with the sometimes-rigorous suppression of parallel markets. In the long run, increased risk tends to reduce production levels, causing less grain to be marketed and real price levels on the open market to rise.

One of the essential characteristics of Tanzanian agriculture is its diversity in agroclimates and crop production. This diversity enables the agricultural sector as a whole to exhibit quite pronounced substitution effects. Such substitution is not only triggered by the usual climatic variability, but also by the type of macroeconomic variability induced by Tanzania's economic crisis and the subsequent economic recovery programs. For instance, the radical changes in the marketing environment have induced producers to shift markedly in and out of official and parallel marketing channels. Moreover, the fact that major agricultural production areas, for export as well as food crops, are situated in closer proximity to Tanzania's borders than to its capital has further amplified the significance of parallel markets.

The adjustment policies of the mid-1980s that could have been relevant to agriculture were market liberalization and the exchange rate devaluation. However, market liberalization only took place for food crops and was never seriously implemented for export crops. The expected food supply reaction did occur, but due to the basic inelasticity of demand, real prices of food immediately plummeted, probably benefiting mainly urban consumers, and producers in regions with a relatively good transportation infrastructure.

Since liberalization with respect to export crops never materialized, only an ephemeral supply reaction was observed, probably caused by a one-time increase in the availability of consumer goods. The monopolistic government marketing structure remained intact. It basically used the exchange rate devaluation to ameliorate its financial position and failed to transmit exchange rate devaluations to the producer level. In other words, it was the political economy of "gradual adjustment" that prevented the supply reaction in the export sector, which continued the pattern of decline that had started in the late 1960s.

6

TRENDS IN INCOMES AND WELFARE OF VARIOUS

INCOME GROUPS

In this chapter we will integrate much of the structural analysis of the previous chapters to assess the impact of the recent stabilization and structural adjustment measures on the poor, as well as on other segments of the population. To the extent possible, we shall try to differentiate impacts by functional income groups.

The intertemporal analyses of incomes that have been done up to now are very few. Bevan et al. (1988; reproduced in Bevan et al. 1990) used information from household surveys conducted in 1969, 1976/77, 1979/80, 1982/83, and 1984 to assess trends in rural and urban incomes in Tanzania during the 15-year period of the "Nyerere experiment." They found an increase in rural per capita real incomes between 1969 and 1976/77, a very substantial drop between 1976/77 and 1979/80, and a very small, further drop in 1982/83. For urban per capita real incomes, their calculations showed a drop of 15 percent between 1969 and 1976/77, and a huge drop of more than 50 percent between 1976/77 and 1984. Their analysis is the only one available that spans such a long period.

Recently, Collier and Gunning (1989) examined changes in rural and urban average real incomes for the period 1983–1989, and they found that the declines indicated by earlier studies have been arrested, but no substantial real income increases have occurred in rural areas. However, the standard of living appears to have improved, primarily because of the increased availability of consumer goods, which enhances welfare by improving consumer choice.

In the following, we will reexamine the above hypotheses and provide some further analysis of differential income changes during the recent period. In the next section we examine the previous analyses of income declines over the post-Arusha-declaration period and find that the earlier conclusions are not supported by other data. We then outline in the next section a theoretical model for tracing the real welfare of different types of households. We then apply this method and show that the poor do not seem to have been significantly affected during or after the crisis.

HOW REAL IS THE DECLINE IN RURAL AND URBAN INCOMES DURING THE "NYERERE EXPERIMENT"?

The paper by Bevan and his colleagues (1988) came to its strong conclusions by examining the structure of income as well as changes in the real value of the various components of income. However, we will show that their results depend heavily on some particular definitions, and that without these, the picture is substantially altered.

Their first assertion concerns the structure of rural incomes circa 1983 by income quintiles, based on the results of a rural survey conducted in 1982/83, which shows that the shares of income derived from cash crop sales are larger for poorer households. However, this result is strongly influenced by the inclusion in total income of livestock, which, as was discussed in Chapter 4, is defined differently across surveys: whether or not asset valuations are included can strongly influence the results.

In Table 50 we reconstruct their reported figures on income and shares leaving out the livestock income that appears to create biases. The table, in the lower section, indicates that among nonlivestock income sources, the rural poor have a very high share of income from crops (especially food), while the rich have a higher share of income from own-business. The assertion of Bevan et al. that cash crops are relatively more important for the poor appears to hold, albeit not as strongly. The regional bias. of that survey, which did not use a national random sample but rather one wherein cash crops are substantial, might account for these results.

TABLE 50

Tanzania: Structure of Rural Incomes in 1982/83 by Per Capita Income Quintiles.

	Quintiles					
Per Capita	*1*	*2*	*3*	*4*	*5*	*Total*
	Tsh/Capita					
Income from:						
Food crops	108.6	293.1	505.3	681.9	2,110.7	642.8
Cash crops	19.1	71.8	98.1	110.2	310.4	108.4
Livestock	−238.2	13.0	136.6	353.0	1,080.2	215.3
Own business	29.9	39.5	66.0	170.5	2,396.3	407.4
Wages	6.6	41.5	38.5	244.5	180.0	99.1
Remittances	1.1	23.1	72.4	161.9	130.4	74.4
Total	−73.0	482.0	917.0	1,722.0	6,208.0	1,547.5
Total without livestock	165.2	469.0	780.4	1,369.0	5,127.8	1,332.1
	Percentages					
Nonlivestock income from:						
Food crops	65.7	62.5	64.8	49.8	41.2	48.3
Cash crops	11.5	15.3	12.6	8.1	6.1	8.1
Own business	18.1	8.4	8.5	12.5	46.7	30.6
Wages	4.0	8.8	4.9	17.9	3.5	7.4
Remittances	0.7	4.9	9.3	11.8	2.5	5.6
Total nonlivestock	100.0	100.0	100.0	100.0	100.0	100.0

Source: Computed from Bevan et al. (1990, 54).

The composition of total incomes, however, is quite different than the composition of cash incomes. Subsistence incomes are a large share of total rural incomes for all expenditure classes, as was seen in Chapter 4. These incomes are largely composed of food consumed out of own-production and, barring weather-induced production fluctuations, will not vary by much in real terms.

In Table 51 we present an analysis of the structure of rural cash incomes in 1982/83 by per capita income quintiles, as revealed by the data of Bevan et al. (1989). The pattern of cash incomes appears more varied than the one exhibited in Table 50. The figures on nonlivestock cash income show that the poorest and the highest-income groups rely substantially on both crops and own-business, while the middle-income quintiles rely relatively more on wage income. In the bottom part of the table, the absolute figures for the various components of income are given. The erratic nature of livestock income is again apparent, while all the other components appear reasonable. Notice that average subsistence

TABLE 51

Tanzania: Shares of Rural Cash Nonlivestock Incomes in 1982/83, by Per Capita Income Quintiles.

| | Quintiles | | | | | |
	1	2	3	4	5	Total
	Percentages					
Crops	48.4	48.6	54.1	31.3	27.9	32.8
Own business	41.1	19.5	17.1	20.3	63.9	47.1
Wages	9.0	20.5	10.0	29.1	4.8	11.5
Remittances	1.5	11.4	18.8	19.3	3.5	8.6
	Per Capita Incomes (Tsh)					
Total cash non-livestock income	72.8	202.6	385.8	839.9	3,752.6	864.9
Livestock cash income	−277.7	−10.8	37.6	−488.9	698.9	−13.4
Total cash income	−204.9	191.8	423.4	351.0	4,451.5	851.5
Subsistence income of which:	131.9	290.2	493.7	1,371.0	1,756.5	696.0
Crop	(92.4)	(266.4)	(394.6)	(529.1)	(1,375.2)	(467.3)
Livestock	(39.5)	(23.8)	(99.1)	(841.9)	(381.3)	(228.7)
Total	−73.0	482.0	917.0	1,722.0	6,208.0	1,547.5

Source: Computed from data in Bevan et al. (1990).

income is 45 percent of total rural income. In the 1976/77 survey (see Table 31) it was 47.6 percent, a very similar figure. However, Table 51 reveals a very different picture of per capita subsistence incomes among various income classes. The ratio of per capita subsistence income between the highest and lowest income quintiles is 13.3; in the 1976/77 survey, the same ratio between the highest and lowest cash expenditure classes (which corresponds to the highest and lower total income classes) was only 0.7. In other words, while the 1976/77 survey reveals a very even pattern of per capita subsistence income among various rural income classes, which is to be expected given the nature of subsistence consumption, the 1982/83 survey indicates a very differentiated pattern—which is very difficult to rationalize unless the higher-income classes consume much more expensive own-produced foods than the lower classes. That such does not appear to be the case is illustrated in the consumption patterns shown in Table 41.

The same, counterintuitive result concerning subsistence incomes also obtains in the 1979/80 survey (Collier et al. 1986). When rural households were divided into two income classes, the lower 50 percent and the upper 50 percent, it turned out that consumption out of own-production in the richer class, per adult equivalent unit, was 2.5 times higher. Again, this is hard to rationalize unless there are widespread differences in subsistence consumption patterns, which, as mentioned, does not appear to be the case.

The conclusion from the above analysis is that some doubt must be cast on the measurement and composition of subsistence incomes revealed by both the 1979/80 and the 1982/83 surveys. Bevan et al. (1989) found substantial declines in real per capita rural subsistence incomes between 1969 and 1982/83, which, given the large share of subsistence income in total income, could account for a significant part of the reported decline in total income. Given that subsistence consumption provides 80 percent of the rural per capita daily calorie intake (see Table 51), a significant reduction in subsistence income, unless accompanied by a large decline in calorie consumption, an unlikely possibility, would be due mainly to lower valuation, but would not necessarily imply lower real consumption. In fact, given that 1978–1983 was a period of shortages and general economic hardship and insecurity, it is very difficult to believe that rural producers would decrease production for subsistence consumption. The most likely reason for a decline in subsistence income would be the use of lower prices in the valuation of subsistence incomes and not lower quantities produced.

In Table 52, we exhibit the composition of average rural per capita cash incomes, as well as the mean value of cash and subsistence incomes in 1969, 1976/77, 1979/80, and 1982/83, as revealed in the same four surveys used by Bevan et al. (1990), namely, the national Household Budget Surveys for 1969 and 1976/77, the ILO survey (Collier et al. 1986), and the 1982/83 survey reported in Bevan et al. (1989). It is immediately apparent that livestock cash income behaves very erratically, and since it can be an important component of income, it influences significantly the structure of total income. In the bottom panel of Table 52 we exhibit the composition of nonlivestock rural cash income in the four survey periods. From that part of the table, the structure of cash income appears much more stable, with crop income accounting for about 32–38 percent of cash nonlivestock income. Noncrop income appears to have declined in 1979/80 but recovers in 1982/83. Within this category, a clear trend appears to be the declining share of wage and salary income, while income from own-business and other sources increased in importance. Finally, remittances seem to have increased in importance after 1976/77.

In the middle part of the table, we exhibit the reported values for the various types of incomes, as well as the NCPI corresponding to the reported periods (adjacent years have been averaged to arrive at a NCPI for a year, such as 1982/83, etc.). Table 53 exhibits the trends in the various components of real income from 1969 to 1982/83. It is apparent that changes in cash and subsistence income

TABLE 52

Tanzania: Composition of Rural Cash and Cash Nonlivestock Incomes,
1969 to 1983.

	1969	1976/77	1979/80	1982/83
Shares of cash income from (percentages):				
Crop sales	31.4	33.0	27.7	32.8
Livestock sales	12.5	4.0	26.2	−1.5
Wages and salaries	22.6	14.7	—	11.5
Own-business	25.0	32.5	38.2[a]	47.1[b]
Other, except remittances	5.1	13.5	—	—
Remittances	4.0	3.3	7.9	8.6
Per capita cash income (Tsh)	213.0	489.0	375.0	851.0
Per capita subsistence income	167.0	445.0	360.0	696.0
Per capita nonlivestock cash income	186.0	469.0	278.0	864.0
National CPI (1976/77=100)	46.0	100.0	146.1	304.1
Cash nonlivestock income from (percentages):				
Crops	35.9	34.4	37.5	32.8
Noncrop, except remittances	60.2	62.3	51.8	58.6
of which:				
Wages	25.8	15.3	n.a.	11.5
Own-business	28.6	33.9	n.a.	47.1[c]
Other	5.8	13.1	n.a.	—
Remittances	4.6	3.4	10.7	8.6

— Data for this item included in another category.
Sources: Computed from Household Budget Survey, 1969 and 1976/77; Collier et al. (1986), and
Bevan et al. (1990).
[a] Nonfarm cash income from all sources, except remittances.
[b] Income from business and other sources, except remittances.
[c] Includes other.

appear to be similar. The ratio of subsistence to total income appears to have
remained remarkably constant over the whole period, at 44–49 percent of total
income. If there was a decline in total real income, as indicated by Bevan et al.,
the share of subsistence income should have risen, as food security concerns
would dictate maintenance of self-produced food consumption. However, no
retreat into subsistence is apparent, as often mentioned in various publications
on Tanzania (e.g., Hyden 1980). The decline in real per capita subsistence
income after 1976/77 was quite problematic, as already mentioned, because no
widespread famine was reported in the rural areas between 1976 and 1982/83
that would be commensurate with the very large decline in subsistence real
income apparent in Table 53.

TABLE 53

Tanzania: Trends in Per Capita Rural Real Incomes, 1969 to 1983 (in 1976/77 prices).

	1969	*1976/77*	*1979/80*	*1982/83*
Total cash income (Tsh)	463.0	489.0	257.0	280.0
Subsistence income	363.0	445.0	246.0	229.0
Cash nonlivestock income	404.0	469.0	190.0	284.0
Total income	826.0	934.0	503.0	509.0
Share of subsistence in total income (percent)	43.9	47.6	48.9	45.0
Percentage changes from previous period in:				
Total cash income		5.6	–47.4	8.9
Subsistence income		22.6	–44.7	–6.9
Cash nonlivestock income		16.1	–59.5	49.5
Total income		13.1	–46.1	1.0

Source: Computed from data in Table 52.

The resolution of this apparent paradox must lie in the deflator used to construct the real income figures. Bevan and his co-authors, and most researchers in Tanzania, use the National Consumer Price Index (NCPI) for deflating nominal income flows. This index uses data collected in 20 urban centers, and it has a high food component (64.2 percent). The price of food, however, ought to be much cheaper in rural areas, as most locally purchased food is also produced locally. On the other hand, the prices of nonfood items ought to be higher in rural areas. Bevan et al. in fact estimated, on the basis of the prices of nonfood items, that the rural CPI was 18.7 percent higher in 1982/83 than the corresponding national CPI.

However, this neglects the differential cost of food in rural areas. In Table 54, we exhibit open market producer prices and open market urban consumer prices for maize, rice, beans, millet, and sorghum, and their ratios to official prices for several regions and zones in Tanzania for 1986/87 and 1987/88. The price differentials between urban and rural areas range from 30 to 80 percent, and this in a period when grain marketing was already partially liberalized. During the period of the surveys, namely, 1979–1983, marketing was very restricted, implying larger urban-to-rural food price differentials. In fact, the ratios of open to official market prices were much higher then, compared with the post-SAP period.

TABLE 54

Tanzania: Open Market Producer and Urban Consumer Prices for Several
Staples, 1986/87 and 1987/88 (all prices in Tsh/kilogram).

	1986/87			*1987/88*		
	Producer	*Urban Consumer*	*Ratio (2) - (1)*	*Producer*	*Urban Consumer*	*Ratio (5) - (4)*
	(1)	*(2)*	*(3)*	*(4)*	*(5)*	*(6)*
Maize grain	8.28	9.74	1.18	10.70	13.86	1.30
Rice	27.07	35.72	1.32	31.88	44.33	1.39
Beans	23.89	32.68	1.37	32.38	43.83	1.35
Finger millet	17.61	25.54	1.45	22.44	35.33	1.57
Sorghum	9.85	17.25	1.75	13.19	23.96	1.82
Ratios of open market to official prices:						
Maize grain	1.31	0.83		1.32	1.13	
Rice	1.32[a]	1.37		1.24[a]	1.39	
Beans	1.66	1.06		1.50	1.09	
Finger millet	3.67	—		3.74	—	
Sorghum	2.05	1.23		2.20	1.32	

— Not available.
Source: Computed from MDB annual reviews of maize, rice, wheat and sorghum, millet, cassava
and beans, 1987 and 1988.
[a] Paddy.

Another problem with the national deflator is that the shares of incomes spent
on food in rural areas is much larger than in urban areas (74.7 percent versus 66.0
percent, as indicated in Tables 33 and 34). This, coupled with the fact that food
is much cheaper in rural areas, implies that the appropriate CPI for rural areas in
1982/83 should be lower, and not higher, than the NCPI.

To obtain an idea of the potential differences, we first estimated the nonfood
prices that would be needed in 1982/83 to achieve a NCPI higher than the official
one by 18.7 percent, as reported by Bevan et al. Using the food and nonfood
weights of the NCPI, prices of nonfood items in rural areas would have to be 71.0
percent higher than in the urban areas. Assuming that food prices are 50 percent
lower in rural areas, however, and using the rural consumption weights of Table
33 instead of the urban weights of the NCPI, implies that the rural CPI in 1982/83
was 25.5 percent lower than the official NCPI. If the price of food is assumed to
be 70 percent lower in rural than in urban areas, then the rural CPI would be 42.7
percent lower than the official CPI. In the first case, the estimated per capita real

subsistence income in 1982/83 would be 307 Tsh (in 1976/77 Tsh) compared to 229 reported in Table 53, while total real income would be 683 Tsh compared to 509 Tsh in Table 53. In the second case, subsistence income in 1982/83 would be 400 Tsh and total income 888 Tsh. These latter figures are comparable to the 1969 and 1976/77 real income levels.

Apparently, then, the use of the national CPI exaggerates the decline in rural real incomes during 1969 to 1982/83. Our analysis casts doubt on this finding because the share of subsistence in total rural income did not increase during the period, and because the proper deflator might be different than the NCPI. Our conclusion is that between 1969 and 1982/83, and certainly between 1976/77 and 1982/83, the decline in rural real incomes was much smaller and less dramatic than reported by Bevan and his co-authors (1988; 1990), and in fact, it is not even clear that there was a real income decline.

This conclusion is reinforced by the observation, often mentioned by Tanzanians and other observers, that during the crisis period there was cross-border trade in agricultural products, and furthermore, there was informal activity in local production of commodities that were unavailable through the official markets (Havnevik 1986). Among parallel exports, coffee would be a case in point, but hides and skins and foodgrains could also have been involved (Maliyamkono and Bagachwa 1990). The 1982/83 survey reported in Bevan et. al. (1990) found from farmers' responses that there were no parallel sales of coffee, even though it reported parallel sales of tobacco, another export crop. Since parallel sales of export crops were illegal, it is to be expected that the responses underestimated those sales. This underestimation ought to be larger in 1979/80 and 1982/83, at the height of the crisis. Hence, compared with the 1976/77 and 1969 surveys, rural cash incomes should have been underreported to a larger degree. This consideration also tends to bring into question the validity of the rural real-income decline thesis.

Turning to urban incomes, our comparison in Chapter 4 of urban incomes in 1969 and 1976/77 (see Tables 22 and 23) revealed an enormous decline in real urban per capita cash incomes of 68 percent between the two periods—and a decline in the share of wage income in total cash income. The Bevan study (1988) mentions that in 1969, wage income was underreported and that this resulted in a 25 percent underreporting of urban income. This would, of course, only make the decline worse.

Bevan and his co-authors (1988) reported the results of an urban survey that they did in 1984. In Table 55, we compare their results with the results of the 1969 and 1976/77 surveys. The first observation that we can make is that between 1976/77 and 1984, the only part of urban cash income that seems to have increased in importance is returns to trade, enterprise, or profession, namely,

TABLE 55

Tanzania: Structure and Levels of Urban Incomes, 1969, 1976/77, and 1984.

	1969	*1976/77*	*1984*
Shares of cash income from different sources (percentages):			
Crops	0.8	1.3	2.7[a]
Animal husbandry	0.4	0.9	—
Wages and salaries	60.4	53.4	54.9
Trade, enterprise, or profession	29.2	25.6	42.3[b]
Other	9.2	18.8	—[b]
Cash income per capita (Tsh)	2,414	1,705	3,777
Subsistence income per capita (Tsh)	—	161	364
Share of subsistence in total	—	(8.6)	(8.8)
Real cash income per capita (1976/77 prices)	5,249	1,705	815
Real subsistence per capita income (1976/77 prices)		161	79
Total real income per capita		1,866	894

— Not available.

Source: Compiled from Tables 36 and 37 of this monograph and Bevan et al. (1988).

[a] All cash farm income.

[b] There is no figure for other income reported in Bevan et al. (1988).

own-business income. The Bevan study (1988) does not mention any figures for other sources of income, which, as can be seen in Table 55, accounted for substantial portions of cash incomes in both the 1969 and 1976/77 surveys. The share of wage income appears to be the same between 1976/77 and 1984. Bevan and his co-authors report a much larger share of wage income in urban income for 1976/77. It is not clear, however, where they obtained these numbers, as the available tables for the 1976/77 Household Budget Survey in the Bureau of Statistics (BOS) suggest the figures analyzed in Chapter 4.

The second observation is that the share of subsistence in total per capita urban income is the same in the two surveys of 1976/77 and 1984. This raises the same issues that were discussed earlier in the context of rural income, namely, if total real urban per capita income declined, one would expect an increase in the share of subsistence income. The Bevan work indeed shows a very large increase in subsistence income, but again, the figures do not match the ones we obtained from the BOS for the same survey. If the subsistence share did not rise, then the substantial urban real income decline evident in the table (52 percent between 1976/77 and 1984) must be questioned. In any case, it is very hard to rationalize the enormous decline in real per capita urban incomes between 1969 and 1984. If the figures in the table are to be believed, urban residents in 1984 enjoyed only 15 percent of their real income in 1969. This seems exaggerated, because throughout the period, no massive famine or starvation was reported.

As was seen in Table 41, the lower urban classes tended in 1976/77 to secure the bulk of their daily calorie needs from subsistence production, and in fact, the bulk of their total food consumption from subsistence activities (see Table 34). The decline in cash incomes would thus tend to influence proportionately more the middle and upper urban classes, which do not have much subsistence income. Table 56 reproduces an interesting table from Bevan et al. (1988), which indicates the structure of income in Dar es Salaam in 1984, compared with that of 1976/77, by income quintiles. What the table shows is that it was the middle- and upper-income classes that increased their income from farming, while wage income declined the least in the poorest class; business income declined the most in the poorest class. However, the comparison of the bottom two quintiles reveals an inconsistency. While the poorest quintile shows declines in all types of income, with the smallest decline in wage income, the next-higher income quintile shows increases in farm and business income and decline in wage income. Given that the bulk of the income of low-income urban households comes from subsistence (see Table 34), it is difficult to see how real farm income for this class could decline in 1984 to 14 percent of its 1976/77 value. It thus appears that the results for the bottom quintile are problematic and should be discarded. The story revealed by the income pattern of the other quintiles, however, is entirely plausible.

Real farm incomes, mainly subsistence, rose between 1976/77 and 1984 for all classes, consistent with the general urban income decline and the rise of subsistence farming; among nonfarm income sources, own-business increased in

TABLE 56

Tanzania: Per Capita Household Incomes in 1984 as Percentage of Their Values in 1977: Dar es Salaam, by Quintiles (comparison is between incomes at 1982/83 prices).

	Quintiles					
	1	*2*	*3*	*4*	*5*	*Total*
Farm income	14	169	279	359	129	150
Own business income	6	121	68	70	86	89
Wage income	76	23	28	20	20	32
Total (per capita) income	40	42	43	38	29	46

Source: Bevan et al. (1988, 79).

importance compared to wage income. There still remains one problem, however, and that is the large underreporting of urban business income throughout the decade of the seventies and early eighties. The severe official discouragement of private activities must have encouraged gross underreporting of clandestine income-generating activities both legal (trade, informal manufacturing and services, etc.) and illegal.

An indication of the magnitude of underreporting can be seen in Table 57, which shows that in the survey of Maliyamkono and Bagachwa (MB) (1990), done in 1986, reported income in urban areas is 39 percent below reported consumption; for rural areas the underreporting is similar, at 36 percent. In fact, since there must be some saving, the underreporting is bound to be even greater. MB (1990) indeed regarded the degree of underreporting as higher than indicated.

TABLE 57

Tanzania: Structure of Rural and Urban Household Income and Consumption in 1986.

	Rural	*Urban*
Shares of income (percent) derived from:		
Self-employment	63.4	21.0
Wages and salaries	19.5	59.0
Interest, dividends, profits	2.9	6.0
Rents, royalties	4.9	7.0
Pensions, annuities, estates, trusts	4.9	3.0
Capital gains	1.2	2.0
Other	3.2	2.0
Average household income (Tsh)	26,525	36,292
Average household income in 1976/77 prices (Tsh)	3,244	4,438
Per capita household income (1976/77 values)	559	888
Shares of expenditure (percent) derived from:		
Food, beverages, and tobacco	65.0	53.9
Clothing and footwear	10.6	11.8
Rent, fuel, water, power	9.0	13.7
Medical care, education, and communication	2.8	5.9
Household durables	3.5	6.9
Recreation and entertainment	7.1	3.9
Miscellaneous	2.0	2.0
Average expenditure per household (Tsh)	41,318	59,495
Average expenditure per household in 1976/77 prices (Tsh)	5,053	7,276
Per capita household expenditures (1976/77 values)	871	1,455

Source: Maliyamkano and Bagachwa (1990, 148), and authors' computations.

If we discount the 1986 household income and consumption reported by MB to 1976/77, using the NCPI, and then use the average household-size figures reported in the 1976/77 Household Budget Survey for rural and urban households (MB do not report their survey's average household size), namely, 5.8 for rural and 5.0 for urban (see Table 31), then for the urban areas real per capita income is 888 Tsh in 1976/77 prices. That figure is practically identical to the 1984 figure for total urban per capita income reported by Bevan et al., (1988) which was 894 Tsh (see Table 55). Real rural per capita income is then 559 Tsh, again quite close to (in fact a little higher than) the figures of 503 and 509 Tsh reported in the 1979/80 and 1982/83 surveys (see Table 53). In other words, the three surveys are quite consistent as far as reported income is concerned.

When total 1986 expenditure is discounted to 1976/77, however, the picture that emerges is different. Per capita real urban consumption is 1,455 Tsh, which is higher by 13.4 percent than the average urban per capita consumption expenditure of 1,283 Tsh observed in 1976/77 (see Table 34; remember consumption and total expenditure are different because the latter includes investment expenditures), and not much lower than the reported total per capita expenditure in urban areas of 1,690 Tsh (again see Table 34). For rural areas, the per capita real consumption expenditure of 871 Tsh in 1986 is 4.3 percent higher than the 1976/77 figure of 835 Tsh and slightly lower than the per capita total expenditure figure of 901 Tsh in 1976/77. Thus, what appears to have happened is that the degree of underreporting of incomes increased substantially after 1976/77, which is entirely plausible and consistent with the evolution of Tanzanian policies in that period.

A further check on our contention that real income declines during the crisis were not as large as previously thought concerns consumption patterns in 1986 (see Table 57) compared with those of a decade earlier (see Tables 33 and 34). In the rural areas, expenditure for food, drinks, and tobacco in 1976/77 accounted for 76.5 percent of total expenditure, while in 1986, according to Table 57, they accounted for only 65 percent. Similarly in the urban areas, the same share in 1976/77 was 68.3 percent, while in 1986, it was 53.9 percent. The decline in this share, according to accepted theory and other country evidence, is not compatible with a decline in real income but in fact, quite the contrary.

The conclusion of our analysis, then, is that real per capita incomes in both rural and urban areas were not seriously declining between 1976/77 and the onset of the ERP in the mid-1980s, as previous studies have indicated. What seems to have happened instead is that both rural and urban households switched their activities from formal, observable ones to informal and unobservable ones, in order to maintain their real incomes. This strategy appears to have met with success for most households, as suggested by the above analysis, but it is quite difficult to observe from published official figures.

A METHOD FOR ANALYZING HOUSEHOLD INCOMES

The previous section illustrated the difficulties of comparing incomes from surveys done in different periods, during which very different policy regimes were in place. In this section we outline a different methodology that we subsequently apply to illustrate the evolution of household incomes.

Consider a household that is representative of a class. The household will derive its income from agricultural and nonagricultural activities. The agricultural activities will be of three kinds: those that produce exportable and other nonfood, tradable cash crops (e.g., coffee, cotton, tobacco, and tea); those that produce tradable, staple food crops (mainly maize and rice); and, those that produce mainly nontradable food products (coarse grains, roots and tubers, fruits and vegetables, livestock products, etc.). In the case of Tanzania, these can be further subdivided among scheduled nontraded crops (sorghum, millet, cassava, beans) and others.

Denote by s_a and s_n, the shares of income derived from agricultural and nonagricultural activities, respectively, in some base year, including transfers and remittances, where of course,

$$s_a + s_n = 1 . \tag{6.1}$$

Also, denote by s_{ai} the shares of agricultural income derived from activity i ($i = e, f, o$) among the three types of activities mentioned above, where e, f, and o denote exportable, tradable staple food, and other nontradable agricultural products, respectively. Among nonagricultural income, we shall distinguish among formal- and informal-sector income. The shares of nonagricultural income that constitute formal- and informal-sector income will be denoted by s_{nf} and s_{nu}. Finally, denote by i the base-year shares of total household consumption expenditures (including subsistence consumption) ($i = f, o, n$) that are used for tradable staple food products, nontradable food products, and nonagricultural products (symbolized by $i = n$), respectively. Changes in the welfare of this type of household can then be monitored by examining the following index of changes of real income:

$$\tilde{Y} = \left(s_a \left[s_{ae} \tilde{P}^P_{ae} + s_{af} \tilde{P}^P_{af} + s_{ao} \tilde{P}^P_{ao} \right] + s_n \left[s_{nf} \tilde{w} + s_v \tilde{r} \right] \right)$$
$$- \left(\delta_f \tilde{P}^c_f + \delta_o \tilde{P}^c_f + \delta_n \tilde{P}^c_n \right) \tag{6.2}$$

where the symbol (~) above a variable denotes percentage change from a given period; Y is real income, P_{ae}, P_{af}, P_{ao} are the price indices of the three (or more) agricultural product groups (as outlined above), relevant for this household, with the superscripts p for producer prices and c for consumer prices, P_n^c is the consumer price of the nonagricultural product, w denotes the unit reward (wage) of formal-sector activities, and r denotes the unit reward to informal (unincorporated) nonagricultural activities of the given class of household.

Expression (6.2) can be derived by taking the derivative of a standard household consumer utility function, which is a function only of quantities consumed, under the assumption that the household earns income by operating on a standard production possibility frontier of agricultural and other activities. As long as smallholder activities are labor intensive, and total labor available per household, as well as technology, do not change, the frontier will not shift outward over time, and hence only substitution among activities, due to relative price changes, will occur. This implies that expression (6.2) does not need to include changes in quantities of total resources available to the household.

While changes that producers and consumers experience in the prices of the three agricultural products and changes in w, as well as in the price of the nonagricultural product P can be observed and monitored relatively easily, the unit reward of the informal production activity r cannot. Given, however, that a large share of household incomes, especially for poor households, is derived from such activities, as seen earlier, it cannot be neglected. In the following, a simple model is outlined by which the change in r can be expressed as a function of the changes in the other observable prices in equation (6.2) above.

Consider an economy composed of two sectors—agriculture and nonagriculture. The agricultural sector produces three products (the same categories outlined above) and, apart from land, uses only labor. The nonagricultural sector produces two products: the formal one that uses labor and an imported intermediate product, and the informal one that uses only labor. Technology is Cobb-Douglas in all sectors. The formal sector, which includes all the public enterprises, is in many analyses modeled as a fix-price nonagricultural sector, namely, one with excess capacity and fixed nominal wages. The informal sector, composed of many individual and small-scale unincorporated enterprises, can be thought of as a flex-price one, with ease of entry and exit and where much self-employment takes place.

Denote by L_{nf} the demand for labor in the formal sector. This sector in Tanzania comprises mostly the public sector and a few large private establishments. While we could assume that it operates in a normal, profit-maximizing fashion, this would hardly represent reality in the Tanzanian case, given various labor laws and other regulations. We, therefore, assume that employment L_{nf} in this sector is exogenously determined.

The informal sector will be assumed to utilize mainly labor. Its production function will be assumed to be Cobb-Douglas

$$X_{nu} = K_{nu} L_{nu}^{\beta} \tag{6.3}$$

where K_{nu} summarizes the contribution to informal sector production of other primary factors, and L_{nu} denotes the labor employed in the informal sector. The unit labor reward for this activity has been defined as r. Denoting by P_{nu} the price for the output of the informal sector and maximizing, we obtain a demand for informal labor. Log-differentiating that (namely, first totally differentiating the resulting expression, and then dividing by itself, so as to produce variables of the form dx/x), we obtain

$$\tilde{L}_{nu} = \frac{1}{1 - \beta} \left(\tilde{P}_{nu} - \tilde{r} \right). \tag{6.4}$$

The other major labor-using sector is agriculture. Agriculture supplies labor to the nonagricultural sector, depending on the relative rewards of agricultural versus nonagricultural activities. At this point, we introduce two structural assumptions that seem to be quite relevant for countries in sub-Saharan Africa in general and Tanzania in particular: first, most agricultural production is organized among individually operated farm units. This implies that the reward of a unit of agricultural labor is, on aggregate, close to the average product of labor in agriculture. The second assumption has to do with the types of nonagricultural activities in which the rural poor engage. Those activities usually involve either informal wage employment in rural or urban areas, or some type of small-scale, owner-operated enterprise. Given capital requirements, risks, and so forth, it seems reasonable to assume that the effective reward offered by the nonfarm enterprise to a unit of nonagricultural labor is not far from the effective reward of farm-operator labor when working on own-account. In fact, there has been empirical evidence confirming this in Tanzania (see Collier et al. 1986).

Given the above reasoning, the behavioral relation that will govern the supply of labor from agriculture to nonagriculture is the following:

$$r = \frac{P_a X_a}{L_a} \tag{6.5}$$

where X_a is the aggregate output of the agricultural sector, L_a is the labor employed in agriculture; and P_a is the aggregate price of agricultural output. If the production of X_a is governed by the following Cobb-Douglas relation

$$X_a = K_a L_a^\alpha, \tag{6.6}$$

then (6.5) gives a relation between L_a and r. Log-differentiating that equation, we obtain a relation between the aggregate use of agricultural labor and the nonagricultural unit reward

$$\tilde{L}_a = \frac{1}{1-\alpha}\left(\tilde{P}_a - \tilde{r}\right). \tag{6.7}$$

Under the Cobb-Douglas assumption, equation (6.7) is also valid if the nonagricultural unit reward is equated to the marginal product of labor in agriculture.

The final consideration has to do with the structure of the aggregate labor market. In sub-Saharan Africa, and also in Tanzania, unemployment rates are very low, and in the rural areas virtually zero, as has been found by household surveys (see Collier et al. 1986). The reason is that people move in and out of various low-skilled activities quite easily. Albeit it is more difficult to find permanent wage work in the rural sector (e.g., as a public employee), even that submarket is not separated from the rest of the labor market. In fact, it is quite prevalent that underpaid civil employees work in other activities by effectively diminishing their labor input into their official activity. The upshot of these arguments is that it is reasonable to suggest that the labor market is characterized by full employment, and it is this that determines informal returns to labor.

The implication of this consideration for our simple model is that we can use equations (6.4) and (6.7) in an aggregate, labor-market-clearing equation to determine $\tilde{r}$. The aggregate labor market equilibrium condition is

$$L_a + L_{nf} + L_{nu} = L \tag{6.8}$$

where L and L_{nf} are exogenously given. Log-differentiating (6.8) and using (6.4) and (6.7), we obtain

$$\tilde{r}\left(\frac{\lambda_a}{1-\alpha} + \frac{\lambda_{nu}}{1-\beta}\right) = \frac{\lambda_a}{1-\alpha}\tilde{P}_a + \lambda_{nf}\tilde{L}_{nf} + \frac{\lambda_{nu}}{1-\beta}\tilde{P}_{nu} \tag{6.9}$$

where L_{nf} is the exogenous growth rate in formal-sector employment. In equation (6.9), λ_a, λ_{nf}, and λ_{nu} are the base-year shares of total labor employed in agriculture, formal and informal sectors, respectively.

Notice that we have abstracted from secular trends in unit rewards caused by changes in the capacity of the three sectors (summarized by the all-inclusive indices K_a and K_{nu} in the model) as well as exogenous growth in the labor force or induced changes in labor supply. These influences could easily be included by adding to the right-hand side of equation (6.9) another term $\tilde{r}^*$, where

$$\tilde{r}^* = \frac{\lambda_a \tilde{K}_a}{1-\alpha} + \frac{\lambda_{nu} \tilde{K}_{nu}}{1-\beta} - \tilde{l}, \tag{6.10}$$

and $\tilde{l}$ is the exogenous natural and induced growth rate of the labor force. Lacking much information on which to empirically estimate $\tilde{K}_a$ and $\tilde{K}_{nu}$, we simply neglect the term $\tilde{r}^*$ altogether.

Before substituting equation (6.9) into our original equation (6.2), we note that the percentage change in the index of agricultural prices P_a can be written as a function of the three agricultural product groups, as follows:

$$\tilde{P}_a = \sum_i \beta_i \, \tilde{P}_{ai}^P \tag{6.11}$$

where β_i ($i = e\ f, o$) are the base year shares of each group's output in the total agricultural output of the country. Notice that β_i is in general different than s_{ai} because a given household group will have different production structure than the average of all agricultural producers. With these conventions, equation (6.9) can be substituted in equation (6.2), yielding the following equation that will be used to trace the real welfare of households:

$$\tilde{Y} = \left(\sum_i \left[s_a s_{ai} + \frac{s_n s_{nu} \lambda_a \beta_i}{(1-\alpha)\Delta} \right] \tilde{P}_{ai}^P + s_n s_{nf} \tilde{w} + \frac{s_n s_{nu} \lambda_{nf}}{\Delta} \tilde{L}_{nf} \right.$$
$$\left. + \frac{s_n s_{nu} \lambda_{nu}}{(1-\beta)\Delta} \tilde{P}_{nu} - \left(\delta_f \tilde{P}_f^c + \delta_o \tilde{P}_o^c + \delta_n \tilde{P}_n^c \right) \right) \tag{6.12}$$

where

$$\Delta = \frac{\lambda_a}{1-\alpha} + \frac{\lambda_{nu}}{1-\beta}. \tag{6.13}$$

Expression (6.12) depends on structural variables that are relatively easy to estimate and on changes of price indices that again can be estimated. There are, nevertheless, several points of clarification and caveats about an expression such as (6.12) that deserve mentioning. The behavioral relation (6.5) is meant to imply that agricultural owner-operators essentially equate the marginal reward to other informal activities with the average reward to their own agricultural activities. In other words, they regard agricultural activities as basic. In practice, considerations such as risk and food security might make any specific test of (6.5) difficult to implement, albeit Collier et al. (1986) provided some evidence that it indeed holds. For instance, agricultural daily wages might appear higher than returns per man day from own-production, but we still do not observe small farmers abandoning their plots to work for large-scale operators or plantations. This implies that the effective reward, or the nominal wage adjusted for other factors, is lower than the apparent, nominal one. This is already well known from the Harris-Todaro model.

Another salient feature of our assumption about sources of income of the rural household is that their reward to nonagricultural activities is basically assumed to be reward to the labor input. In other words, they do not share much in the aggregated profits of the nonagricultural sector. This basically means that because of ease of entry in the informal sector, whatever business the rural poor engage in will be mostly own-labor intensive and owner operated, earning effective rewards, that, when adjusted for risk and so forth, will be roughly equivalent to those from other labor activities.

Notice that inside the first bracket of (6.12) the weights multiplying prices (namely, except the one that multiplies $\tilde{L}_{nf}$) sum to one. The same, of course, holds for the consumption weights. In other words, real income can be looked at as the ratio of an index of nominal income (assuming that the term multiplying the quantity of formal labor is zero in the base year) and an index of consumer prices with weights specific to each class of households. It is the weights s_a, s_n, s_{nf}, s_{nu}, s_{ai}, and δ_i that will differ among households.

If we use fixed weights in the numerator and denominator of expression (6.12), this will bias the results. The numerator, which represents nominal incomes, will be smaller than true nominal incomes because no consideration is given to shifts between activities. The denominator, which represents the nominal cost of a unit of expenditures, will be larger than the true one because consumers will substitute among goods as relative prices change. The upshot is that the fixed weight ratio will always underestimate real income gains or overestimate real income losses. In Appendix B we propose a method to deal with the problem, which is subsequently applied.

CLASSIFICATION OF HOUSEHOLDS

In order for the method outlined in the previous section and Appendix B to be applied, we need to classify households and derive their characteristics for a base year. Given the analysis of the structure of incomes and consumption set out in Chapter 4, it is natural to take 1976/77 as the base year for the projections.

In Chapter 4 we estimated poverty lines for urban and rural households in 1976/77 and classified households according to household cash expenditure. Table 31 gives a good classification of households according to this criterion. We shall attempt to define a "typical poor," a "typical middle-class," and a "typical rich" household in rural and urban areas and outline their structures of income and consumption. From Table 46 we can choose a poverty line, and conservatively we choose the one for which the ratio of food to total expenditure is 0.70 or higher. According to Table 47, this implies that in 1976/77 50 percent of households and 60 percent of people were below the poverty line. Examining Table 31 in light of these assumptions, it can be seen that the lowest three household cash expenditure classes in both rural and urban areas have average per capita total incomes below the chosen poverty levels. These groups represent 78.3 percent of rural households and 32.5 percent of urban households. We shall choose as close-to-representative of rural and urban poor households those that in 1976/77 had annual household cash expenditures between 1,000 and 1,999 Tsh. This is the middle among the three cash expenditure classes assumed to represent the poor. Ideally we should try to estimate the weighted average profiles of income and consumption for each class, but this turned out to be impossible, given the assumptions that had to be made in subsequent stages. For the rural and urban middle class, we took as representative the class with household cash expenditure in the range of 6,000–7,999 Tsh. This is the second-lowest among the six "nonpoor" classes, and comprises a fair share of "nonpoor" rural and urban households. Given the skewness of the distribution evident in Table 31, this seems reasonable. For the "rich" rural and urban classes, we chose the ones with annual household cash incomes in the range of 25,000–39,999 Tsh. Given some anomalies for the highest expenditure class as discussed in Chapter 4, this seems reasonable. Since there are nine cash expenditure categories of Table 31, our choice amounts to dividing rural and urban households into three classes; each is represented by three cash expenditure classes, and we have chosen the middle among the three as representative of the whole class. If we regard this assumption as a reasonable approximation, then we can also associate with each a proportion of all households that the class represents.

The allocation of the total average household incomes of the three classes from Table 31 to agriculture, formal wages, and unregulated and other sources utilizes Table 32, which gives sources of income for all households in a given expenditure class without distinguishing rural and urban, and Table 22, which gives the sources of income for farm and nonfarm rural and urban households in

1976/77. It was assumed that in the lower class, the share of wages and salaries in rural cash income is that indicated in Table 22 for rural farm households. For urban poor households, it was assumed that the share of cash income from crop and animal husbandry was what is indicated in Table 22 for urban farm households. It was assumed that agricultural income comprises crop and animal husbandry. All other income sources were lumped under "other." Furthermore, all subsistence income was assumed to originate in agriculture. Tables 33 and 34 indicated that this is very nearly true for all classes, rural and urban. With these assumptions it is possible to estimate the shares of income from various sources for poor rural and urban households. For the middle-level households it was assumed in both rural and urban areas that the share of their cash income coming from wages and salaries is that for the average household in Table 22. For the rich households it was assumed that the share of wages and salaries in their total cash incomes is that stated under nonfarm households in rural and urban areas in Table 22. The resulting allocation of income is given in Table 58.

The differences in income structure evident in Table 58 are quite substantial. In rural areas, agriculture is the main income source of the poor and middle households but not of the rich ones. The main income sources of that class are wages and other (mainly income from business and profession). In the urban areas, the poor draw most of their income from subsistence agriculture and from other sources (again, mainly business) and a very small share from wages. It is for the middle group that wages are most important, while for the rich it is business that is the chief income source. Notice that agriculture is a major cash income source only among poor and middle rural households; it is negligible as a cash source among rich rural households. Agriculture is a minor source of cash income for poor and middle urban households and a negligible one for rich urban households.

COMPOSITION OF AGRICULTURAL INCOME

We now turn to the composition of agricultural income. First, we will split cash or export crop income from total agricultural income. In Tanzania the term "cash crops" means income from exportable, nonsubsistence crops; hence the terms "export" and "cash crops" will be used interchangeably. Given that urban households are not expected to produce many cash crops, and that Table 58 implies that most of urban agricultural income is subsistence income, it seems reasonable to assume that all the agricultural income of urban households is income from food crops and livestock. The same will also be assumed for rich rural households, for which, as Table 58 indicates, almost all agricultural income is for subsistence consumption. This leaves only the poor and middle

TABLE 58

Tanzania: Sources of Income of Representative Poor, Middle, and Rich
Rural and Urban Households, 1976/77.

	Rural		*Urban*	
	Value	*Shares*	*Value*	*Shares*
	(Tsh)	*(percent)*	*(Tsh)*	*(percent)*
Poor households				
Share of all households (percent)		66.6		4.9
Share of all people		63.8		3.9
Per capita total income	804	100.0	603	100.0
From agriculture	654	81.3	337	55.8
(Subsistence)	(537)	(66.8)	(303)	(50.2)
Wages and salaries	15	1.9	77	12.7
Other	135	16.8	189	31.5
Middle households				
Share of all households (percent)		15.6		6.7
Share of all people		18.2		5.7
Per capita total income	1,285	100.0	1,523	100.0
From agriculture	708	55.1	165	10.8
(Subsistence)	(397)	(30.9)	(75)	(4.9)
Wages and salaries	131	10.2	977	64.1
Other	446	34.7	381	25.1
Rich households				
Share of all households (percent)		2.9		3.3
Share of all people		4.3		4.1
Per capita total income	3,375	100.0	4,668	100.0
From agriculture	384	11.4	72	1.5
(Subsistence)	(337)	(10.0)	(31)	(0.7)
Wages and salaries	1,382	41.0	276	5.9
Other	1,609	47.6	4,320	92.6

Sources: Computed from data in Tables 22, 33, and 34.

rural households (which, of course, comprise 82.2 percent of all households) as
producers of cash export crops. To estimate the amount of cash crop income for
these two classes, we utilize Tables 50 and 51. Taking from these tables the
difference between income from food crops and subsistence crop income, we
obtain an estimate of cash income from sales of food crops. Comparing this with
income from cash crops in Table 50 across income quintiles, we obtain the data
in Table 59.

TABLE 59

Tanzania: Shares of Cash Crop Income from Food and Cash (Export) Crops.

| | *Quintiles* | | | | | |
	1	*2*	*3*	*4*	*5*	*Total*
Total cash crop income						
(Tsh/capita)	35.3	37.2	208.8	263.0	1,045.9	283.9
Percent from food crops	45.9	27.2	53.0	58.1	70.3	61.8
Percent from cash crops	54.1	82.8	47.0	41.9	29.7	38.2

Source: Computed from Tables 50 and 51.

The interesting observation is that the proportion of cash income from crop sales that arises from the sale of food crops is higher among wealthier rural households than among poor ones. We chose the share representative of the highest quintile as that to apply to our middle rural households, and adjusted the share for the poor households so that the weighted average for the two classes is equal to .8 percent, which is the average in Table 59.

The result is that the share of food crop sales in total cash income from crops is 70.3 percent for the rural middle, as assumed, and 55.7 percent for the rural poor. Note that agricultural income includes livestock income and not only crop income. Given the erratic nature of livestock income revealed in Tables 50 and 51, we assumed that 16 percent of rural agricultural income arises from livestock, as implied by the national accounts data for 1976 and 1977, which is close to the figure implied by Table 51.

With these assumptions, the share of total agricultural income that arises from sales of cash crops is 6.6 percent for poor rural households and 11.0 percent for middle rural households. As a check on the calculations, the 1979/80 rural income survey (Collier et al. 1986) reported that, on average, 11.95 percent of net crop income was from the sale of export crops. If we assume that livestock income is 16 percent of total agricultural income, this implies that 10.0 percent of total agricultural income was from export crop sales, comparable to the 7.6 percent implied by our calculations. The discrepancy could be due to the assumptions about livestock income, or to the nonrepresentative sample in Collier et. al.

The next step involves the breakdown of non-export, agricultural nonlivestock income among tradable food and other food crops. Livestock income will be lumped with other agricultural income. While the distinction between tradable and nontradable crops is conceptually clear, it is not so clear at the practical level. In Tanzania many agricultural products can be considered as traded given the vast borders with neighboring countries and the concentration of production in border areas. Given, however, that the interesting questions in the context of adjustment concern the issues of marketing interventions and parallel markets, we shall lump under the category "traded food" (namely, the one with subscript *f*) in the model the main scheduled staple food crops, that is, those for which an official marketing system existed for a long time. These crops, in turn, can be split into internationally traded ones, and mainly domestic staples. In the context of Tanzania, the internationally traded scheduled staple food crops are maize, rice, and wheat (which will be referred to as traded scheduled crops). The largely domestic scheduled staples are sorghum, millet, cassava, and beans. The latter will be referred to as nontraded scheduled crops.

The procedure used to split the crop income into the two categories was first to identify from the 1976/77 Household Budget Survey the proportion of subsistence income that is accounted for by traded and nontraded scheduled crops. Then these shares were multiplied by total income from non-export food crops (monetary and subsistence). In other words, the assumption was made that the structure of non-export crop income from sales is the same as the structure of subsistence crop income. The assumptions then summed up imply the structure of agricultural income that is indicated in Table 60.

It must be noticed that traded scheduled crops (maize, rice, wheat) make up a relatively large share of total agricultural income (about 36 percent), compared with the approximately 20 percent that the national accounts indicate as the share of these products in total agricultural GDP in 1976 and 1977. However, even if we assumed that a zero share of cash income from food crops originated in these products, the proportion of agricultural income from this category of products would be higher than 20 percent because of their major share in subsistence production. The nontraded scheduled crops make up about 20 percent of agricultural income, compared with the 14 percent indicated by the national accounts. It must be noted, however, that the national accounts use official prices to value production. They would naturally tend to underestimate the share since official prices are almost always below the open market ones.

Another way to check the figures is to use the two surveys reported in Collier et al. (1986) for 1979/80 and Bevan et al. (1990) for 1982/83. The 1979/80 survey indicated that, on average, traded scheduled crops accounted for 24.8 percent of crop income (or about 21 percent of total agricultural income, if livestock is assumed to make up 16 percent of agricultural income), and nontraded scheduled crops accounted for 20 percent of crop income (17 percent of agricultural income). The 1982/83 survey, on the other hand, showed that, on average, traded

TABLE 60

Tanzania: Structure of Per Capita Agricultural Income of Representative
Poor, Middle, and Rich Rural and Urban Households, 1976/1977.

	Rural		Urban	
	Value	Shares	Value	Shares
	(Tsh)	(Percent)	(Tsh)	(Percent)
Poor				
Agricultural income	654	100.0	337	100.0
Export crops	43	6.6	0	0.0
Traded scheduled crops	234	35.8	88	26.1
(of which subsistence)	(206)	(31.5)	(79)	(23.4)
Nontraded scheduled crops	154	23.5	112	33.2
(of which subsistence)	(135)	(20.6)	(101)	(30.0)
Other, including livestock	223	34.1	137	40.7
(of which subsistence)	(196)	(30.0)	(123)	(36.5)
Middle				
Agricultural income	708	100.0	165	100.0
Export crops	78	11.0	0	0.0
Traded scheduled crops	253	35.7	75	45.5
(of which subsistence)	(159)	(22.5)	(34)	(20.6)
Nontraded scheduled crops	105	14.8	29	17.6
(of which subsistence)	(66)	(9.3)	(13)	(7.8)
Other, including livestock	272	38.5	61	36.9
(of which subsistence)	(172)	(24.3)	(28)	(17.0)
Rich				
Agricultural Income	384	100.0	72	100.0
Export crops	0	0.0	0	0.0
Traded scheduled crops	167	43.5	27	37.5
(of which subsistence)	(147)	(38.3)	(12)	(16.7)
Nontraded scheduled crops	44	11.5	8	11.1
(of which subsistence)	(38)	(9.9)	(3)	(4.2)
Other, including livestock	173	45.0	37	51.4
(of which subsistence)	(152)	(39.6)	(16)	(22.2)

Source: Computed by authors.

food crops made up 51.6 percent of crop incomes (43.3 percent of all agricultural
income with the same livestock income assumption), while nontraded scheduled
crops made up 14.5 percent of crop income (12.2 percent of total agricultural
income). By these comparisons, it appears that the figures indicated in Table 60
are reasonable.

CONSUMPTION PATTERNS

The next set of figures concerns the consumption patterns of the representative households. These can be easily derived from the 1976/77 Household Budget Survey, and they are indicated in Table 61. The most interesting thing that

TABLE 61
Tanzania: Expenditure Shares of Representative Households (percentages).

	Rural	*Urban*
Poor		
Food	82.1	83.6
Monetary	14.7	35.2
Traded scheduled	(2.4)	(8.8)
Nontraded scheduled	(1.0)	(3.4)
Other	(11.3)	(23.0)
Subsistence	67.4	48.4
Traded scheduled	(25.8)	(12.6)
Nontraded scheduled	(17.0)	(16.1)
Other	(24.6)	(19.7)
Nonfood	17.9	16.4
Middle		
Food	66.5	70.4
Monetary	32.4	65.2
Traded scheduled	(6.8)	(18.9)
Nontraded scheduled	(2.5)	(4.2)
Other	(23.1)	(42.1)
Subsistence	34.1	5.2
Traded scheduled	(13.7)	(2.4)
Nontraded scheduled	(5.7)	(0.9)
Other	(14.7)	(1.9)
Nonfood	33.5	29.6
Rich		
Food	56.0	51.6
Monetary	37.5	50.9
Traded scheduled	(5.7)	(11.3)
Nontraded scheduled	(2.1)	(1.8)
Other	(29.7)	(37.8)
Subsistence	18.5	0.7
Traded scheduled	(8.0)	(0.3)
Nontraded scheduled	(2.1)	(0.1)
Other	(8.4)	(0.3)
Nonfood	44.0	48.4

Source: Computed from Tables 3C and 3D in the Household Budget Survey, 1976/77.

emerges from the table is that the poor households, both rural and urban, allocate very low shares of their total consumption expenditures for monetary purchases of the scheduled staple crops, both traded and nontraded, while for middle and rich households, particularly in urban areas, these shares are quite high. This implies that the bulk of the benefit from subsidies of scheduled staple crops accrues to middle- and upper-income urban households.

PRICES

Given that the objective is to trace real income of households according to the model outlined earlier, we need producer price series for export crops, traded scheduled crops, nontraded scheduled crops, other crops, and a series for formal wages and salaries, since the return to other nonofficial activities will be estimated. Also we need consumer price series for traded scheduled staple foods, nontraded scheduled staples, other foods, and nonfoods. We compiled indices of all these prices from 1976 to 1989 as follows. Official producer prices for the traded scheduled crops (maize, rice), nontraded scheduled crops (sorghum, millet, cassava, beans), and five export crops (coffee, cotton, cashew nuts, tea, and tobacco) were used to construct Laspeyres official producer price indices using 1976/77 average production value shares as weights. Official consumer prices for the same products (except the export crops) were also used to construct official consumer price indices for traded scheduled, and nontraded scheduled, staples.

To construct open market price indices for the food categories, we used monthly open market prices for 1982–1990, provided by MDB for urban markets, and averaged the months within a crop year so as to obtain annual average open market consumer prices. For years before 1982, we used the information provided for some of the crops in Odegaard (1985). For maize and rice, the open market prices obtained were complete. For nontraded staples, the index before 1982 consists only of bean prices. For the nonscheduled products for years after 1982, we built an index composed of the prices of sweet potatoes, cooking bananas, tomatoes, and beef meat. Of these, prices for the first two were taken from Odegaard to continue the index back to 1976. Based on the three indices constructed, we also built an aggregate index of open market food prices. In all cases the weights were expenditure shares derived from the 1976/77 HBS.

Assuming that the unofficial marketing margins did not change much, and given that the open market prices are normally averages from about 30 to 40 urban centers dispersed among all regions in Tanzania, it is reasonable to consider the trends in these open market consumer prices as representative of trends in open market producer prices for food.

For a price for official wages and salaries, we used the series for average wages published by the Bureau of Statistics, which covers official wage employment. The official nonfood consumer price index was computed by weighing the published components by their published shares. It turns out that the published official consumer food price index and the nonfood CPI thus computed do not add up to the overall published National CPI, and hence we used the computed nonfood CPI in our computation.

Table 62 indicates trends in the ratios among several of these prices. It is clear that between 1976 and 1984 (the first year of liberalization) official export prices declined substantially with respect to both official traded staple prices (column 1) and open market food prices (columns 3 and 4). Since 1984 they have recovered appreciably, however, and in fact by 1988/89, they were above their 1976/77 levels vis-à-vis food crops. Turning to competition between the traded and nontraded scheduled staples, the official prices indicate an improvement in their terms of trade between 1976 and 1984 and a relative stability after that (column 2). However, the open market price signals show large fluctuations, with a negative trend, between 1976 and 1984, and a clear negative trend after that (column 5).

The terms of trade between official and open market prices of traded scheduled staples are indicated in column 8, and the same ratio for nontraded scheduled staples is shown in column 9. In the case of traded staples, there are fluctuations but no major trend between 1976 and 1984, implying that the ratios between open and official prices did not widen much over the period, or equivalently, that open markets for the traded staples were functioning all along and were not a feature only of the crisis. From 1984 on, it appears that the official prices have gained, compared with open market prices, and this is evidenced by the large increase in maize production after the marketing liberalization.

The picture is not the same, however, for nontraded scheduled crops. In that case, it clearly appears that the official market prices declined substantially, compared with open market prices, between 1976 and 1984, and that since 1984 they have recovered somewhat, but not to the levels of the late 1970s.

An interesting ratio is indicated in column 6 between the official food CPI and the open market consumer food price index compiled by the procedure explained earlier. If the two price indices measure the same thing, their ratio ought to stay constant. It indeed stays relatively constant between 1985 and 1989, but it shows a sharp drop during the crisis period 1979–1984, implying that during that period, the official food CPI increasingly underestimated the true cost of food.

TABLE 62

Tanzania: Terms of Trade (Ratios) between Several Price Indices (1984=100).

	Official Producer Export/ Official Producer Traded Staples (1)	Official Producer Traded Staples/ Official Producer Nontraded Staples (2)	Official Producer Export/ Open Market Traded Staples (3)	Official Producer Export/ Open Market All Food (4)	Open Market Traded Staples/ Open Market Nontraded Staples (5)	Official Food CPI/ Open Market All Food (6)	Official Nonfood CPI/ Nonagricultural GDP Deflator (7)	Official Producer Traded Staples/ Open Market Traded Staples (8)	Official Producer Nontraded Staples/ Open Market Nontraded Staples (9)
1976	.186.2	71.1	158.7	201.5	139.6	—	—	85.3	167.4
1977	149.0	51.0	128.4	161.2	165.7	111.8	59.2	86.2	279.7
1978	137.1	50.0	140.1	165.8	133.5	157.5	59.0	102.2	272.8
1979	138.5	59.5	218.2	233.2	76.1	204.5	63.8	157.6	201.5
1980	152.6	66.5	141.7	170.0	132.4	166.4	70.5	92.8	184.9
1981	120.7	94.7	110.5	138.6	156.9	145.5	80.0	91.6	151.7
1982	119.5	95.4	130.3	120.8	97.5	142.2	90.4	109.1	111.5
1983	129.2	90.9	96.6	97.0	116.3	105.3	91.2	74.7	95.6
1984	100.0	100.0	100.0	100.0	100.0	100.0	100.0	100.0	100.0
1985	113.1	91.7	172.6	162.9	80.0	140.3	112.7	152.6	133.9
1986	127.2	91.7	224.3	203.0	80.4	175.9	123.0	176.3	154.7
1987	133.8	93.3	231.9	216.9	83.3	173.7	119.0	173.3	154.9
1988	148.6	94.7	222.5	202.2	76.0	175.3	104.3	149.7	120.2
1989	174.6	—	293.3	247.0	67.7	189.2	102.0	167.9	—

— Data were not available to compute relevant values.

Source: Computed by authors.

Another ratio exhibited in Table 62 is that between the official nonfood CPI (as calculated by the authors) and the implicit nonagricultural GDP deflator. It can be seen (column 7) that the nonfood CPI increased considerably relative to the nonagricultural GDP deflator between 1977 and 1986, but has declined since then. The implication is that the nonagricultural GDP deflator, which is based on prices for formal-sector activities, continuously fell behind even the nonfood cost of living, which in turn includes several controlled prices, such as rents and fuel.

The figures indicated in Table 62 obscure somewhat the extent of distortion between open and official markets. In Table 63 we exhibit the ratios of annual average open market (urban) prices to the official consumer and producer prices. Both sets of prices are computed for crop years (so that 1982 refers to the June 1982–May 1983 crop year and the open market prices are computed accordingly). The ratios of open market to producer prices were very high until 1984, in excess of 300 percent in many cases. They seem to have declined for maize and rice, but continue to be quite high for the other scheduled staple crops. If the open market urban prices are discounted to farm level, with a 100 percent marketing margin (an exaggeration, given the data in Table 54), they still indicate that the open market prices have been and still are much more attractive than the official price. In the empirical model, we constructed indices of traded and nontraded scheduled staple prices by, for rural areas, weighing the indices of official producer prices and open-market urban prices 0.25 and 0.75, respectively; for the urban areas we weighted the index of official consumer prices and open-market prices by the same weights. Given that both sets of prices are

TABLE 63

Tanzania: Ratios of Open Market Urban Prices to Official Consumer and Producer Prices.

	Consumer			Producer					
	Maize	*Rice*	*Bean*	*Maize*	*Paddy*	*Sorghum*	*Millet*	*Cassava*	*Beans*
1982	1.84	2.88	1.84	2.63	3.34	4.81	7.63	2.58	3.79
1983	1.09	3.81	2.05	3.95	4.46	6.60	8.93	3.22	3.93
1984	0.82	2.67	2.17	2.82	3.87	5.80	8.21	3.35	3.95
1985	0.48	2.51	1.40	1.77	2.96	4.38	6.23	3.56	2.68
1986	0.32	1.89	1.05	1.56	2.43	3.66	5.25	3.69	2.24
1987	0.44	1.38	1.07	1.68	2.00	4.15	6.01	3.22	1.99
1988	0.41	1.03	1.09	1.96	2.31	5.33	7.62	4.04	2.57
1989				1.68	2.22	6.06	7.26	4.77	2.80

Source: Computed by authors.

indexed to 100 for a base year, the combined indices show the direction of price changes in each product category from a mixture of both markets. However, we did not allow for changing weights over time between official and open markets in the computation of price indices.

The model specified in the section, "A Method for Analyzing Household Incomes" needs two more series—namely, prices for the output of the informal sector and a series for formal-sector employment. For the price of the informal sector, we used the open market price index for all foods which was discussed above, or the official food consumer price index. Formal-sector employment data from 1975 to 1984 were obtained from the World Bank (1989) and extended to 1989 by using the index of real GDP of public administration from the national accounts.

OTHER DATA

The remaining information needed to implement the model of "A Method for Analyzing Household Incomes" and Appendix B concerns the initial shares of labor engaged in agriculture, formal, and other unincorporated activities, the shares of the three categories of agricultural products in total agricultural output (the β_i), the technological parameters α and β, which represent labor shares of output, the transformation elasticity parameters T, T_a, T_n, and φ, and the demand parameters η_b, ε_{bb}, and σ.

For the shares of labor in the three sectors, we used the 1978 population census. We found there both the number of people in the work force (7,686 thousand) and the number whose main activity is agriculture (6,752 thousand). From other surveys (e.g., Collier et al. 1986), it turns out that 92 percent of farmers' labor is engaged in agriculture (mostly on own plots, but also some communal). However, some of those engaged mainly in nonagricultural work also engage in agricultural activities; we assume that 5 percent of the labor time of nonagricultural workers is engaged in agriculture. These assumptions imply that 82 percent of all labor, circa 1978, was occupied in agriculture. To allocate the remaining labor between the formal and informal sectors, we used the figures for the number of people employed in nonagricultural work in 1978 (935,000), and from this we subtract the number of employees reported in 1978 in the formal employment statistics of the BOS (536,000). We apply the resulting shares to the 18 percent of labor that is nonagricultural and obtain a figure of 10.3 percent of the labor force engaged in formal types of activities, while the remaining 7.7 percent of the labor force was engaged in informal, unincorporated activities.

To compute the shares of the three categories of products in the output of the agricultural sector, we averaged the national accounts 1976 and 1977 detailed data on the makeup of the agricultural GDP. We find that scheduled crops make up 33.4 percent of total agricultural output (19.4 traded scheduled, 14.0 percent nontraded scheduled), export crops 12.3 percent, and the rest, including livestock, 54.3 percent.

Turning to the technological coefficients, for agriculture we utilize the production function estimated by Collier and his co-authors (1986), which related crop output to land, labor, and other inputs. Under the assumption that input of land is directly proportional to labor, we obtain a value of α equal to 0.73. As far as the informal sector is concerned, we assume that it is less labor intensive than agriculture and more labor intensive than formal nonagriculture. We assume a value of β equal to 0.6, which is the simple average of the two labor coefficients (the labor coefficient for nonagriculture, 0.47, is computed from the 1976 input-output table).

Turning to demand parameters, the procedure we use is the following. We start by using the expenditure elasticities of demand for food reported for rural and urban Tanzania by Okunade (1985), which are 0.92 for rural Tanzania and 1.15 for urban Tanzania. By making the assumption that poor households have food expenditure elasticities 20 percent higher than middle households, and that rich ones have elasticities 20 percent lower than middle ones, we can specify expenditure elasticities for each of the three rural and urban household classes so that the weighted average of the three group elasticities correspond to those reported above. Aggregate, own-price elasticities of demand for maize, rice, and beans are reported in Amani et al. (1989), and these, when weighted by the expenditure shares for each group, give figures for the aggregate price elasticity of demand for food. When a formula such as (B.47) is used to implicitly derive values for the elasticities of substitution σ, we obtain values between 0.5 and 1.1. We then assume that the values of σ are 0.6 for poor households (rural and urban), 0.8 for middle households, and 1.0 for rich households.

Turning to supply parameters, we utilize the estimates for long-run price elasticity of total supply of maize (0.423) and rice (0.362) as reported by Gerrard and Roe (1983). Assuming, as is apparent in Tables 58 and 59, that the overwhelming bulk of traded scheduled staples is produced by poor and middle rural households, and that these two classes of households have the same price elasticities of supply for maize and rice, as reported above, we can derive figures for the price elasticity of supply of traded scheduled staples for poor rural households (0.412) and middle rural ones (0.414). Using these and the shares of traded staples in total agricultural income, and the share of agriculture in total income, formula (B.24) can be used to derive figures for the transformation elasticity T_a if we assume a value for T. We assume a value for T equal to 0.3 for rural poor, which implies a value of T_a equal to 0.61. For rural middle households, we assume T equal to 0.5, which implies T_a equal to 0.57.

For urban poor and middle households, we assume $T = 0.3$ and $T_a = 0.5$. For urban rich households, we assume $T = 0.1$ and $T_a = 0.5$, and for rural rich, we assume $T = 0.1$ and $T_a = 0.5$.

Concerning T_n, the elasticity of transformation between the two types of nonagricultural income, we assume that for poor rural households it is 0.1, for poor urban ones 0.3, for middle households (rural and urban) 0.5, and for rich households (rural and urban) 0.8.

The final value that needs to be specified is φ, the aggregate elasticity of transformation among the three types of agricultural products. Given the assumed values for T_a in Table 64, we assume a value of 0.5 for φ.

Table 64 summarizes the demand, supply, and other parameters derived and/or assumed, and Table 65 summarizes all the remaining parameters.

TABLE 64

Tanzania: Demand and Supply Parameters for the Six Representative Households.

	Rural	*Urban*
Poor		
η_b	0.97	1.38
ε_{bb}	−0.87	−0.88
σ	0.60	0.60
T	0.30	0.30
T_a	0.61	0.50
T_n	0.10	0.30
Middle		
η_b	0.81	1.15
ε_{bb}	−0.91	−1.02
σ	0.80	0.80
T	0.50	0.30
T_a	0.57	0.50
T_n	0.50	0.50
Rich		
η_b	0.65	0.92
ε_{bb}	−0.93	−1.02
σ	1.00	1.00
T	0.10	0.10
T_a	0.50	0.50
T_n	0.80	0.80

Note: Symbols are explained in the text.
Source: Computed by authors.

TABLE 65

Tanzania: Values of Other Model Parameters, Circa 1976–77.

λ_a	0.820	α	0.73	β_e	0.123
λ_{nf}	0.103	β	0.56	β_f	0.334
λ_v	0.077			β_o	0.543
				φ	0.5

Note: Symbols are explained in the text.
Source: Computed by authors.

RESULTS

The model and data described in the three previous sections were implemented for the period 1975–1989. To avoid spurious effects resulting from yearly price variations, the period was divided into five, three-year periods, and averages for each three-year period were used for the model. The results are exhibited as a series of indices for the five periods.

Table 66 indicates the results obtained from the model under the assumption of fixed shares (at the initial levels) and under the assumption of variable shares, as analyzed in Appendix B. The results confirm the analysis presented in the section, "How Real is the Decline in Rural and Urban Incomes?" First, in the rural areas, under the fixed-share assumption, it is only the middle and rich households that appear to have experienced a significant decline in income, while the poor seem to have experienced only a very small decline. When adjustment in household and overall shares is allowed, the income decline for all rural classes disappears. This implies that households adjusted so as to counteract the declines in formal-sector employment and production. The major adjustment was in moving out of formal, into informal, activities, as will be seen below.

Turning to urban households, while under fixed shares they all exhibit significant declines in real incomes, when variable shares are considered, it is the middle-income urban households that seem to have experienced the worst income decline—this despite the fact that we have assumed a relatively high elasticity of tansformation, T_n of 0.5, between the two nonagricultural sectors. This result seems quite reasonable, as it is this group that has the highest initial income share from wages and salaries (see Table 58), and it is real wages that have declined the most over the last 15 years. The results set out in Table 66 change only very marginally when, instead of the index of open market food prices as a proxy for the price of the informal sector, we use the official food CPI.

It is worthwhile exhibiting several of the driving variables of the model, as well as the implied changes in some of the shares, in the case of the variable-share

TABLE 66
Tanzania: Impact of Changing Prices on Household Real Incomes.

	Rural			Urban		
	Poor	*Middle*	*Rich*	*Poor*	*Middle*	*Rich*
Fixed shares						
1975–1977	100.0	100.0	100.0	100.0	100.0	100.0
1978–1980	98.2	96.4	91.0	97.0	86.5	98.2
1981–1983	98.0	94.2	77.1	92.8	60.2	101.1
1984–1986	97.1	90.2	67.2	90.6	49.8	96.1
1987–1989	96.7	88.5	63.8	89.8	47.3	94.1
Variable shares						
1975–1977	100.0	100.0	100.0	100.0	100.0	100.0
1978–1980	100.2	98.9	94.1	99.2	88.5	100.7
1981–1983	104.6	107.3	104.9	102.6	80.0	113.2
1984–1986	100.0	99.5	98.0	100.7	81.8	102.9
1987–1989	99.8	98.4	97.0	100.3	82.2	101.0

Note: Symbols are explained in the text.
Source: Computed by authors.

model. Table 67 exhibits in index form several key model prices, all deflated by the official CPI, as well as the official data for wage and salary employment. It is quite apparent that official real producer and consumer prices for both traded and nontraded staples, as well as real producer prices for export crops, declined significantly between the periods 1976–1978 and 1981–1983. Real prices in the open market increased over the same period, especially during the peak crisis years 1981–1983.

Since 1984, official real producer prices have stabilized, or shown increases as in the case of export crops, while official real consumer prices significantly increased. Open market prices declined. The worst performance is exhibited by the average real wage, which has declined enormously over the last 15 years. It is reasonable under these conditions to expect that employees started looking for parallel, income-generating activity.

Finally, notice that formal-sector wage employment increased substantially until the 1981–1983 period, stabilized during 1984–1986, and declined during the SAP period, 1987–1989. However, this does not reflect the real level of labor input in the formal sector. Given the decline in real wages, the true labor input must have been much lower than exhibited in the official employment statistics. We tried an experiment wherein the exogenous, formal labor series L_{nf} was

TABLE 67

Tanzania: Evolution of Several Key Price Indices and Wage Employment, 1975 to 1989.

	Official Export Crop Prices	Official Producer Traded Staple Crop Prices	Official Producer Nontraded Staple Crop Prices	Open Market All Food Prices (same as prices of informal sector)	Official Traded Staple Consumer Prices	Official Nontraded Staple Consumer Prices	Average Wage	Food CPI	Wage and Salary Employment
1975–1977	100.0	100.0	100.0	100.0	100.0	100.0	100.0	100.0	100.0
1978–1980	83.8	95.9	106.6	86.6	79.6	106.8	80.6	115.8	121.2
1981–1983	70.1	92.8	64.6	119.3	61.0	85.3	43.7	114.3	131.5
1984–1986	78.1	110.8	76.9	96.7	133.0	105.7	20.5	103.1	129.2
1987–1989	88.9	94.4	63.3	76.2	139.8	111.4	15.2	105.8	124.7

Note: All prices are deflated by the official CPI.
Source: Computed by authors.

adjusted by assuming an elasticity of formal labor input with respect to real wage of 0.5. This only marginally changed the results shown in Table 66.

Table 68 exhibits the changes in several share parameters for the variable-share case. Under the assumptions concerning parameter substitution and transformation elasticities, it appears that the share of formal wage labor in total labor has gone down, after the significant, post–1977 rise, while the share of labor

TABLE 68

Tanzania: Evolution of Aggregate and Household Shares Parameters, 1976 to 1989, under the Influence of Price and Formal Employment Trends (percentages).

	1975–1977	1978–1980	1981–1983	1984–1986	1987–1989
Share of labor employed in					
Agriculture	82.0	77.5	82.9	82.7	80.6
Formal employment	10.3	11.6	11.6	10.3	9.1
Informal sector	7.7	10.9	5.5	7.0	10.3
Share in total agricultural output					
Export crops	12.3	8.9	4.2	6.5	9.2
Traded scheduled staples	19.4	14.2	13.5	15.4	13.5
Nontraded scheduled staples	14.0	13.9	10.4	14.8	14.7
Other agricultural products	54.3	63.0	71.8	63.3	62.6
Shares of total household income					
Rural poor					
Agriculture	81.3	81.0	81.3	82.3	82.1
Informal	16.8	17.5	18.2	17.4	17.6
Rural middle					
Agriculture	55.1	55.4	58.4	59.6	59.5
Informal	34.7	37.0	40.3	39.7	39.8
Rural rich					
Agriculture	11.4	12.2	15.1	15.5	15.2
Informal	47.6	55.6	76.9	80.4	81.4
Urban poor					
Agriculture	55.8	57.3	61.6	64.5	65.3
Informal	31.5	32.8	35.4	33.6	33.1
Urban middle					
Agriculture	10.8	12.0	17.7	21.4	22.5
Informal	25.1	30.4	46.8	53.2	55.2
Urban rich					
Agriculture	1.5	1.5	1.5	1.6	1.6
Informal	92.6	94.7	98.5	98.4	98.4

Source: Computed by authors.

employed in agriculture, after an initial decline in 1978–1980, recovered during the crisis, and declined after the onset of the SAP, but still stays at levels above 80 percent. The share of labor employed in informal activities has gone up, especially after the SAP.

As far as composition of agricultural output is concerned, the model shows that the share of export crops went down during the crisis but has recovered since 1984, while the share of traded scheduled crops declined after 1975–1977 and has not recovered yet. Other products seem to have increased their share in agricultural output, which is to be expected as their prices are not controlled. All households exhibit significant change in their income structure in the form of increases in income shares originating in agriculture and, more pronouncedly, in informal activities. All these changes, of course, occur at the expense of formal-sector income.

The foregoing results turn out to be quite robust in terms of the parameter values assumed. Table 69 exhibits the evolution of real household incomes under the variable-share case, under the assumptions, first, that all substitution and transformation parameters are equal to zero and, second, that all such parameters are twice their base-case values.

TABLE 69

Tanzania: Evolution of Household Real Incomes under Alternative Parameters Assumptions in the Variable-Share Case.

	Rural			*Urban*		
	Poor	*Middle*	*Rich*	*Poor*	*Middle*	*Rich*
	All Elasticity and Transformation Parameters Equal to Zero					
1975–1977	100.0	100.0	100.0	100.0	100.0	100.0
1978–1980	98.5	97.1	92.0	97.4	86.7	98.8
1981–1983	99.8	100.6	91.1	97.2	70.2	106.6
1984–1986	98.9	96.9	87.4	98.7	72.1	101.1
1987–1989	98.3	95.8	86.6	98.2	71.9	99.8
	All Elasticity and Transformation Parameters at Twice Their Base–case Values					
1975–1977	100.0	100.0	100.0	100.0	100.0	100.0
1978–1980	101.9	100.8	96.3	101.0	90.5	102.7
1981–1983	109.5	114.0	119.1	108.1	90.9	119.5
1984–1986	101.2	101.5	103.2	102.4	90.4	103.8
1987–1989	101.3	100.4	101.4	102.1	90.5	101.2

Source: Computed by authors.

In the first case, the results are intermediate between the fixed- and variable-weight cases of Table 66 but the trends are the same. The rural and urban poor do not exhibit any marked decline in their welfare, and the same holds for the urban rich. Rural middle, and especially rich, households exhibit real income declines, while urban middle-income households show the worst declines, as was the case in the base scenario.

The second sensitivity case indicates that only urban middle-income households have experienced declines in real incomes, while real incomes for all other groups increased until 1984 and then declined to the 1975–1977 level.

The results also do not change much if, instead of the weighted average prices used for traded and nontraded scheduled staples (25 percent official and 75 percent open market), we use only official or only open market prices.

The results change somewhat if we assume not only open market prices for traded and nontraded scheduled staple crops but also parallel export markets. This was done by multiplying the official export crop prices by the ratio of period average parallel, to official, exchange rates (see Table 8) and using the resulting prices to compute the relevant export price index. Table 70 summarizes the results. What most distinguishes these results from those shown in Table 66, which indicates the base case, is that in this case the early SAP period, 1984–1986,

TABLE 70

Tanzania: Impact on Household Welfare When All Prices, Including Those for Export Crops, Are Open Market Prices.

	Rural			*Urban*		
	Poor	*Middle*	*Rich*	*Poor*	*Middle*	*Rich*
	Fixed Shares					
1975–1977	100.0	100.0	100.0	100.0	100.0	100.0
1978–1980	96.4	93.8	89.7	96.1	85.9	95.7
1981–1983	99.8	96.6	78.7	93.7	60.6	104.2
1984–1986	102.4	97.3	71.3	93.2	52.1	103.2
1987–1989	94.9	86.0	62.6	88.6	46.7	89.8
	Variable Shares					
1975–1977	100.0	100.0	100.0	100.0	100.0	100.0
1978–1980	100.0	98.2	93.5	98.8	88.1	99.9
1981–1983	104.0	107.5	106.5	101.5	79.5	113.9
1984–1986	108.4	111.1	108.5	105.5	89.2	113.3
1987–1989	101.5	98.9	98.1	100.5	80.4	99.6

Source: Computed by authors.

appears to be a period of significant, real income gains, especially for rural households and especially in the variable-share case. However, these gains appear to have diminished substantially after 1986. The point is that households that operated wholly in the parallel market could have taken advantage of the significant overvaluation over the 1981–1986 period, while after 1986, overvaluation declined significantly and with it the real gains from operating in the parallel market.

The major conclusion of this chapter is that despite the major crisis that afflicted the Tanzanian economy from 1979 till 1986, the poor in both rural and urban areas seem to have been shielded from major real income declines on account of their large agriculture and subsistence orientation. The rural middle and rich households also do not seem to have been greatly affected and, if any, it is the rich that paid the most in terms of real income declines. In the urban areas, however, the middle classes that comprise the bulk and the most vocal segment of urban residents seem to have suffered during the crisis, while the rich do not seem to have done very badly. During the period of the adjustment program, none of the rural or urban household classes seems to have either benefited significantly or become worse off in real terms.

7

EVALUATION AND CONCLUSIONS

Our analysis in the previous chapters offers several conclusions, generalizations, and hypotheses for further research that we wish to summarize in this chapter.

Perhaps the first general conclusion that can be drawn from the Tanzanian experience is that in an economy that is poor and does not have a well-developed infrastructure and bureaucracy, it is next-to-impossible to impose a complete, top-down, bureaucratic system of economic control. In an undeveloped system such as prevailed in Tanzania after independence, economic institutions such as product markets, the system of agricultural production, manufacturing production, and others, were organized along dual lines, with a small, modern sector typified by private plantations, large private manufacturing establishments, and so forth, operating alongside a diverse traditional sector.

The nationalization of the late 1960s affected largely the modern part of the economy and created a large number of additional economic and bureaucratic units, patterned along the lines of the modern sector, and initially leaving much of the traditional sector unaffected. The effort to expand the modern sector under different ownership (public as opposed to private) continued throughout the 1970s. It appears, however, that it was the attempt to destroy the traditional sector that created the major problems in Tanzania. That attempt took the form of efforts to control marketing centrally and to organize production according to concepts quite different than the ones that had prevailed until the early-to-mid-1970s. In manufacturing, small-scale activities were discouraged, and in services almost all activities were taken over by the state.

The traditional sector in Tanzania had very long and strong roots, however. It was organized on the basis of a subsistence, agrarian economy, which in turn was oriented along food-first lines and on nonagricultural products and services catering to this agrarian economy. The gradual commercialization of largely subsistence-oriented farm operations had not been completed at the time that the state attempted to take over the institutions supporting this traditional sector, especially the many private agents operating along the agricultural marketing chain. Furthermore, the state did not have the means to fully substitute for the range of products and services provided to the peasants (and also to urban residents) in exchange for their marketed surplus. The result appears to have been a gradual "disappearance" of the traditional sector (but only from official eyes) and its re-emergence as an unobserved but important "second economy." This second economy appears to have been responsible for the maintenance of the real welfare of most inhabitants of Tanzania, despite indications by official statistics that the economy had collapsed by the early 1980s.

It appears that a traditional economy in the early stages of development and commercialization, such as existed in Tanzania in the 1960s and 1970s, is not easily amenable to centralized bureaucratic control. Perhaps the reasons are social as well as economic. The traditional, extended-family system in Tanzania and other African countries provides economic and social security that cannot be easily and suddenly substituted by Western-type, centralized welfare institutions when the economy is not more developed. These considerations, however, are beyond the scope of this report and are subjects for future research. Our analyses in Chapters 3 and 5 illustrated the importance of the parallel economy and the diversity of signals sent to economic agents by the official and the second economies.

Another aspect of the parallel economy that has direct distributional implications is the allocation of rents generated through the bureaucratic control mechanisms. It was seen in Chapters 5 and 6 that parallel-economy prices (including that for foreign exchange) throughout the period of crisis were substantially higher than official prices. This implies that recipients of goods or foreign exchange at official prices were receiving economic rents, the size of which were, to a first approximation, proportional to the price differences in the two markets. The existence of rents must have generated a large amount of rent-seeking activities that potentially could have created substantial transfers among economic agents. Given the official discouragement of wealth accumulation in Tanzania, an obvious vent for the surplus appropriated through rent seeking is capital flight, and this is quite consistent with the enormous premium between parallel and official exchange rates that prevailed during the crisis period. These premiums, as was seen in Chapter 3, were much greater than was justified by price parity calculations.

Another lesson that appears to be consistent with the Tanzanian experience is that for an economy that relies for its foreign exchange earnings on agricultural cash crops produced largely by peasants, it is probably not good policy to build a manufacturing and tertiary sector that is dependent on a steady stream of imported inputs. The reason is that, on the one hand, external markets for Tanzanian exports are volatile, and hence the supply of foreign exchange is variable. Peasants, on the other hand, rely to only a limited extent on export cash crops for their cash income. They can easily switch to other activities, agricultural or not, if the price signals warrant it. Thus the domestic control of export crop prices, and the gradual widening of the marketing margin to the benefit of marketing boards, can easily backfire, as is well-evidenced by the Tanzanian experience. The lesson is that a variable flow of export earnings must be counterbalanced by equally easily variable import requirements.

The analysis in Chapter 4 revealed that poverty is widespread in Tanzania. At least 40 percent of households or 50 percent of people were most conservatively estimated to be below an empirically estimated poverty line in 1976/77, a year that was probably one of the best, from an income perspective, of all years since 1970. Our estimates are much higher than previous poverty estimates and are consistent with the generally acknowledged fact that Tanzania is one of the poorest countries in the world. Our further finding was that poverty is rather evenly spread, as evidenced by low Gini coefficients. While this observation should be tempered by the generally acknowledged difficulty of capturing very low and very high incomes and consumption with accuracy in any survey, it is nevertheless evidence of the low level of commercialization in Tanzanian agriculture.

It was clearly seen in Chapter 4 that subsistence farming provides the bulk of income for rural households and, rather surprisingly, for poor urban households. In a land-abundant economy such as the one in Tanzania, farming is easy, since land is easily available and the major constraint on farm production is labor. Several surveys have indicated that land is not a major differentiating factor among peasants in Tanzania. This implies that, at a minimum, most people can ensure their food needs through subsistence production, and it is that circumstance that probably accounts for the low degree of inequality.

While poverty is widespread in both rural and urban areas, it is not clear whether or not poverty increased during the period of crisis. An increase in poverty can occur either because more households join the ranks of the poor or because the incomes of those already classified as poor decline further. Our analysis in Chapter 6 suggested that the average incomes of those already classified as poor did not change much during the period of the crisis, while the incomes of middle-class households (especially the urban ones) experienced severe declines. This suggests that some of the households that were earlier (in the mid-1970s) classified as middle class must have fallen below the poverty line by the mid-to-late 1980s. This implies that aggregate poverty, as measured, for instance, by the number of households falling below the poverty line, must have increased during the last 10 years.

Our analysis of poverty in Chapter 4 also found that the bulk of the food needs of most rural, and a large number of urban, households were satisfied through subsistence production. This implies that food price policy, especially at the consumer level, does not have much impact on poverty. Such an observation, of course, does not mean that agricultural price policy does not have implications for producer incomes.

In Chapter 5 we first showed that official agricultural statistics in Tanzania must be seriously questioned, especially those for years after 1974. Comparisons with independent production and consumption surveys suggest that food output has not grown as fast as suggested by official figures—this despite the fact that official producer food prices tended to appreciate, in terms of cash crop prices, until 1984. Since 1984 the official agricultural terms of trade have turned in favor of export crops, and staple food marketing has gradually been liberalized. This has been accompanied by increased food production and a sharp decline in open market staple food prices. The increase in staple food marketing in the face of declining real prices could be due to increased market access through liberalization or an increase in the availability of consumer goods that necessitates an increase in farmers' cash needs.

The analysis of farm and production structures in 1971/72 and 1986/87, before and after the crisis, revealed that the size distribution of farms did not change much despite the upheavals of the intervening period. Furthermore, total cropped, as well as staple, food area per holding appears to have declined, not increased, over this period, as would be inferred from official staple food production data.

There also appears to be a distinct pattern among different farm size classes, with larger farms increasing their area under food, as well as permanent, crops. Furthermore, larger farms also appear to have increased their labor input per unit of farm area. If these trends are confirmed by further research, they would suggest that it was mainly middle-size and larger farmers that benefitted from the crisis by increasing their output supply of both food, and possibly cash, crops, especially for the parallel market. This latter hypothesis appears to be corroborated by our analysis in Chapter 6. In the empirical results discussed in that chapter (see Table 68), it can be noticed (in the variable shares case) that during the crisis years, especially the period 1981–1983, middle-income and rich rural households increased their shares of income from agriculture. In fact, as is shown in Table 70, middle and rich rural households operating in parallel agricultural markets significantly increased their real incomes only during the period 1981–1986.

Our analysis in Chapter 6 challenges the belief that real incomes declined enormously during the Nyerere experiment from 1967 to 1985. Based on analysis of several surveys of incomes and consumption, we concluded that the apparent decline in real incomes must have been largely due to a growing tendency of households to rely on parallel activities, and hence a reluctance to reveal their true incomes. Data on consumption expenditures in fact suggested that real household consumption hardly declined between 1976/77 and 1985, despite an apparent, enormous drop in stated real incomes.

The analytical framework developed in Chapter 6 allowed the investigation of real income changes for representative poor, middle, and rich rural and urban households over the period 1975–1989. The results, which were subjected to sensitivity analysis without major changes in conclusions, suggested that the poor, both in rural and in urban areas, appear not to have been seriously affected by either the crisis or the adjustment policies after 1984. It was, rather, the urban, middle-income households that bore the brunt of the crisis in terms of real income losses. In the period since 1984, the real income decline for those households appears to have stopped, but no improvement appears to have occurred as yet. It is quite interesting that the period 1984–1986 appears to have resulted in significant real income declines for rural middle- and high-income households, compared with 1981–1983, with the same holding true for urban, high-income households; the most recent period, 1987–1989 has not resulted in any further change, positive or negative.

The finding that the poor appear not to have been affected very much during either the crisis or the adjustment period cannot be attributed directly to the policies followed during those episodes. Policies certainly affect economic signals such as prices, but at this point we are unable to ascertain whether the observed price signals and quantity responses are strictly due to the policies followed or to exogenous and underlying factors. The formal sector, from which many of the observed signals come, is the one that has been most affected by adjustment policies. However, the informal, traditional sector is the one where most people, and certainly most poorer operate; it appears that sector has continued operating in some fashion throughout the examined period, despite official efforts to diminish its importance. Our analysis has revealed that it is the interaction between this unofficial sector and the more readily observed, formal sector that provides the main clues to understanding the evolution of the Tanzanian economy, as well as household welfare. It also sets the agenda for subsequent empirical research, as neglect of the duality characteristic of the Tanzanian economy can lead to seriously misleading conclusions and policy interventions based on them.

APPENDIX A

COMPUTATION OF THE REAL EXCHANGE RATE FOR TANZANIA

The method used for computing the real exchange rate is a simplified version of the IMF methodology (Maciejewski 1983), as follows.

First, we choose the major hard-currency countries that are the main import and export trade partners of Tanzania (excluding trade in mineral fuels). According to Foreign Trade Statistics 1987 (Bureau of Statistics, Dar es Salaam), there are six such countries that account for the bulk of Tanzanian trade. They are the Federal Republic of Germany (FRG), U.K., Italy, Netherlands, U.S., and Japan. Italy is included because it is a large trade partner, although its currency is not as hard as those of the other countries. These six countries bought 49.2 percent of total domestic exports in 1980, and 41.3 percent of exports in 1987. They were the source of 53.2 percent of total imports in 1980 (69.0 percent without mineral fuels), and 56.1 percent in 1987 (64.8 percent without mineral fuels). The remaining exports and imports are spread among a large number of trade partners, many of which are soft-currency countries.

Denote by e_{Tit} the official exchange rate vis-à-vis country i (in Tsh per currency of country i) in year t, by $e_{i\$t}$ the exchange rate vis-à-vis the U.S. dollar of country i's currency (in units of foreign currency per U.S. dollar) in year t, and by $e_{T\$t}$ the Tanzanian shilling official exchange rate versus the U.S. dollar in year t (in Tsh per US\$). Then if the Tanzanian authorities keep the cross-exchange rates, at the same levels as the internationally determined ones, to avoid arbitrage, it should hold that

$$e_{Tit} = \frac{e_{T\$t}}{e_{i\$t}}. \tag{A.1}$$

Our computations of implied cross-exchange rates, using official Tsh/US Dollar and IMF published exchange rates, showed that on average the Tanzanian cross rates are kept reasonably close to their international values. For this reason, and lacking long-term information on Tsh rates versus the various currencies, the relevant rates are computed by using formula (A.1).

Denote by P_{it} the consumer price index (CPI) in country i and by P_{Tt} the Tanzanian national CPI, both in year t. The index of the real exchange rate for Tanzania (RER_{Tt}) will then be defined as follows:

$$RER_{Tt} = 100 \cdot \sum_{i=1}^{6} w(i) \frac{e_{Tit} \left(\dfrac{P_{it}}{P_{Tt}} \right)}{e_{Tio} \left(\dfrac{P_{i0}}{P_{T0}} \right)} \tag{A.2}$$

where $w(i)$ are fixed weights described below, and 0 denotes a base year. By applying (A.1), we obtain:

$$RER_{Tt} = 100 \cdot \frac{e_{T\$t} \left(\dfrac{P_{1t}}{P_{Tt}} \right)}{e_{T\$0} \left(\dfrac{P_{10}}{P_{T0}} \right)} \sum_{i=1}^{6} w(i) \frac{e_{i\$0} \left(\dfrac{P_{it}}{P_{1t}} \right)}{e_{i\$t} \left(\dfrac{P_{i0}}{P_{10}} \right)} \tag{A.3}$$

where index 1 is meant to represent the exchange rate vis-à-vis the US\$. The expression (A.3) indicates that the real exchange rate of Tanzania can be written as the product of a real exchange rate vis-à-vis the U.S. dollar, and a "correction factor" that depends on Tanzania's trade composition (the weights $w(i)$) and on cross movements between foreign currencies and the US\$, relative to their respective inflation rates.

The weights $w(i)$ are computed as follows. First, define the following aggregates: X = total merchandise exports of Tanzania (in value terms) to the six countries over a given base period; M = total merchandise imports of Tanzania (in value terms) from the six countries (over the same base period). The base period could be one or more years. In the following, reference to the base period will be omitted for convenience. It will also be understood that all magnitudes are in value terms. Define the following additional magnitudes: $X(i)$ = exports from Tanzania to country i; $M(i)$ = Tanzanian imports from country i.

The weights $w(i)$ are defined as follows:

$$w(i) = \frac{X(i) + M(i)}{X + M} \ . \tag{A.4}$$

Note that a decline in $RERTt$ implies an appreciation of the Tanzanian shilling. We can compute a nominal equivalent exchange rate (NEER) that would compensate for over- or undervaluation and that can be visually or otherwise compared with the official or parallel rate as follows:

$$NEER_t = 100 \cdot e_{T\,\$t}\,/RER_{Tt} \ . \tag{A.5}$$

APPENDIX B

VARIABLE SHARES IN THE INDEX OF REAL HOUSEHOLD INCOMES

Expression (6.2) in Chapter 6 could be considered to hold quite accurately for predicting real income changes from one period t to the next $t+1$. However, in period $t+1$ price changes will induce shifts in the shares, and hence the expression will progressively lose its accuracy over time.

The original expression (6.2) presupposes that the household operates along a production possibility frontier of agricultural and nonagricultural activities. Suppose that this frontier is given by the following constant elasticity of transformation (CET) separable expression:

$$Q = \left(a A^{\frac{T+1}{T}} + b N^{\frac{T+1}{T}} \right)^{\frac{T}{T+1}} = g\left(K_h, L_h \right) \tag{B.1}$$

where A, N are the quantities of agricultural and nonagricultural products produced, Q is the index of total household real product, L_h and K_h are the amounts of labor and capital supplied by the specific household, T is the elasticity of transformation, and a, b are parameters. If P_{ah} and P_n are the prices of A and N faced by the household (notice P_{ah} is not the same as P_a), then profit maximization subject to (B.1) implies that the quantities supplied are equal to

$$A = Q \, a^{-T} \left(\frac{P_{ah}}{P_h} \right)^T \qquad N = Q \, b^{-T} \left(\frac{P_n}{P_h} \right)^T \tag{B.2}$$

where

$$P_h = \left(a^{-T} P_{ah}^{1+T} + b^{-T} P_n^{1+T} \right)^{\frac{1}{1+T}} \tag{B.3}$$

and the nominal income of the household is equal to

$$Y_h = P_{ah} \, A + P_n \, N . \tag{B.4}$$

Furthermore, we assume that A is a CET index of the three classes of agricultural products, while N is a CET index of formal and informal products:

$$A = \left(\sum_i a_i A_i^{\frac{T_a+1}{T_a}} \right)^{\frac{T_a}{T_a+1}} \tag{B.5}$$

$$N = \left(b_1 N_f^{\frac{T_n+1}{T_n}} + b_2 N_u^{\frac{T_n+1}{T_n}} \right)^{\frac{T_n}{T_n+1}} \tag{B.6}$$

The allocation of A to the A_i's and N to the N_i's will be done according to the formulas

$$A_i = A \, a_i^{-T_a} \left(\frac{P_{ai}^P}{P_{ah}} \right)^{T_a} \tag{B.7}$$

$$N_i = N \, b_i^{-T_n} \left(\frac{P_{ni}}{P_n} \right)^{T_n} \tag{B.8}$$

where

$$P_{ah} = \left(\sum_i a_i^{-T_a} \left[P_{ai}^P \right]^{1+T_a} \right)^{\frac{1}{1+T_a}} \tag{B.9}$$

$$P_n = \left(\sum_i b_i^{-T_n} P_{ni}^{1+T_n} \right)^{\frac{1}{1+T_n}} \tag{B.10}$$

under the nested CET structure.

Log-differentiating expression (B.4), we obtain the term in the first bracket in (6.2) if we assume that K_h, and in particular L_h, stay unchanged, so that the amount of the total product Q does not change. If, however, we assume that there is a short-run aggregate labor supply response of the sort, for instance,

$$\tilde{L}_h = \lambda \left(\left[s_a \tilde{P}_{ah} + s_n \tilde{P}_n \right] - \sum \delta_i \tilde{P}_i^c \right) \tag{B.11}$$

then expression (6.2) would have to be multiplied by $1 + \lambda$ where λ is the elasticity of labor supply with respect to real income. In the empirical part later, the value of λ is assumed to be equal to zero.

The issue, however, is to derive expressions for the next period weights s_a, s_{ai}, s_n, and s_{ni} given the imposed structure. The log-change in the share of household income deriving from agriculture between two periods can be written from the above structure, as follows:

$$\tilde{s}_a = \tilde{P}_{ah} + \tilde{A} - \tilde{P}_h - Q. \tag{B.12}$$

Utilizing (B.2) and (B.4), this can be written as

$$\tilde{s}_a = (1+T)\left(\left[1 - s_a \right] \tilde{P}_{ah} - s_n \tilde{P}_n \right). \tag{B.13}$$

The change in s_n will obtain as a residual from (6.1).

The log-change in s_{ai} is given by the following expression in view of (B.7) and (B.9):

$$\tilde{s}_{ai} = (1 + T_a)\left(\tilde{P}_{ai}^P - \tilde{P}_{ah} \right) \tag{B.14}$$

where in accordance with (B.9)

$$\tilde{P}_{ah} = \sum s_{ai} \tilde{P}_{ai}^P. \tag{B.15}$$

Similarly, for the nonagricultural shares

$$\tilde{s}_{ni} = (1 + T_n)\left(\tilde{P}_{ni} - \tilde{P}_n \right) \tag{B.16}$$

where

$$\tilde{P}_n = \sum_{s_{ni}} \tilde{P}_{ni}. \tag{B.17}$$

The price P_{nf} is the formal-sector average wage rate, while P_{nu} is the unit labor reward r of the informal sector.

The above expressions can be used for period-to-period updating of shares, as follows:

$$s_{a,t+1} = \left(1 + \tilde{s}_a\right) s_{a,t} \tag{B.18}$$

$$s_{n,t+1} = 1 - s_{a,t+1} \tag{B.19}$$

$$s_{ai,t+1} = \left(1 + \tilde{s}_{ai}\right) s_{ai,t} \qquad i = e, f \tag{B.20}$$

$$s_{ao,t+1} = 1 - s_{ae,t+1} - s_{af,t+1} \tag{B.21}$$

$$s_{nf,t+1} = \left(1 + \tilde{s}_{nf}\right) s_{nf,t} \tag{B.22}$$

$$s_{nu,t+1} = 1 - s_{nf,t+1}. \tag{B.23}$$

The above expressions depend on only three parameters, namely, T, T_a, and T_n. Given the lack of empirical information on these, we could examine alternative values. Notice that under the assumptions made, the short-run agricultural supply response can be derived by log-differentiating the expressions (B.7) and (B.2). Utilizing also the corresponding price expressions (B.3) and (B.9), we can write the following:

$$\tilde{A}_i = \left(T_a + s_{ai}\left[T\{1 - s_a\} - T_a\right]\right)\tilde{P}^P_{ai}$$
$$+ \sum_{j \neq i} s_{aj}\left(T\left[1 - s_a\right] - T_a\right)\tilde{P}^P_{aj} - T s_n \tilde{P}_n. \tag{B.24}$$

The expression multiplying $\tilde{P}^P_{ai}$ in (B.24) above is the short-run, own-supply price elasticity, while the expressions multiplying $\tilde{P}^P_{aj}$ are the cross-price elasticities.

Notice that the analysis up to now concerned the period-to-period changes in the various shares that pertain to the typical household. For the analysis of share changes relevant to the whole agricultural sector, the analysis of Chapter 6 holds, that is based on the assumption of equilibrium in the aggregate labor market by equality of relative rewards in agricultural and nonagricultural informal activities. Given, however, the changes in relative prices, the shares λ_a, λ_{nf}, and λ_{nu}, as well as β_i, are also bound to change. The changes in the shares of total labor going to agriculture and the informal sector can be derived with the help of expression (6.7):

$$\lambda_{a,t+1} = \left(1 + \tilde{\lambda}_a\right)\lambda_{a,t} \tag{B.25}$$

$$\lambda_{nf,t+1} = \left(1 + \tilde{\lambda}_{nf}\right)\lambda_{nf,t} \tag{B.26}$$

$$\lambda_{nu,t+1} = 1 - \lambda_{a,t+1} - \lambda_{nf,t+1} \tag{B.27}$$

where

$$\tilde{\lambda}_a = \tilde{L}_a = \frac{1}{1-\alpha}\left(\tilde{P}_a - \tilde{r}\right) \tag{B.28}$$

$$\lambda_{nf} = \tilde{L}_{nf} - \tilde{l}. \tag{B.29}$$

In (B.29) $\tilde{l}$ is the growth rate of the labor force (equal to the population growth rate). Implicit in (B.28) is the assumption that the exogenous growth of labor in agriculture is equal to $\tilde{l}$, the exogenous growth in the labor force.

A different problem is presented by potential changes in the aggregate agricultural product mix shares β_i ($i = e, f, o$). These are not the same as s_{ai} mentioned earlier. However, we could make an assumption that the allocation of total agricultural supply among the three classes takes place along a CET transformation frontier, much as was done for the smallholder. The analysis of share changes then follows the analysis done in arriving at (B.14). The resulting changes in β_i would then be given as follows:

$$\tilde{\beta}_i = (1 + \varphi)\left(P^P_{ai} - \tilde{P}_a\right) \tag{B.30}$$

where

$$\tilde{P}_a = \sum \beta_i P^P_{ai} \tag{B.31}$$

and φ is the elasticity of transformation for the whole agricultural sector. In this case, period-to-period changes in β_i would be given as follows:

$$\beta_{i,t+1} = \left(1 + \tilde{\beta}_i\right)\beta_{i,t} \qquad i = e, f \tag{B.32}$$

$$\beta_{0,t+1} = 1 - \beta_{e,t+1} - \beta_{f,t+1}. \tag{B.33}$$

Turning to the weight changes in the expenditure index δ_i, these cannot, of course, be ascertained unless a demand system is specified. Consider a nested demand system whereby utility is derived from food, denoted by b, and other goods, denoted by n. Food in turn is a composite good of traded food (f) and other food (o). By the assumptions already made, the nominal income of a household with labor endowment L_h is

$$YN_h = r\left(L_{ha} + L_{hu}\right) + w\, L_{hf}, \tag{B.34}$$

and we assume that it is all consumed. In (B.34), L_{hi} is the absolute amount of labor devoted by the household to the i'th activity, and the sum of all these is equal to L_h, which is assumed fixed. Given (B.34), the share of food in total consumption expenditures δ_b is defined as follows:

$$\delta_b = \delta_f + \delta_o = \frac{P_b^c Q_b}{Y_h} \tag{B.35}$$

where P_b^c is the consumer price index of the composite commodity food, and Q_b is the corresponding quantity index of food consumed. Hence changes in δ_b from period to period will be given as follows (remember L_h stays fixed):

$$\tilde{\delta}_b = \tilde{P}_b^c + \tilde{Q}_b - \tilde{Y}N_h. \tag{B.36}$$

The proportional change $\tilde{Q}b$ is given by the following standard demand expression, where use has been made of the homogeneity restriction:

$$\tilde{Q}_b = \eta_b\left(\tilde{Y}N_h - \tilde{P}_n^c\right) + \varepsilon_{bb}\left(\tilde{P}_b^c - \tilde{P}_n^c\right) \tag{B.37}$$

where η_b is the income elasticity of demand for food and ε_{bb} is the own-price elasticity of demand for food of the household.

If a constant elasticity of substitution σ is assumed between traded food and other nontraded foods in the consumption of Q_b, then we can easily derive the share changes of δ_f and δ_o, as follows:

$$\tilde{\delta}_f = \tilde{\delta}_b + (1 - \sigma)\left(\tilde{P}_f^c - \tilde{P}_b^c\right) \tag{B.38}$$

$$\tilde{\delta}_o = \tilde{\delta}_b + (1 - \sigma)\left(\tilde{P}_o^c - \tilde{P}_b^c\right) \tag{B.39}$$

where

$$\tilde{P}_b^c = \delta_f' \tilde{P}_f^c + \delta_o' \tilde{P}_o^c \tag{B.40}$$

with

$$\delta'_f = \frac{\delta_f}{\delta_b} \qquad \delta'_o = \frac{\delta_o}{\delta_b}. \qquad (B.41)$$

We, therefore, obtain the following expressions for the period-to-period changes in consumption shares:

$$\delta_{b,t+1} = \left(1 + \tilde{\delta}_b\right)\delta_{b,t} \qquad (B.42)$$

$$\delta_{n,t+1} = 1 - \delta_{b,t+1} \qquad (B.43)$$

$$\tilde{\delta}_b = \left(\eta_b - 1\right)\tilde{Y}N_h - \left(\eta_b + \varepsilon_{bb}\right)\tilde{P}^c_n + \left(1 + \varepsilon_{bb}\right)\tilde{P}^c_b \qquad (B.44)$$

$$\delta_{f,t+1} = \left(1 + \tilde{\delta}_f\right)\delta_{f,t} \qquad (B.45)$$

$$\delta_{o,t+1} = \delta_{b,t+1} - \delta_{f,t+1} \qquad (B.46)$$

$$\tilde{\delta}_f = \tilde{\delta}_b + (1 - \sigma)\left(\tilde{P}^c_f - \tilde{P}^c_b\right). \qquad (B.47)$$

It is, therefore, seen that to implement the changes in the various shares into the expression (6.12), we need as a minimum three parameters for the consumption system—namely, η_b, ε_{bb}, and σ—and three parameters for the production system—namely, T, T_a, and T_n—as well as a value for the aggregate transformation parameter φ. Notice that the nominal income required for implementing (B.44) is nothing but the term in the first bracket of (6.14).

The above assumptions imply that the percentage change in the quantity consumed of a given food good can be written as follows:

$$\tilde{Q}_i = \eta_b\left(\tilde{Y}N_h - \tilde{P}^c_n\right) + \left(-\sigma + \delta_i\left[\sigma + \varepsilon_{bb}\right]\right)\tilde{P}_i$$

$$+ \sum_{j \neq i}\left(\varepsilon_{bb} + \sigma\right)\delta'_j\,\tilde{P}^c_j - \varepsilon_{bb}\,\tilde{P}^c_n.$$

$$(B.48)$$

The above expression shows how information about aggregate elasticities of food demand, along with information on elasticities of demand of specific food groups, can be used to obtain some estimates of the substitution elasticity σ.

REFERENCES

Agland Investment Services. 1989. *Coffee Sub-Sector Study Tanzania. An Analysis.* Prepared for the African Development Bank, Coffee Sub-Sector Study Tanzania. Larkspur, California: Agland Investment Services, Inc.

Amani, H.K.R., S. M. Kapunda, N.H.I. Lipumba, and B. J. Ndulu. 1987. "Effects of Market Liberalization on Food Security in Tanzania." Dar es Salaam: University of Dar es Salaam, Economics Department. Mimeo.

_____. 1989. "Impact of Market Liberalization on Household Food Security in Tanzania." In *Household and National Food Security in Southern Africa.* Edited by G. D. Midimu and R. H. Bernsten. Proceedings of the Fourth Annual Conference on Food Security Research in Southern Africa, October 31–November 3, 1988, University of Zimbabwe and Michigan State University, Food Security Research Project, Harare.

Bagachwa, M.S.D., and A. Naho. 1990a. "Estimates of the Second Economy in Tanzania." University of Dar es Salaam. Mimeo.

_____. 1990b. "The National Accounts Statistics." Dar es Salaam. Mimeo.

Bagachwa, M.S.D., and B. J. Ndulu. 1988. "The Urban Informal Sector in Tanzania." Dar es Salaam. Mimeo.

Bagachwa, M.S.D., N. E. Luvanga, and G. D. Mjema. 1990. "Tanzania: A Study on Non-traditional Exports." Report prepared for the Ministry of Finance, Dar Es Salaam, Tanzania.

Bank of Tanzania. 1984. *Tanzania: Twenty Years of Independence (1961–1981): A Review of Political and Economic Performance.* Dar es Salaam: Bank of Tanzania.

Bevan, D. L., A. Bigsten, P. Collier, and J. W. Gunning. 1988. "Incomes in the United Republic of Tanzania During the Nyerere Experiment." In *Employment and Labor Incomes.* Edited by W. van Ginneken, 61–83. Geneva: International Labor Organization.

Bevan, D. L., P. Collier, and J.W. Gunning, with A. Bigsten and P. Horsnell. 1989. *Peasants and Governments, An Economic Analysis.* Oxford: Clarendon Press.

_____. 1990. *Controlled Open Economies: A Neoclassical Approach to Structuralism.* Oxford: Clarendon Press.

Bhattacharyya, D. K. 1990. "An Econometric Method of Estimating the Hidden Economy, United Kingdom (1960–1984): Estimates and Tests." *Economic Journal* 100 (September): 703–717.

Biermann, W., and J. Campbell. 1989. "The Chronology of Crisis in Tanzania, 1974–1986." In *The IMF, the World Bank, and the African Debt: The Economic Impact.* Edited by B. Onimode. London: ZED Publishers.

Bienenfeld, M. 1989. "Structural Adjustment and Rural Employment in Tanzania." Paper submitted to ILO/EMP/RU project on Structural Adjustment and Rural Labour Markets in Five African Countries. Geneva: International Labour Office.

Collier, Paul, and Jan Willem Gunning. 1989. "The Tanzanian Recovery, 1983–1989." Mimeo.

_____. 1991. "Money Creation and Financial Liberalization in a Socialist Banking system: Tanzania, 1983–89." *World Development* 19(5): 533–538.

Collier, P., S. Radwan, and S. Wangwe, with A. Wagner. 1986. *Labour and Poverty in Rural Tanzania: Ujamaa and Rural Development in the United Republic of Tanzania.* A study prepared for the International Labour Office within the framework of the World Employment Programme. Oxford: Clarendon Press.

Cornia, A.P.R., R. Jolly, and F. Stewart. 1987. *Adjustment With a Human Face.* Oxford: Clarendon Press.

Coulson, A. 1982. *Tanzania: A Political Economy.* Oxford: Clarendon Press.

Ellis, F. 1983. "Agricultural Marketing and Peasant State Transfers in Tanzania." *Journal of Peasant Studies* 10 (4): 214–242.

Ellis, F. 1982. "Agricultural Price Policy in Tanzania." *World Development* 10 (4): 263–283.

Food and Agriculture Organization/International Bank for Reconstruction and Development. 1975. *Raising the Productivity of Small Farmers.* Cooperative Research Project. Dar es Salaam.

Frey, B. S., and W. W. Pommerehne. 1982. "Measuring the Hidden Economy: Though This be Madness, There is Method in It." In *Underground Economy in the United States and Abroad.* Edited by V. Tanzi. Lexington, MA: Lexington Books.

Gerrard, Christopher D., and Terry Roe. 1983. "Government Intervention in Food Grain Markets: An Econometric Study of Tanzania." *Journal of Development Economics* 13 (1–2, August/October): 109–132.

Gordon, Henry. 1988a. "Incentives to Export in Private Tanzanian Maize Markets." Mimeo.

_____. 1988b. "Open Markets for Maize and Rice in Tanzania: Current Issues and Evidence." Medford, MA: The Fletcher School, Tufts University. Mimeo.

_____. 1989. "An Overview of Basic Data on Grain Marketing in Tanzania, 1974/75 to the Present." Mimeo.

Green, H. R., D. G. Rwegasira, and B. van Arkadie. 1980. *Economic Shocks and National Policy Making: Tanzania in the 1970s.* The Hague: Institute of Social Studies.

Greer, J., and E. Thorbecke. 1986. "A Methodology for Measuring Food Poverty Applied to Kenya." *Journal of Development Economics* 24: 59–74.

Guttman, P. M. 1977. "Subterranean Economy." *Financial Analysis Journal* 33 (November/December): 26–27.

Gwyer, G. D. 1971. "Perennial Crop Supply Response: The Case of Tanzanian Sisal." London: University of London, Wyseley College.

Havnevik, K. J. 1986. "A Resource Overlooked - Crafts and Small Scale Industry." In *Tanzania Crisis and Struggle for Survival.* Edited by J. Bosen, K. J. Havnevik, J. Koponen, and R. Odgaard. Uppsala: Scandinavian Institute of African Studies.

Hyden, G. 1980. *Beyond Ujamaa in Tanzania: Underdeveloped and an Uncaptured Peasantry.* London: Heinemann.

International Labour Office (ILO). 1982. "Basic Needs in Danger. A Basic Needs Oriented Development Strategy for Tanzania." Addis Ababa: JASPA.

International Monetary Fund. Various years. *International Financial Statistics.* Washington, D.C.: IMF.

Jamal, Vali. 1986. "Economics of Devaluation: The Case of Tanzania." *Labor and Society* II (3 September): 379–393.

Kristjanson, P., D. Newman, C. Christensen, and M. Abel. 1990. *Export Crop Competitiveness: Strategies for Sub-Saharan Africa.* Agricultural Policy Analysis Project, Phase II, Technical Report No. 109. Bethesda, MD: Abt Associates Inc.

Krugman, P., and L. Taylor. 1978. "Contractionary Effects of Devaluation." *Journal of International Economics* 8 (3, August): 445–456.

Land Resources Development Centre. 1987. *Tanzania: Profile of Agricultural Potential.* Surrey, UK.

Lipumba, N., B. Ndulu, S. Horton, and A. Plourde. 1988. "A Supply Constrained Macroeconometric Model of Tanzania." *Economic Modelling* (October): 354–375.

Lofchie, Michael F. 1988. "Tanzania's Agricultural Decline." In *"Coping with Africa's Food Crisis."* Edited by Naomi Chazan and Timothy M. Shaw, 144–168. Boulder and London: Lynne Rienner Publishers.

————. 1989. *The Policy Factor: Agricultural Performance in Kenya and Tanzania.* Boulder, CO: Lynne Rienner Publishers Inc.

Loxley, J. 1989. "The Devaluation Debate in Tanzania." In *Structural Adjustment in Africa.* Edited by B. K. Campbell and J. Loxley. New York: St. Martins Press.

Lundahl, M., and B.J. Ndulu. 1987. *Market-Related Incentives and Food Production in Tanzania: Theory and Experience.* From Incentives and Economic Systems: Proceedings of the Eights Arne Ryde Symposium, Frostvalen, August 26–27, 1985. Stockholm: Stockholm School of Economics.

Maciejewski, E. B. 1983. "Real Effective Exchange Rate Indices." *IMF Staff Papers* 30 (3, September).

Malima, K. A. 1971. "The Determinants of Cotton Supply in Tanzania." Economic Research Bureau Paper No. 71.4. Dar es Salaam.

Maliyamkono, T. L., and M.S.D. Bagachwa. 1990. *The Second Economy in Tanzania.* London: James Currey.

Mtetewaunga, S. D. 1986. "Social Implication of Land Reforms in Tanzania." In *Land Policy and Agriculture in Eastern and Southern Africa.* Edited by J. W. Arntzen, L. D. Ngcongco, and S. D. Turner. Tokyo: United Nations University.

Ndulu, B. J. 1980. *The Impacts of Inter-regional Transport Subsidy Policy on Commercial Supply of Food Grains in Tanzania: The Case of Paddy and Maize.* Economic Research Bureau Paper 80.1. January 1980. Dar es Salaam.

————. 1988. *Stabilization and Adjustment Policies and Programmes.* Country Study 17, Tanzania. Helsinki: World Institute for Development Economics.

Ndulu, B. J., and M. Hyuha. 1986. "Inflation and Economic Recovery in Tanzania: Some Empirical Evidence." Report to the World Bank. Dar es Salaam. Mimeo.

Odegaard, Kurt. 1985. "Cash Crop Versus Food Crop Production in Tanzania: An Assessment of the Major Post-Colonial Trends." *Lund Economic Studies* 33. Lund, Sweden.

Okunade, A. A. 1985. "Engel Curves for Developing Nations: The Case of Africa." *East African Economic Review* 1 (1, December): 13–22.

Renkow, M. A., J. B. Leonard, and D. L. Franklin. 1983. "The Potential Effects of Alternative Structures and Pricing Policies in the Markets for Maize in Tanzania." Raleigh, NC: Sigma One Corporation.

Sabai, M. T., L. A. Msambichaka, D. S. Dandi, T. W. Maembe, E. L. Mkusa, and J.M.T. Maserele. 1989. "Redeployment of Human Resources in Tanzania: Report on Informal Sector Constraints and Opportunities." Dar es Salaam. Mimeo.

Sahn, David E., and Alexander Sarris. 1991. "Structural Adjustment and Rural Smallholder Welfare: A Comparative Analysis from Sub-Saharan Africa." *World Bank Economic Review* 1 (2, May): 259–289.

Sharpley, J. 1985. "External Versus Internal Factors in Tanzania's Macroeconomic Crisis: 1973-1983." *Eastern African Economic Review* 1 (1, December): 71–85.

Singh, A. 1986. "Tanzania and the IMF: The Analytics of Alternative Adjustment Programmes." *Development and Change* 17: 425–454.

Stewart, F. 1986. "Economic Policies and Agricultural Performance: The Case of Tanzania." Paris: OECD Development Center.

Tanzania, United Republic of (URT). 1974. *Bureau of Statistics Agricultural Census 1971/72*. Dar es Salaam.

_____. 1978. *Bureau of Statistics Household Budget Survey 1976/77*. Dar es Salaam.

_____. *1978 Population Census: Preliminary Report*. Dar es Salaam: Hassan Printers Ltd.

_____. 1983. "Preliminary Report on the Parallel Market for Grains in Tanzania." Dar es Salaam: Marketing Development Bureau, Ministry of Agriculture and Livestock Development.

_____. 1986. "Aspects of the Open Market for Food Commodities in Mainland Tanzania." Dar es Salaam: Marketing Development Bureau, Ministry of Agriculture and Livestock Development.

_____. 1987a. *Annual Review of Cocoa*. Dar es Salaam: Marketing Development Bureau, Ministry of Agriculture and Livestock Development.

_____. 1987b. "Agriculture and Livestock Development, Food Self-Sufficiency Policy, and Food Needs Assessment in Tanzania." Food Policy Analysis paper. Dar es Salaam: Food Strategy Unit.

_____. 1988. *1988 Population Census: Preliminary Report*. Dar es Salaam: Bureau of Statistics. Ministry of Finance, Economic Affairs and Planning.

_____. Various years a (1981-1989). *Basic Data—Agriculture and Livestock Sector*. Dar es Salaam: Marketing Development Bureau, Ministry of Agriculture and Livestock Development.

_____. Various years b (1987, 1988). *Annual Review of Tea*. Dar es Salaam: Marketing Development Bureau, Ministry of Agriculture and Livestock Development.

_____. Various years c (1987, 1988). *Annual Review of Cotton*. Dar es Salaam: Marketing Development Bureau, Ministry of Agriculture and Livestock Development.

_____. Various years d (1987, 1988). *Annual Review of Tobacco*. Dar es Salaam: Marketing Development Bureau, Ministry of Agriculture and Livestock Development.

_____. Various years e (1987, 1988). *Annual Review of Cashewnuts*. Dar es Salaam: Marketing Development Bureau, Ministry of Agriculture and Livestock Development.

_____. Various years f (1987, 1988). *Annual Review of Coffee*. Dar es Salaam: Marketing Development Bureau, Ministry of Agriculture and Livestock Development.

_____. Various years g (1987, 1988). *Annual Review of Pyrethrum*. Dar es Salaam: Marketing Development Bureau, Ministry of Agriculture and Livestock Development.

_____. Various years h (1987, 1988). *Annual Review of Sorghum, Millet, Cassava and Beans*. Dar es Salaam: Marketing Development Bureau, Ministry of Agriculture and Livestock Development.

_____. Various years i (1987, 1988). *Annual Review of Maize, Rice and Wheat*. Dar es Salaam: Marketing Development Bureau, Ministry of Agriculture and Livestock Development.

_____. 1989. *Agricultural Sample Survey of Tanzania Mainland 1986/87: Main Report*. Vol. 3 (December). Dar es Salaam: Bureau of Statistics, President's Office.

Tanzania, Bureau of Statistics. 1982. *Economic Survey*. Dar es Salaam: BOS.

_____. 1987. *Selected Statistical Series, 1951-1985*. Dar es Salaam: BOS.

_____. 1989. *Foreign Trade Statistics, 1987*. Dar es Salaam: BOS.

Tanzi, V. 1983. "The Underground Economy in the United States: Annual Estimates, 1930-80." *IMF Staff Papers* 30 (2, June): 283-305.

Tanzi, V. (ed.). 1982. *The Underground Economy in the United States and Abroad*. Lexington, MA: Lexington Books, DC: Heath.

University of Dar es Salaam. Various years. *Tanzanian Economic Trends (TET)*. Various issues. Published in collaboration with the Ministry of Finance, Economic Affairs, and Planning. Dar es Salaam: University of Dar es Salaam, Economic Research Bureau.

van Arkadie, B. 1983. "The IMF Prescription for Structural Adjustment in Tanzania: A Comment." in *Monetarism, Economic Crisis and the Third World*. Edited by K. Jansen. London: Frank Cass.

Weaver, J. H., and A. Anderson. 1981. "Stabilization and Development of the Tanzanian Economy in the 1970s." In *Economic Stabilization in Developing Countries*. Edited by W. R. Cline and S. Weintraub. Washington, DC: Brookings Institution.

World Bank. 1983. *Tanzania: Agriculture Sector Report*, August 19, 1983. Washington, DC: World Bank, Eastern Africa Projects Department, Southern Agriculture Division.

_____. 1987a. "Report to the Consultative Group for Tanzania on the Government's Economic Recovery Program." Washington, DC: World Bank. Mimeo.

_____. 1987b. *Tanzania: An Agenda for Industrial Recovery* (2 volumes). Report No. 6357-TA. Washington, DC: World Bank.

_____. 1988. *Parastatals in Tanzania: Towards a Reform Program*. Report No. 7100-TA. Washington, DC: World Bank.

_____. 1989a. *Tanzania Public Expenditure Review* (3 volumes). Report No. 7559-TA. Washington, DC: World Bank.

_____. 1989b. *Tanzania Population, Health and Nutrition Sector Review*. Report No. 7495-TA. Washington, DC: World Bank.

_____. 1990. *World Development Report 1990*. Oxford: Oxford University Press.

_____. 1991. *Tanzania Economic Report. Towards Sustainable Development in the 1990s*. Report No. 9352-TA. Washington, DC: World Bank, Country Operations Division, Southern Africa Department.

Yambi, Olivia, F. P. Kavishe, and W. Lorri. 1990. "Malnutrition and Household Food Security in Tanzania." Prepared for the World Bank/FAO Mission on Household Food Security. Dar es Salaam.

INDEX